A DOUBTER'S GUIDE TO WORLD RELIGIONS

OTHER BOOKS BY JOHN DICKSON

Bullies and Saints

A Doubter's Guide to Jesus

A Doubter's Guide to the Ten Commandments

A Doubter's Guide to the Bible

Hearing Her Voice, Revised Edition

Humilitas

Life of Jesus

The Best Kept Secret of Christian Mission

The Christ Files

A DOUBTER'S GUIDE TO WORLD RELIGIONS

JOHN DICKSON

A FAIR AND FRIENDLY INTRODUCTION TO THE HISTORY,
BELIEFS, AND PRACTICES OF THE BIG FIVE

ZONDERVAN
REFLECTIVE

ZONDERVAN REFLECTIVE

A Doubter's Guide to World Religions
Copyright © 2022 by John Dickson

Requests for information should be addressed to:
Zondervan, *3900 Sparks Dr. SE, Grand Rapids, Michigan 49546*

Zondervan titles may be purchased in bulk for educational, business, fundraising, or sales promotional use. For information, please email SpecialMarkets@Zondervan.com.

ISBN 978-0-310-11833-6 (softcover)
ISBN 978-0-310-11835-0 (audio)
ISBN 978-0-310-11834-3 (ebook)

Cover design: Studio Gearbox
Cover photos: Shutterstock
Interior typesetting: Sara Colley

Printed in the United States of America

22 23 24 25 26 27 28 29 30   /TRM/   12 11 10 9 8 7 6 5 4 3 2 1

For Buff
my truest thing on this earth

THANKS TO

Jenny Glen, for your tireless efforts as my personal assistant for more than fifteen years, allowing me to write and teach—on all subjects, including this one—out of all proportion to my natural abilities. May your retirement be filled with shalom.

Cornay Sinac, for reading everything and reminding me to keep it clear and simple.

Duncan Giles, for influencing the direction of this book more than you know.

My new executive assistant, Lyndie Leviston, for valuable research assistance.

Those who kindly read draft chapters and offered insights and corrections: Dr. Richard Shumack, Marie Graber, Dr. Sheevalee Patel, Kelsang Sudhana, Simon Smart, Dr. Kankesu Jayanthakumaran, Harry (†) and Olive Cotter, Simona Barukh, and Rahil Patel.

All inadequacies are my own.

CONTENTS

PART 4: JUDAISM, THE WAY OF THE TORAH

PART 5: CHRISTIANITY, THE WAY OF THE CHRIST

PART 6: ISLAM, THE WAY OF SUBMISSION

PART 7: LETTING THE RELIGIONS HAVE THEIR SAY

PREFACE
THE FEAST OF IDEAS

My introduction to religion came not through family tradition, Sunday school, church, or any other formal means of religious instruction, but through the irresistible power of good food.

One of the relics of Australia's semi-Christian heritage is the once-a-week "Scripture lesson" offered in many state schools around the country, especially in the state of New South Wales where I grew up. Usually, the person running the lesson was an elderly volunteer from the local church, synagogue, mosque, or temple. I took my chances with these harmless old ladies because "non-Scripture" involved doing homework under the supervision of a real teacher.

One of these Scripture teachers had the courage one day to invite the entire class to her home on a Friday afternoon after school for discussions about "God." This would be illegal nowadays, but it seemed plausible at the time. Anyway, the invitation would have gone unnoticed, except that she added: "Oh, and if anyone gets hungry, I'll be making hamburgers, milkshakes, and scones." Looking back, this was perhaps an unfair offer to a bunch of ravenous teenagers!

Several weeks later, I was sitting on a comfy lounge in this woman's home with half a dozen classmates, feasting on her food and bracing myself for the "God bit." I had never been to church or even had a religious conversation of any length, so this was an entirely new experience. I remember thinking at the time that there was nowhere to run. I had eaten so much of her food, I couldn't have left the couch if I'd tried.

My fears were unfounded. This woman's style was relaxed. She knew she was speaking to a room full of religious spectators and sceptics rather than believers, so she never pushed us. She asked us what we thought, she let us ask her what she thought, and she read to us from some relevant parts of the Bible. For me, and several others from that class, this was the beginning of a very interesting journey into the wonders of faith.

Life has changed a lot since those days. Whereas I once prided myself on "not being the religious type," I suppose now I appear about as "religious" as a modern Australian can get. I have recorded songs about faith, written books about it, given talks on it, completed degrees in it, and even went so far as to get myself ordained as an Anglican (or Episcopalian) priest.

Yet for all this "religion" in my life, I still wince when people ask, "Are you religious?" It is not that I am embarrassed about spirituality—far from it. It is just that the word "religion" sometimes conjures up images of formality, close-mindedness, and strictness, and these are the last descriptions I would attach to my convictions.

I guess those early hamburger discussions as a teenager set the course of my spiritual journey in subtler ways than simply convincing me of the merits of Christianity. Whether in song, speech, or print, I have always felt more in tune with religious spectators than players. Almost everything I have tried to do over the last thirty years has sought to help the not-so-religious gain a clearer picture of the "brand" of faith that has convinced me.

Although my topic in this book is much broader—five major faiths instead of just one—the same thing motivates me: I want to help the person on the street explore the big questions in a non-pushy way. There is no religious "sell" here. It is not even a minor purpose of this book to criticise the different world faiths. As will soon become clear, my aims are far simpler. I hope to encourage understanding, tolerance, and appreciation of the five great world religions. I also hope to expose a couple of the "Chardonnay myths" about religion that have become popular in broader secular society.

I hope you will take a seat on your comfortable mental lounge and join me as a welcome guest as we sample the feast of ideas found in the world's great religions.

A NOTE ON THE TEXTS OF THE WORLD RELIGIONS

There is a bewildering array of English translations of the various scriptures of the world religions. I have tried to give readers the clearest rendition of any given text under discussion, and so I have employed a range of standard translations.

English Translations of the Hindu Scriptures

Doniger, Wendy. *The Rig Veda*. Penguin Classics, 1981; Goodall, D. *Hindu Scriptures*. Berkeley: University of California, 1996; Sutton, N. *The Bhagavad Gita: A New Translation and Study Guide* (Oxford Centre for Hindu Studies). San Rafael, Mandala Publishing, 2020.

English Translations of the Buddhist Scriptures

Takakusu, J., Müller, F. Max Müller, and E. B. Cowell. *Buddhist Mahāyāna Texts*. Delhi: Motilal Banarsidass, 1965; Rahula, W. *What the Buddha Taught*. The Grove Press, 1974; Horner, I. B. *The Collection of the Middle Length Sayings*, Vol. 2. London: The Pali Text Society, 1989; Warren, H. C. *Buddhism in Translation*. Cambridge, Mass.: Harvard University, 1900; Bodhi, Bikkhu. *The Connected Discourses of the Buddha: A New Translation of the Samyutta Nikaya*. Somerville: Wisdom Publications, 2003; Thanissaro, Bhikkhu. *Digha Nikaya, The Long Collection. Access to Insight (BCBS Edition)*. Online: https://www.dhammatalks.org/suttas/DN/index_DN.html; Smart, N. *Sacred Texts of the World: A Universal Anthology*. New York: Crossroad, 2002; Reeves, G., *The Lotus Sutra: A Contemporary Translation of a Buddhist Classic*. Wisdom Publications, 2008; Jones, J. J. *The Mahavastu*. Vol.1. Luzac & Company, 1949.

English Translations of the Jewish Scriptures

Unless otherwise noted, all quotations from the Jewish Bible (the Tanakh or Christian "Old Testament") are from *Tanakh: The Holy Scriptures*. Jewish Publication Society, 1985. All quotations from the Jewish Prayer book or Siddur are from *The Complete Artscroll Siddur*. Mesorah Publications, 2001. All quotations from the Mishnah are from Neusner, J. *The Mishnah: A New Translation*. Yale University Press, 1988. Quotations from the Talmud are either from Rodkinson, M. L. *The Babylonian Talmud*. Vol. 1–10. Boston: Boston New Talmud Publishing Company, 1903–18; or Neusner, J. *The Babylonian Talmud: A Translation and Commentary*. Vol. 1–22. Hendrickson, 2005.

English Translations of the Christian Scriptures

All quotations from the Christian Bible (Old and New Testaments) are from *The Holy Bible: New International Version*. Zondervan, 2011.

English Translations of the Muslim Scriptures

Khan, M. M. *Sahih al-Bukhari. Summarised Sahih al-Bukhari: Arabic-English.* Maktaba Dar-us-Salam Publishers, 1994; Dawood, N.J., trans. *The Koran,* Penguin Classics. Penguin Books, 2003; Peters, F. E. *A Reader on Classical Islam.* Princeton University Press, 1994; Ali, A. Yusuf. *The Holy Quran: Text, Translation and Commentary.* Amana Corporation, 1983; Fakhry, M. *An Interpretation of the Quran: English Translation of the Meanings, A Bilingual Edition.* New York University Press, 2000.

PART 1
A WORD OR TWO TO SPECTATORS

1

SO YOU'RE GOING TO WRITE A BOOK ON RELIGION

How can someone possibly write a book on the world religions when he is already a devoted follower of just one of them? This is a question I have grappled with from the very beginning of this project. The book itself, I guess, will prove whether or not I have managed to resolve it.

The dilemma is made more complicated because of my particular education. At first glance, being a student of both theology and history might seem like a good background for someone trying to discuss the spiritual traditions of the centuries. Yes and no.

THE PROBLEM WITH THEOLOGY AND HISTORY

Theology can at times be overly theoretical in its discussion of religious issues. As the "study of the divine," theology tends to focus on doctrines and philosophy, and can sometimes leave aside the equally important issues of a religion's place in history, or (perhaps more importantly) its significance in the lives of those who practise it.

There is a danger in being a Christian theologian in particular.

We are tempted to ask the wrong questions about other religions. Asking, for example, "What does Buddhism teach about sin?" might be interesting to the average churchgoer, but it doesn't help the many spectators out there to appreciate what Buddhism is really about. Buddha didn't have much to say about "sin." Asking Christian questions of Buddhism is a bit like asking football questions of cricket. How do you score a touchdown? When is someone offside? How do you tackle? None of these questions applies to cricket, just as cricket questions don't really apply to football: How do you get caught out? How many points for a boundary? Where is silly mid on? (US readers may like to google these important cricket issues!)

Being a student of history has its own peculiarities, and if these are not kept in check, they can easily make the historian irrelevant in the quest to understand religion. Historians pride themselves on being critical in the study of history. But when it comes to spiritual matters, this is not always a good thing. Lengthy discussions about whether the Christian Gospels were written after the Roman invasion of Jerusalem (AD 70) or before, or whether Israel's exodus from Egypt occurred in the thirteenth century BC or the fifteenth century BC, or at all, do not enhance our understanding of what it is like to be a Christian or Jew. And yet historians love talking about these things. The historical emphasis can obscure the very obvious personal dimensions of religious faith.

A Note on Dating Conventions

My preference in both academic and popular writing is to use the traditional Western dating convention of BC ("before Christ") and AD (*anno Domini*, "the year of our Lord"). This convention is still widely accepted in secular ancient history and classics journals.

However, throughout the rest of the book, I will only use BC and AD when talking about Christian history and doctrine. When talking about other religions, I will use the recent alternative convention of BCE ("before the Common Era") and CE ("Common Era"). It somehow feels more polite not to force my Jewish readers, for example, to read that their second holy book, the Mishnah, was compiled "in the year of our Lord" 200. I hope in doing this I will not annoy Christian readers.

THE IMPORTANCE OF THEOLOGY AND HISTORY

Let me explain why theology and history might not be completely useless perspectives from which to write a book on the world religions.

First, most religions do have a bit to say about God, creation, salvation, and philosophical questions. A theological perspective is crucial for getting inside the head of a religious faith. By contrast, I have read books about Islam that gave lots of names and dates but very little about the things that make Muslims tick—things like God and God's will for our lives. One of the most famous books on the world religions—a textbook used in schools and universities around the world—reduces religions to sociological phenomena without offering any insight into the way religion helps the adherent cope with suffering or make sense of science or live morally. Theology counts, and this book will hopefully show why.

The historical perspective also proves helpful, so long as we don't get carried away with it. Religions are historical things. Each of them developed at a certain point in time and as a result of particular cultural forces. Understanding these historical influences can help us appreciate more fully what was distinctive about a particular religion and what early believers found attractive about it. For example, I only appreciated Buddha's emphasis on what he called the "middle path" when I understood the poles of extravagance and asceticism in the sixth- and fifth-century BCE Hinduism he was trying to "correct." More about that later. My simple point for now is that I intend to point out interesting connections between the religions and their historical backgrounds.

THE PROBLEM OF BIAS

But what about the Christian tag I wear? Is it possible for a believer in Christ to write about, say, Judaism without letting his bias get in the way? Don't Christians believe the Jews killed Jesus? Won't that colour the way a Christian presents the Jewish faith?

It may seem at first that the more confident you are in a particular religion, the more likely you are to "fudge" your description of another religion. I think the reverse is true. Bias in the description of other faiths is a sure sign of a lack of confidence in one's own faith. I can't speak for other Christian writers, but it seems to me perfectly obvious that if someone feels the need to misrepresent, say, Islam, in order to make Christianity look good, that person's Christian belief is anything but confident.

If Christianity is uniquely true, its beauty will be best seen only when viewed amidst a full and fair account of the alternatives. Let me give you an analogy that comes to mind. Imagine yourself as an art curator who is convinced that one piece in his collection has an unequaled truth and beauty. What will you do? Will you dim the lights on the "competitors" in the gallery and put the spotlights on your favourite piece? I think not. That would be a sure sign you were not actually convinced about the special quality of your treasured masterpiece. If you have to obscure the other pieces in order to make your favourite one appear better, something is clearly wrong. A truly assured curator, one with a deep confidence in the excellence of his prized item, will place all the gallery lights on full, confident that as careful art lovers inspect the whole collection, viewing all the works in their best light, one painting in particular will draw people's attention.

This is how I felt as I wrote this book. I am more than ever convinced that each of the world's religions is a "work of art," worthy of a public showing in the best light. At the same time, I am also more than ever confident of the unique quality of the Christian faith. I can think of no better way to embody confidence and help readers see that quality for themselves than to turn all the gallery lights on full and let you view the whole collection for yourself.

In the next chapter, I want to offer a few tips on how to get the most out of a book on world religions.

2

TIPS FOR READING
THE RELIGIONS

As the title makes clear, this book is not written for religious devotees but for spectators and doubters, those with a simple curiosity about Hinduism, Buddhism, Judaism, Christianity, and Islam.

Few things provide a better window into a culture's views than its religion. When you sit in your local Thai restaurant, wouldn't it be nice to know why there is a little shrine on the wall? This is not simply a decoration or good luck charm. It's not there to appear "authentically Asian." If you happen to ask the owner, you will probably find that the shrine represents an important part your Buddhist restauranteur's life. If nothing else, by the end of this book, you will be able to eat at your local Indian, Thai, Chinese, Persian, and Kosher restaurants and explain to your friends what makes Buddhism different from Hinduism, and how Islam responded to the Jewish and Christian communities of its time. Hopefully, there will be some additional spin-offs as well.

THE IMPORTANCE OF THE WORLD RELIGIONS

Of course, religion is far more than a dinner party topic of conversation. It is fair to say that nothing has influenced the world—for good and ill—more than the world religions. Much of the world's art and music grew out of religious devotion. Music historians will often tell you how rock 'n' roll grew out of gospel, and how classical grew out of medieval church music. It is also clear that many of the social laws of various societies were shaped decisively by religion.

The big questions addressed by the world religions are truly universal: Who are we? What is our worth? How should we live? Are we alone? Because of this, I've often described the religious inclinations of humanity as common sense. My atheist friends don't like this description very much, but I think it is nonetheless true. The human fascination with religion is like the human interests in music, art, and learning. They are all found throughout the world. They are, if you like, among the few universally shared pursuits of Homo sapiens throughout time. I cannot speak authoritatively for art or music, but it is no exaggeration to say that every single society about which anthropologists and historians know anything significant has made religion a central part of its cultural life.

The oldest rock art in the world, whether the paintings found in the Kimberley in Western Australia or those from Lascaux in southern France, almost always depict a spiritual, shamanistic world where spiritual forces operate alongside material realities. Recent research has found that this religious urge may be innate in human beings, not something that even needs to be taught. I interviewed Olivera Petrovich from the Department of Experimental Psychology at Oxford University about her investigations into the beliefs of young children in Japan and Britain. It turns out that kids across different cultures tend to believe that someone (rather than something) is responsible for the operations of the universe. You might expect this in Britain, where talk of God is still relatively common, but Petrovich found that children in Japan, where a creator is rarely discussed, believed in this "someone" at roughly the same rates as British children.[1]

Petrovich's research pre-empted a major three-year project exploring children's innate religious beliefs: 57 researchers were involved across 40 separate studies conducted in 20 countries. They concluded, among other things, that "the natural default position seems to be for children to think a nonhuman someone or someones are the best explanation for the apparent purpose and order in nature all around."[2]

This religious hunch in children is not like believing in Santa, as some of my sceptical friends like to joke. After all, no kid believes in Santa without being told about Santa, whereas the research suggests that children tend to believe in God or gods behind nature without being taught the idea. Moreover, plenty of people only come to believe in God in a meaningful way as adults. I'm not sure Santa has any adult converts! "That such belief [in God or gods] begins in childhood and typically endures into adulthood," writes Dr. Justin Barrett in *New Scientist*, "places it in the same class as believing in the permanence of solid objects, the continuity of time, the predictability of natural laws, the fact that causes precede effects, that people have minds, that their mothers love them and numerous others. If believing in gods is being childish in the same respect as holding these sorts of beliefs, then belief in gods is in good company."[3]

---

1 See the series of interviews at https://www.publicchristianity.org/person/olivera-petrovich/.

2 See Justin L. Barrett, *Born Believers: The Science of Children's Religious Belief* (Atria Books, 2012), 73.

3 Justin L. Barrett, "The God Issue: We are all born believers," *New Scientist*,

All of this is to say that religious questions are common sense—they are *common* to our humanity.

I want now to offer a few tips about how to get the most out of our exploration of the world religions. Some of the suggestions will be immediately obvious, whereas others may only appear helpful as you progress through the book.

TIP 1: ASSUME NOTHING

When studying religion, I have found it helpful—even if only as an experiment—to assume nothing about what the various faiths teach. Of course, we all have a vague idea of what they're on about: Jews avoid pork, Buddhists burn incense, and Muslims say prayers. But sometimes these obvious expressions of faith tell you very little about what the religion really teaches. In fact, they can even give entirely the wrong impression. Buddha would roll in his grave if he heard me say Buddhism has "something to do with burning incense." He was perhaps the least religious and ritualistic of all the founders of the great faiths.

Making assumptions about other religions can have the effect of lowering our tolerance for difficult concepts. When faced with an idea that appears a little complex—say, the central Buddhist belief that the human *self* does not exist—we may well give up trying to understand it and revert to our easier, perhaps simplistic, ideas about what the religion teaches: "Oh, Buddhism is all about tranquility and world peace!"

---

https://www.newscientist.com/article/mg21328562–000-the-god-issue-we-are
-all-born-believers/.

Unless you happen to be an expert in comparative religion, try to suspend all assumptions and preconceptions about religion as you make your way through this book. From experience, I think you might be surprised by the happy result.

TIP 2: THROW OUT THE CATEGORIES

Some books and courses on world religions try to fit the teachings of the various faiths into categories which are thought to be common to all world religions.

I've come across two forms of this approach. The first is found in Christian books about world religions. When I first became interested in the major faiths, twenty or so years ago, I read numerous books about Buddhism, Islam, and so on, all written by Christians, for Christians, and from the Christian perspective. Such books tend to describe non-Christian religions using the mental categories of Christianity, as I mentioned earlier. Because Christianity has a lot to say about sin, forgiveness, and eternal life, these books set out to analyse religions on the basis of these topics. Christian categories are imposed on non-Christian faiths. The authors asked questions such as: What does Buddhism teach about sin? How do Hindus understand forgiveness? What does a Jew do to receive eternal life? and so on.

This approach certainly succeeds in helping Christians feel better about their particular views on sin, forgiveness, and eternal life, but it does not help readers understand the world religions on their own terms and in their own categories. I've often wondered what it would look like if an author set out to describe Christianity from the perspective of the Buddhist concepts of self, karma, and rebirth. I imagine Christianity would be almost unrecognisable.

My point is that approaching the world religions on their own terms is the only way really to understand them. For my fellow Christian readers, I would add that this is also the only way to engage in meaningful conversation about Christ with those from other religions.

There is also a secular version of the attempt to fit all religions into predetermined categories. It, too, can obscure rather than clarify. One influential textbook in front of me describes the major faiths using the same six categories: sacred narrative, doctrine, ritual, institutional expression, experience, and ethics.

The categories are sometimes helpful. Most of the religions do have something to say about ethics, for instance. The problem is, presenting the faiths in these neat categories leaves the impression that the great world religions are all asking exactly the same questions, just arriving at different answers.

The reality is quite different. To give just one example, many forms of Hinduism have a lot to say about ritual—set prayers, regular offerings, mandatory ceremonies, and so on. Many forms of Christianity are, by comparison, ritual-less. Christianity's fastest-growing movements are the Evangelical and Pentecostal movements throughout Africa and Asia. In these traditions, "ritual" is almost looked down upon as inauthentic and merely traditional. So if I provided a chapter on Hinduism's rituals, followed by one on Christianity's rituals, I would obscure the relative emphases of the two religions. Readers would be left with the false impression that these faiths are simply different expressions of the same ritual instinct common to religion.

Imagine if I were to set out to write a book on five world sports— soccer, rugby, racing, judo, and synchronised swimming—and tried to explain them using a set of predetermined categories, let's say scoring, speed, force, training, playing field, and so on. I may be able to squeeze all the sports into these categories. But would this help readers understand each sport from its own perspective? I doubt it. The categories might help the appearance of coherence in my table of contents: The Use of Force in Judo; The Use of Force in Synchronised Swimming, and so on. But they probably would not help readers appreciate what it's like to perform the awesome Tomoe-nage on an opponent, or to execute a synchronised leg lift with twirl (I have only performed one of these manoeuvres). The concepts of force, scoring, and so on mean quite different things in each case. The various sports, you could say, are asking different things of their participants.

You will notice as you read on that very few of the same terms make an appearance across chapters, except where these terms are explicitly shared by the religions themselves. This may prove frustrating at times, since our natural tendency is to want to organise disparate ideas into coherent concepts. But it is my firm belief that in order to understand the world religions, we must resist the temptation to file their various teachings into predetermined categories.

TIP 3: ALLOW THE DIFFERENCES

I was asked at dinner party just last weekend about the similarities between the religions. It had come up in conversation that I was writing a book on the topic, and this rather sophisticated middle-aged gentleman, with white wine in hand, piped up: "If one set out the beliefs of the world religions in a kind of spreadsheet grid and shaded in those boxes where their teachings overlapped, would there be any unshaded areas?" I surprised him by replying, perhaps a little provocatively, "There would be far more unshaded boxes than shaded ones—not much overlap at all!"

As it turns out, this gentleman's wife was due to attend a day-long course on world religions the very next weekend. She was hoping, she explained to me, to discover what all the great faiths had in common. I think I disappointed her. The topic of conversation changed very quickly.

It was perhaps a little mischievous of me to say that the imagined religious spreadsheet would be mostly white spaces, but it is not far from the truth. One of the real keys to understanding the world religions, I believe, is to allow them to have their differences.

It is very popular today to emphasise the sameness of the great faiths. This is partly motivated by a desire to get along with and to connect to each other as fellow members of the human family. It is also partly motivated by ignorance of the blissful kind. At a great distance, most people look pretty much the same. Close up, however, it's a different story. Along similar lines, I find it humorous whenever I hear people from Asia say that Westerners "all look the same" (there is also a reverse Western-Asian claim, of course). It reminds me that if you don't mix with people from different races, you will have no eye for detail. The same is true with religion. The statement, "All religions are basically the same," is born of the same lack of acquaintance as "All Asians look the same."

At a distance, it probably does seem as though Hinduism, Buddhism, Judaism, Christianity, and Islam teach many of the same things. They all have beautiful buildings of worship, they all teach that we should be nice to people, and they all offer prayers to a divinity (well, almost all of them). When one begins to look more closely, however, it becomes clear that the religions are only superficially similar. They are substantially different.

By seeking to affirm the sameness of the world religions, modern societies like ours are in danger of honouring none of them. If we squash distinctions between them and quash debate about them, we are not really listening to them. As unpopular as the idea appears to have become, we simply must allow the world religions to have their distinct voices and to express their (often very) different points of view.

WHY THE "BIG FIVE"?

You've probably worked out already that I intend to focus on just five religions: Hinduism, Buddhism, Judaism, Christianity, and Islam. The rationale for including four of these is simple. Numerically, they are the largest world religions: in descending order, Christianity, Islam, Hinduism, and Buddhism. The fifth largest religion is actually Sikhism, with an estimated 28 million Sikhs in the world as of 2020 (according to Boston University's prestigious World Religions Database [WRD], from which I will draw my numbers[4]).

So why include Judaism over Sikhism, when Jews comprise the sixth largest religion with just 15 million adherents? First, despite its smaller numbers, Judaism is found in reportable numbers in 147 countries worldwide, making it more "international" than both Sikhism (64 countries) and even Hinduism (140 countries). Buddhism is found in 150 countries, Islam in 218 countries, and Christianity in all 234 countries listed by Boston University's World Religions Database (2020).

---

4 Visit www.worldreligiondatabase.org.

Tradition	Number of adherents	Percentage of world population	Number of countries in which it is found
Christianity (Christians)	2.5 billion	32 percent	234
Islam (Muslims)	1.9 billion	24 percent	218
Hinduism (Hindus)	1.1 billion	14 percent	140
Agnostic / Atheist	879 million	11 percent	234
Buddhism (Buddhists)	546 million	7 percent	150
Sikhism (Sikhs)	28, million	0.36 percent	64
Judaism (Jews)	15 million	0.19 percent	147

The second reason for including Judaism (over Sikhism) in our Western context is perhaps a little more subjective. The words *Israel* and *Jew* feature almost every day on our TV screens, as we hear of increased tensions, peace deals, and anti-Semitic attacks (which, sadly, have been on the rise in recent years). A deeper knowledge of the Jewish worldview is, I think, necessary in our times.

A third reason for including Judaism is its significance for the two largest world religions. Islam and especially Christianity grew out of Jewish belief. The faith of Israel, in other words, has influenced the religious landscape of the world out of proportion to its numerical size.

So with humble apologies to my Sikh readers (who, fortunately for me, believe in showing mercy), let's begin this doubter's guide to world religions with an account of the oldest of the great faiths.

PART 2
HINDUISM, THE WAY OF RELEASE
IN A NUTSHELL

Hinduism is a terrifically diverse way of life which has thrived mainly throughout India for millennia. At its heart, Hinduism teaches the wisdom and duties necessary to be released from the tragic cycle of life-death-rebirth so that one's true self may return to Brahman, the ultimate source of life.

3
ORIGINS OF THE "ETERNAL RELIGION"

When someone mentions Christianity, you know immediately it has something to do with a person known as "Christ." When we say "Buddhism," we think of that happy round fellow of many famous Asian statues (actually, Buddha was probably not "round" at all, but let's not worry about that now).

When we come to Hinduism, things are not so simple. The name tells you nothing about the content. There was no such person as "Hindu." To complicate things further, people in India don't typically refer to their religion as "Hinduism." It is strange to think that the average Hindu (and there are about a billion of them, by the way) living in, say, rural Uttar Pradesh may never have heard of a thing called "Hinduism."

The term *Hinduism* came into Western usage via British writers in India in the 1800s who couldn't think of an appropriate term to describe the array of spiritual beliefs and practices they saw around them. To get technical for a moment, the word *Hindu* comes from the name of the great Indus River, which runs along the entire northwest border of India (the word *India* also comes from *Indus*). Calling Hinduism "Hinduism," then, is about as helpful as calling

Native American beliefs "Mississippism" or Indigenous Australian beliefs "Murrumbidgism."

The fact that these nineteenth-century writers could not come up with a better name for Indian religion perhaps illustrates something important to this chapter: Hinduism is not one neat, easily understood religious system. More than any other tradition discussed in this book, Hinduism is a cocktail of rituals, beliefs, practices, and exercises (yoga, remember!) with no historical founder and no institutional hierarchy—there is no pope or Dalai Lama in Hinduism.

"Cocktail" is not intended as a flippant description, because the official religion of India can be compared (hopefully without any offence to Hindus) to an enormous party full of colours, music, food, and dancing. Some at the party are loud and boisterous, others are deep in conversation. Still others are sitting by themselves, gazing into the air—and they are perfectly happy about it, too.

For simplicity's sake, we're going to use the word "Hinduism" throughout this book, but please keep in mind that the collection of traditions described here is just that—a "collection," a fascinating, daring, and (for some Westerners) bewildering assortment of ideas and activities.

So where did it all begin?

THE OLDEST RELIGION IN THE WORLD?

What is called "Hinduism" in the West is known as *sanatana dharma* in India. These words—which come from ancient Sanskrit—mean "eternal law/religion." Whether or not the religion is literally "eternal" is for others to judge. One thing is certain: Hinduism is very,

very old. In fact, scholars usually identify Hinduism as the oldest of the world religions. Orthodox Jews might have a problem with this description, since the fathers of the Jewish faith—Joseph (1700s BCE), Abraham (1800s BCE), and Noah (well, who knows?)—are also very ancient. Nevertheless, it is conventional to think of Judaism in the official sense as beginning with Moses (of the Ten Commandments fame) sometime in the 1300s–1200s BCE.

Hinduism pips Judaism at the post, then, by just a few hundred years, with the story of the formalisation of Indian religion beginning around 1500 BCE. In secular scholarship, it has been common to state that Hinduism started when nomadic or invading Aryan tribes (originally from Persia) settled in the Indus Valley in the northwest of India, bringing their religion with them. This Aryan religion (*aryan* means "noble") is known as Vedism, and is said to be the basis, or first layer, of what we would eventually call "Hinduism."

This theory—which I myself used to teach—is viewed with suspicion by many Hindu scholars, who argue instead that the "noble ones," or Aryans, were indigenous to the Indus Valley region, and that they developed their own rituals and beliefs, which then spread throughout India.

From the Vedism of these early "noble ones" to the full-blown religion of Hinduism, there was a long history of reflection and development. The best way to appreciate this development is to think of Hinduism as being made up of three layers (or ingredients in a cocktail, to push my metaphor perhaps too far). These layers correspond to three slightly overlapping periods in Indian history, each with its own set of sacred writings: the Vedas (1500–500 BCE), the Upanishads (1000–300 BCE), and the Smriti writings (500

BCE–300 CE). Don't worry about these names and dates right now; just remember that, taken together, these three interlocking traditions constitute India's "eternal religion."

We begin with the first ingredient in the cocktail that is Hinduism, the ancient writings known as the Vedas.

4

GODS, DRUGS, AND
SACRIFICE: THE VEDAS

The word *veda* means something like "wisdom" of the sacred kind. Because of this, the term Vedas (with a capital *V*) is often used to refer to all of the Hindu scriptures, a little like the way Christians talk about the Bible (a word that really just means "book").

But there is a stricter meaning of the term Vedas. Many Hindus use the word to refer only to the earliest writings of Hinduism, those formally compiled between 1500–500 BCE and reflecting the original vedic religion of the "noble ones" of the Indus Valley mentioned in the last chapter. This is the way I will use the word throughout this chapter. The later writings, which we will explore in a moment, have their own important names and categorisation.

There are four basic Vedas (in this strict sense), which in published form would fill a bookshelf:

1. Wisdom of Verses (Rig-veda). This is a collection of about one thousand hymns that were sung in connection with ancient rituals designed to keep the gods in favour. Animal sacrifices and fire offerings, as well as the drinking of hallucinogenic

> plant juice, were all part of the highly complex "liturgy" (or act of worship) described here.

2. Wisdom of the Sacrificial Formulas (Yajur-veda). This contains the words that were to be said by a priest as these rituals took place. The words often involved praise of the gods.

3. Wisdom of the Chants (Sama-veda). This mainly contains verses from the first Veda (*Rig-veda*) but with indications of how they are to be chanted with fixed melodies.

4. Wisdom of the Atharvan Priests (Atharva-veda). This is a little bit different from (and was probably written later than) the first three. It is a collection of hymns, prayers, and curses of a more "magical" nature.

Attached to these four Vedas are various discussions, explanations, and amplifications of the rituals. These extensions are known as the Brahmanas, the Aranyakas, and the Upanishads, and they were written later than the original collections. These extensions mark a clear development in the outlook of the early vedic material. This is particularly the case in the Upanishads, which will be discussed in the next section.

For now, we should ask, what aspects of Hinduism are revealed in this first layer, the Vedas? Two ideas deserve mention.

LOTS OF GODS

One of the most striking aspects of the religious outlook of the Vedas is a belief in a great variety of gods or expressions of God. This is sometimes called *polytheism* (Greek for "many gods"), but the Hindu concept of God and gods is more complicated than it first appears. Hinduism is different from both traditional monotheistic ("one God") religions like Judaism and Islam, and from traditional polytheistic religions, such as those of ancient Greece and Rome, where each deity had its own individual existence and personality.

The world of the Vedas is full of powerful, unpredictable beings, usually called *devas*. There are about one thousand devas mentioned by name in the Vedas. Some are decent, some are evil, and all of them deserve the respect of human beings. The main devas of early Hindu thought include Indra, the warrior and storm god; Agni, the god of fire; and Soma, a god associated with the plant juice the priest drinks in one of the main vedic rituals. Other deities such as Vishnu and Siva (also spelt Shiva) make minor appearances in the Vedas but will later come to dominate the religious landscape. Indeed, in later Hinduism, Vishnu will come to be seen by many as the supreme god who manifests himself through various *avatars* (meaning "descent" or "incarnation"), such as Krishna or Rama. Krishna and Rama are not additional "gods" but manifestations of supreme Vishnu. But that's getting ahead of ourselves.

For now, it is just worth noticing that Indian religion began with a belief in many divine beings, each with its own role to play in the cosmos. This feature still exists in modern Hinduism but in a quite different way, as we will see.

RITUALS AND SACRIFICE

At least two rituals were vitally important in the ancient Vedas. The first is the Soma ritual. This involved a priest taking the juice of a now-unknown plant and pouring it over an altar. The priest also drank some of the drug and literally got high. The intoxicating effect of the juice was believed to be divine. It thus gave special powers and favours to the worshippers: "We have drunk the Soma; we have become immortal; we have gone to the light; we have found the gods" (Wisdom of the Verses, or Rig-veda 8:48.1–8 [Doniger]).

The second important ritual in the Vedas is the fire ritual. A priest places an animal on the altar and sets it alight. The fire is considered to be the manifestation of Agni (the fire deva), who consumes the sacrifice on behalf of the other divine beings. When the sacrifice is accepted by Agni deva (burnt up by the flames), divine blessings will be granted to the worshippers. To this day in India, many upper-class families (or Brahmans) maintain a small household fire in honour of the Agni deva. It is amazing to think that a custom which started three and half thousand years ago is still practised today.

The Vedas on the Fire Deity Agni

Now get dressed in your robes, lord of powers and master of the sacrificial food, and offer this sacrifice for us. Young Agni, take your place as our favourite priest with inspirations and shining speech. The father sacrifices for his son, the comrade for his comrade, the favourite friend for his friend. May Varuṇa, Mitra and Aryaman, proud of their powers, sit upon our sacred grass, as upon Manu's. You who were the first to invoke, rejoice in our friendship and hear only these songs. When we offer sacrifice to this god or that god, in the full line of order, it is to you alone that the oblation is offered. Let him be a beloved lord of tribes for us, a favourite, kindly invoker; let us have a good fire and be beloved. For when the gods have a good fire, they bring us what we wish for. Let us pray with a good fire. So let praises flow back and forth between the two, between us who are mortals and you, the immortal. Agni, young spawn of strength, with all the fires take pleasure in this sacrifice and in this speech.

Wisdom of the Verses, or Rig-veda 1:26.1–10 (Doniger).

Other rituals from the Vedas which still exist in Hinduism today include the Indian wedding ceremony (the oldest in the world) and the common Hindu practice of ceremonially cremating the dead. Temple worship and offerings, reminiscent of the ancient vedic rituals, still feature prominently in Indian religious life.

Indian religion developed out of the Vedas, and belief in these writings is still a basic tenet of Hinduism. However, Hinduism did not limit itself to the ideas found in these ancient scriptures. Some of the most important themes of Hinduism were still to come. These emerged not out of the vedic material but out of what Hindus call the Vedanta, or "conclusion of the Vedas," a term used to describe another set of written traditions known as the Upanishads.

5

GOD, THE SOUL, AND ENTRAPMENT: THE UPANISHADS

The term Upanishad literally means "sitting near." It is an allusion to sitting in a class, learning from the great teachers of India. And that is exactly what these writings are about. During the period after the writing of the early Vedas, many Indian gurus began to reflect deeply on the content of their religion and sought to make sense of the world in light of that tradition. What these gurus came up with is recorded in the twelve classical Upanishads (composed between 1000–300 BCE). These are regarded by many as the real sacred writings of Hinduism. Certainly in terms of their philosophical contribution to Hinduism, the Upanishads far outweigh the Vedas.

The Upanishads contain parables and anecdotes, dense philosophical argumentation, dialogues, poems, and proverbs. Behind it all, however, stands the claim that reading this material (and, of course, understanding it) will give you ultimate insight into life, the universe, and (literally) everything. My little book can't promise you that much, but I can point you in the direction of four of the most important beliefs that crystallise in the Upanishads.

BRAHMAN: THE ONE BEHIND THE MANY

Already in the Wisdom of the Verses, the oldest of the Hindu writings, there is occasional reference to a mysterious background force in the universe known as *brahman*. Think perhaps of the "force" in the Star Wars movies. Little is made of brahman in these early scriptures, except that the priest who conducts the rituals is himself also called a brahman. The idea is that the priest is connected to the life force of the universe. He is, therefore, able to harness its power for the sake of the worshippers.

In the later Upanishads, however, brahman experiences something of a magnification. From the status of a cosmic background power, Brahman (now it needs a capital B) is elevated to the level of the ultimate and (for many) only reality in the universe. From Brahman everything in the universe came; to Brahman everything in the universe will return.

Brahman is a difficult concept to grasp for people brought up in the Western world. Westerners can cope with the idea of a physical universe, and they can cope with the concept of a universal personal God. But when these two concepts are brought together into one mega idea, we begin to scratch our heads. In India, however, the idea of the One (Brahman) is a key aspect of a person's upbringing. It is part of the way Hindus look at the world. This is sometimes called *pantheism*, from the Greek for "God as everything." Whether or not this Western philosophical terminology is strictly accurate can be debated—Western categories are not always sufficient for Eastern concepts, and vice versa. For now, it is probably accurate enough to say that most Hindus see the divine reality in and through everything.

The analogy of a fire might help. A fire produces sparks which flit about for a while and then disappear, perhaps back into the flame from which they came. There is a sense in which the spark and the flame are both separate and not separate. They are separate in the sense that the spark is visible independently of the flame, but they are not separate inasmuch as the spark came from the flame, is made of the same stuff as the fire, and ultimately returns to the flame, where it is absorbed back into its source. This is something like the way Hinduism understands the universe. Brahman is the flame from which everything originates—creation, humans, the gods, and so on. All these things flicker for a while, and then they return to their source where they are absorbed into the ultimate and true reality.

Is Brahman "God" in the Western sense of that word? In some texts, some of the time, it comes close. There are "monotheistic" versions of Hinduism, where only one god (Brahman, worshipped as Vishnu) exists and is worthy of praise. In other texts, not so much. It is not consistently clear in the Upanishads whether or not we are to think of Brahman as a conscious and personal being. Most Hindus do believe in personal gods, but they don't usually have Brahman in mind or on their lips. Instead, they focus their worship on one of Brahman's emanations, such as Vishnu, who embodies the *preserving* aspects of ultimate reality, or Siva, who embodies both the *fertile* and *destructive* aspects of ultimate reality. According to the teaching of the Upanishads, these more personal deities are themselves "sparks" from the ultimately unfathomable flame which is Brahman. No single deva or god could fully embody the boundless nature of ultimate reality.

Fairly consistently in the Upanishads, Brahman is beyond attributes, beyond description, and therefore impersonal. This posed philosophical issues for those Hindus who wanted to maintain the notion of relationship with the ultimate. How do you have a relationship when there is ultimately only one thing? There are three traditional answers to this dilemma.

Trimurti: Some teachers proposed that the gods Brahma, Vishnu, and Siva (a kind of Hindu trinity, called *Trimurti*) were the three ultimate manifested aspects of Brahman. This trinity brought the indescribable into focus so as to allow some form of personal relationship with ultimate Brahman through Brahman's three fundamental manifestations.

Visist-advaita school: Others proposed that Brahman somehow bears within itself the characteristic of relationship—that relationship is part of the unified reality of the ultimate. *Visist* means "distinct" and *advaita* means "not-dual." So this Visist-advaita school of Hinduism holds that while Brahman is everything (not-dual), other beings have a measure of "distinct" existence which wholly depends upon Brahman. Other beings, including ourselves, are modes of Brahman's existence; they are like Brahman's "body" in the universe. The school of thought is usually associated with Ramanuja (1017–1137 CE), a great South Indian Brahman theologian and philosopher. His writings were influential in the rise of the practice of *bhakti*, or devotion to gods, which we will discuss later. This school is a modification (one might say rejection) of the absolute non-dualist understanding of Brahman known as the Advaita school.

Advaita school: this non-dual school insists that notions such as relationship and particularity are illusions. The leading proponent of Advaita Hinduism is the great Sankara (circa 700–750 CE). His influence is probably unparalleled in the history of the development of Hindu thought. Even today, his philosophical framework is pervasive in India.

Sankara wrote vast commentaries on the Upanishads in which he outlined his belief in one eternal unchanging reality, Brahman, and his rejection of notions such as differentiation and plurality. Helping people to realise that there is nothing but Brahman was the goal of his philosophical program.

As I have hinted at already, it should be noted that many contemporary Indians choose to believe in the existence of a single God, and they regard the traditional emanations of God (Siva, et al.) as metaphors of different aspects of the divine character. It can be debated how much this approach depends on themes internal to historic Hinduism and how much it owes to the complex interactions between India and Britain (and, therefore, British monotheism) since the late 1700s.[1]

ATMAN: THE SOUL AND THE SOUL

Connected to the idea of Brahman is the concept of the *atman*, or soul. This is the "inner you," the real, eternal life force which exists in every living creature.

The Upanishads teach that this real you—as opposed to your mere physical and psychological characteristics—is a reflection of the ultimate force, Brahman. It is a "spark" from the big flame.

The Hindu concept of the atman mustn't be confused with Western ideas about the human soul or spirit, which is thought to

---

1 See the discussion in P. Mitter, "Rammohun Roy and the New Language of Monotheism," *History and Anthropology* 3, no. 1 (1987): 177–208.

go to heaven when we die. Atman is more a life-principle which animates your existence. It is the eternal YOU which lies behind your everyday consciousness, and survives your personal existence. If you think this sounds vaguely like the concept of Brahman, you are right. The atman is that part of you which is from Brahman.

The Upanishads on Brahman and the Atman

What is called Brahman, that is what this space outside a man is, and what that space outside of a man is, that is what this space within a man is; and what that space within a man is, that is what this space within the heart is. That is the "full"—inactive, undeveloping. Whoso knows this wins good fortune, full inactive, undeveloping . . . All works, all desires, all scents, all tastes belong to it: it encompasses all this universe, does not speak and has no care. This my Self within the heart is that Brahman. When I depart from hence I will merge into it. He who believes this shall never doubt.

Chandogya Upanishad 3.12–17 (Goodall).

It is very important that we get our heads around the idea that this real you (the atman) corresponds to the ultimate reality behind the universe (or Brahman). But as I pointed out above, the great "schools" of Hinduism disagree over the precise connection between atman and Brahman. In the non-dualism school (Advaita), these are not two things but one. Your atman really is Brahman, and its destiny is absorption into Brahman. However, in the distinct non-dualism school (Visist-advaita), your atman and Brahman are not completely identical. The "spark"—while constitutionally existing through the "flame"—is not exactly the same thing as the "flame."

Understanding that atman and its connection with Brahman provides the basis for understanding the Hindu concepts of entrapment and liberation. In Hinduism, the goal of life is to free the atman (the real you) from the impurities of worldly existence so that it might return to Brahman as a spark returns to its flame. First, we will talk about the "trap" we are all in according to Hinduism, and then we will explore the escape.

SAMSARA: ENTRAPMENT IN AN ENDLESS CYCLE

In Western cultures, reincarnation (bodily re-existence in this world after death) is often thought of as an exciting experience: "I was an Amazon Queen in a former life," or "I hope I come back as an eagle," and so on. From the point of view of Hinduism, statements like these involve a basic misunderstanding of the important idea of *samsara* ("the running around"). Samsara refers to the potentially endless snare of being born in this physical world, dying, and then having to be reborn. It is a snare that catches all living beings, even insects. It is an "entrapment."

The Upanishads describe this cycle of birth-death-and-rebirth not as an opportunity to "come back and have another go" but as a regurgitation into the harsh realities of physical existence. At best, this existence is fleeting and false; at worst, it is evil and impure. The realities of earthly existence (and re-existence) are described by the gurus of the Upanishads as a foul stench unpleasantly attaching themselves to your true soul (your atman) which is trapped in this physical world.

At this point, you may be thinking, "But I like my life: it's rich, fun, and full of friendship and things to learn." The teachers of the Upanishads would reply that such thinking is short-sighted and ultimately tragic. Why would a little "spark" want to remain a spark when it could return to the great flame from which it had come? Why would it not want to experience the fullness of its own true nature by uniting with its source?

So what is the cause of this entrapment in the cycle of birth, death, and rebirth? What is it that makes the "stench" fix itself upon our souls, preventing us from returning to the purity of our source, Brahman? The answer: karma.

KARMA: THE POWER BEHIND ENTRAPMENT

The concept of being "trapped" is better understood when we look at the connected idea of *karma*. Literally, this word means "action," but it includes the idea of the consequences of action as well. Karma is sometimes translated in the Hindu scriptures (in English) as "fruititive action"—action which bears fruit.

Karma is one of those well-used words in Western society: people experience a bit of bad luck and sometimes say, "Oh, bad karma." Or they may witness someone doing a "good deed" and declare, "There's some good karma waiting for you!"

This popular understanding of karma is actually not too far off the mark. In short, the Hindu teaching about karma (Buddhism has its own version) insists that all of your actions in life "attach" themselves to you. They stick to your soul in such a way as to determine your soul's re-existence, your next incarnation.

The Upanishads on Karma and Reincarnation

As a man acts, as he behaves, so does he become. Whoever does good, becomes good: whoever does evil, becomes evil. By good works a man becomes holy, by evil he becomes evil. On this there is this verse: To what his mind and character are attached, to that attached a man goes with his works. Whatever deeds he does on earth, their rewards he reaps. From the other world he comes back here—to the world of deed and work.

Brhadaranyaka Upanishad 4.4.5–6 (Goodall).

You may have heard people joke about someone deserving to come back as a cockroach: in orthodox Hinduism, this is a real possibility.

To understand all these ideas properly, we have to realise that coming back as something a little bit better in the next life (let's say a wealthy rock star or a beautiful princess) is not, strictly speaking, a good thing. It is just the lesser of two evils. The ultimate goal for the Hindu is not to come back as something better next time around; it is to escape the need to come back at all. According to the teaching of the Upanishads, even wealthy rock stars and princesses (not a topic of discussion among the gurus) are trapped in the unreality of existence. The rich and famous, just like the rest of us, are unable to feel the warmth or see the light of the ultimate flame of Brahman. Something better than "good karma" is needed for true liberation.

MOKSHA: RELEASE INTO ULTIMATE REALITY

If karma and entrapment are the bad news of Hinduism, what's the good news? The answer lies in another important teaching of the Upanishads, the idea of *moksha*.

Once we understand the concepts of karma and entrapment, the idea of moksha doesn't require much explanation. Moksha is simply "release" from the futile cycle of re-existence (caused by karma), so that you can enter into the reality of Brahman, the source of true existence. As Svetasvatara Upanishad 1.7 says: "Brahman-knowers become merged in Brahman, intent thereon, liberated from the womb (i.e., from rebirth)."

This liberation is likened in the Upanishads to a snake shedding its skin, a drop of water falling into the ocean, and, as I have already said, a spark returning to its flame. Your previously trapped soul is reabsorbed into the ultimate reality of Brahman. For Hindus who maintain some distinction between your atman and Brahman (Visist-advaita), this "release" is not so much a reabsorption which smothers the atman's existence; it is more like a unifying of the atman and Brahman.

Is this release like Western notions of heaven? Yes and no. Usually, when people speak about heaven (more about that later), they mean a place where individuals consciously enjoy each other and God as wholly distinct beings in relationship with one another. This is not typically what Hinduism envisages when it speaks of release from entrapment. In fact, according to some forms of orthodox Hinduism, the notion of individual personality is part of your ignorant separation from Brahman. According to other forms, however, being released to Brahman does destroy one's own sense of existence. Release, or moksha, at its heart involves the unity of your soul with the ultimate soul.

Will you be conscious in this experience of release? Hinduism gives different answers to this question, and it depends on what you mean by *you* and *conscious*. It is probably true to say that the *you* reading this book, complete with all your memories of this life, will not be individually conscious when unified with Brahman. However, since Brahman is "pure consciousness," being united to that reality will be more about gaining true consciousness (Brahman's consciousness) than losing your current consciousness. A spark returning to the flame may lose something of its individual shape, colour, and warmth, but it gains the greater shape, colour, and warmth of the flame. The Hindu concept of release (moksha) is somewhat similar—though, as I have been stressing, the Advaita and Visist-advaita schools have different ways of conceiving these things.

The Upanishads on Moksha, "Release"

Now we come to the man without desire: He is devoid of desire, free from desire; all his desires have been fulfilled: the Self alone is his desire . . . Being very Brahman to Brahman does he go. On this there is this verse: When all desires which shelter in the heart detach themselves, then does a mortal man become immortal: to Brahman he wins through. As the slough (i.e., the cast off skin) of a snake lies on an ant-hill, dead, cast off, so too does this body lie. Then is this incorporeal, immortal spirit Brahman indeed, light indeed . . . Free from evil, free from doubt, immaculate, he becomes a Brāhman (in very truth, for Brahman now indwells him). This, sire, is the Brahman-world, (this is the state of being which is Brahman). This it is which has been granted you.

Brhadaranyaka Upanishad 4.4.5–23 (Goodall).

How can we experience this *moksha*? What is the path to liberation? That is the subject of our next chapter.

6

CASTE, DUTY, AND SALVATION: THE SMRITI LITERATURE

So far we have been discussing ideas that emerge in the earliest and most authoritative writings of Hinduism, the Vedas and the Upanishads. These make up the first two layers of Hindu tradition. Hindus call this material *sruti*, which literally means "heard." This is a reference to the conviction that these teachings existed from eternity and were simply "heard" (and recorded) by certain gurus through a kind of divine revelation.

As a Trivial Pursuit™ aside, Hindus believe that the universe appears and disappears every twenty-four million years (twelve million years of existence followed by twelve million years of non-existence). According to Hindus, the Vedas (along with the Upanishads) are revealed to human teachers at the beginning of each new cosmic cycle.

"REMEMBERED" WRITINGS

The final scriptures to be discussed in this chapter are known as the *smriti* or "remembered" writings. These teachings have been passed down in a long line of human tradition. These "remembered" scriptures are usually regarded as less authoritative than the "heard" scriptures, but they are every bit as popular. Many would say even more so. These texts have had an enormous influence on the beliefs and practices of modern Hindus.

Most important among these "remembered" writings are two great epic poems known as the Romance of Rama (Ramayana), written sometime after 300 BCE, and the Great Epic of the Bharata Dynasty (Mahabharata), composed a century or more later.

The Romance of Rama is, of course, a "romance." It is a love story about Rama, a royal and divine figure, and his wife, Princess Sita. Throughout the narrative, there are contests with the gods, accusations of adultery, kidnapping (of Sita) by demons, and a daring rescue conducted by Rama and a warrior-monkey named Hanuman (It would make a marvellous film on the big screen. In fact, the 1990s movie version of Frances Hodgson Burnett's *A Little Princess* includes a delightful little film-within-the-film of part of the Ramayana). On the basis of this narrative, many in India still worship Rama as the god of virtue and chivalry. Hanuman, the monkey god, is also worshiped in India today, and monkeys (actual living ones) are widely revered as sacred. Type "temple monkeys" into Google, and you'll see what I mean.

THE BHAGAVAD-GITA, OR SONG OF THE LORD

Of more interest for understanding the key beliefs of Hinduism is the Great Epic of the Bharata Dynasty (*Mahabharata*). At the centre of this massive traditional epic is a battle between cousins, after which almost the entire race is destroyed. Just before the bloody battle, an extraordinary conversation breaks out between the hero of the story, Prince Arjuna, and his advisor, Krishna, who turns out to be an incarnation of the god Vishnu (one of the premiere emanations of ultimate Brahman, along with Siva and Brahma).

The poetic account of this conversation runs about seventy pages in my copy, and it forms what is known as the Bhagavad-gita ("the Song of the Lord"). This text is regarded by many as the most treasured portion of all the Hindu scriptures. It is certainly the most widely published. For this reason, it is important to talk a little more about the Bhagavad-gita and what it teaches.

Just before Prince Arjuna gets ready to slay the opposing armies, he pauses for a moment and begins to wonder whether it would be better to lay down his weapons and avoid shedding blood. Enter: the divine Krishna, the Prince's charioteer, who reveals to Arjuna the wisdom he needs to fulfil his duty. Taking Krishna's advice, Arjuna launches into battle and emerges the winner.

We mustn't think of the Bhagavad-gita as a simple justification of warfare. Many Hindus reject the path of violence. The purpose of this popular part of the Hindu scriptures is more religious than political. In the next few pages, we will discover just how much the Bhagavad-gita has influenced modern Hinduism.

THE FOUR CASTES OF PEOPLE

One of the important themes in the Bhagavad-gita is a concept that sounds quite foreign to egalitarian societies, such as my native Australia aspires to be. Here is one of those moments when understanding another person's point of view requires humility and open-mindedness.

As early as the first Vedas, the Hindu scriptures talked about human society (Indian society, at least) in four categories, or castes. In the Bhagavad-gita, the god Krishna endorses this hierarchical view of humanity in an important way.

The four *varnas*, or castes, of people are as follows:

1. Priests (Brahmans). Brahmans, sometimes spelled Brahmins, are regarded as the descendants of the original Vedic priests (1500 BCE). They form the top layer in Indian society and are considered blessed with nearness to the ultimate life principle of the universe, Brahman. They maintain a high level of religious purity by not participating in human activities—such as warfare or working the land—that cause spiritual uncleanness.

2. Warrior-kings (Ksatriya). Also prominent in the Vedas, and especially prominent in the Bhagavad-gita, are those who make up the second layer of Indian society, the "warrior-kings." These are thought by Hindus to be the descendants of the original commanders of the ancient Vedic state. Arjuna, the princely hero of the Bhagavad-gita, belonged to this caste. "Warrior-kings" in contemporary Indian society tend to occupy what we would call the "upper middle class."

3. Common people (Vaisyas). Still regarded as descendants of the original Indus Valley peoples, the "common people" make up the bulk of Indian society and are meant to be occupied with industry and economy. They are the "workers" of society, you might say: for example, farmers, merchants, bookkeepers, and so on.

4. Servants (Sudras). Hindu society regards the fourth caste of person as sharing little of the Vedic heritage. Their role is simply to serve the three upper castes of India. A "servant" can only hope that his or her karma will cause a "promotion" in the next life. Only by being born a "priest," "warrior-king," or "common person" does a person have a direct share in Brahman and a chance at release (moksha). If this sounds a little unfair, the Hindu scriptures would explain that the place of the "servant" at the bottom of Indian society is simply the outworking of universal karma. (In addition to these four main castes, there are also people classed avarna, those without a caste. These are below even the sudras or servants and are sometimes called "untouchables.")

The early Rig-Veda (Wisdom of the Verses) explains that these four varnas were created by the gods out of the body of the first (primal) man, Purusa. From his head came the Brahmans, from the arms came the Ksatriyas, from his thighs the Vaisyas, and from his feet the Sudras (other divisions within these varnas were also developed).

CASTE AND THE "TWICE-BORN" CEREMONY

The partial exclusion of the "servants" from Indian society (the "feet" of the primal man) is emphasised by the fact that only those from the three upper castes of India undergo the most important ceremony of a Hindu boy's life. The "twice-born" ceremony (the *dvija*) is perhaps the equivalent of baptism in Christianity, or the bar mitzvah in Judaism. The ceremony involves placing a sacred thread (like a sash) over the left shoulder of the child (eight years old for Brahmans, eleven for Ksatriyas, and fourteen for Vaisyas) and across his right hip. The ritual symbolises the child taking on his duties as a member of Hindu society. This is thought of as a "second birth." The servant caste in India, however, has no opportunity in this life for a second birth.

Having said all this, it must be pointed out that since the time of the (controversial) Indian activist Mahatma Gandhi (who died in 1948), traditional Hindu ideas about the castes have been greatly moderated among those who love him. Influenced by Gandhi, many modern Indians endorse a more egalitarian view of society than that advocated in these sacred writings. As a result, the popularity of the dvija ceremony has waned somewhat in contemporary Indian society. Some Hindus even reject the ritual as overly exclusive. On the other hand, it is also worth noting that many traditional Hindus do not accord Mahatma Gandhi—or these revisions—the same respect often accorded him in the West.

BACK TO THE BHAGAVAD-GITA

The idea of four castes, or varnas, is important to the Bhagavad-gita and provides the rationale for Krishna's instruction to Prince Arjuna that he should go into battle. After all, the prince belonged to the caste of warrior-kings: it was his place in life to work and fight for matters of state. To do otherwise would be to try to defy karma and reject his universally appointed duty, his dharma. Rejecting one's dharma forfeits one's hope of release (moksha).

In the process of instructing Arjuna about his duty (dharma), the god Krishna explains to the prince the three paths to liberation that are available to the faithful Hindu. Here is where the Bhagavad-gita makes its most significant contribution to Indian religion. Faithful Hindus today hope eventually to experience release by following one (or a combination) of these three *margas*, or paths.

The three paths are ways of escaping birth and rebirth and so returning to ultimate Brahman. Each path has the name yoga attached to it, because yoga means "oneness" or "unity," that is, unity with Brahman. Let me briefly explain the three paths.

PATH OF DUTIES (KARMA-YOGA)

As already mentioned, Krishna explained to Prince Arjuna that it was his duty in life, his *dharma*, to fight for the interests of the state. One of the paths of salvation open to Arjuna—and to all Hindus—is faithfully to continue performing one's duty.

Two aspects of this duty have to be kept in mind to understand this path to liberation. First, one's dharma ("duty/law") is largely governed by what caste you're from. Even a so-called good deed, says Krishna in the Bhagavad-Gita is of no value if it is not a deed appropriate to your caste. Hence, although Arjuna's desire to lay down arms seemed like a nice thing to do, it was not beneficial to his liberation. Why? Because it would have been a rejection of his duty as a member of the warrior-king caste. Only actions in accordance with the duties of your caste lead to your release.

The second thing to keep in mind is that one's actions must be performed with *detachment*. In other words, your actions must be done *without desire or intention for a particular outcome*. This is a difficult concept, but Krishna in the Bhagavad-Gita insists on it: "Remaining always unattached, you should therefore perform your prescribed duty. A person who performs such duty without attachment attains the highest goal" (*Bhagavad-Gita* 3.19 [Sutton]).[1] The logic goes like this: The thing that traps you in this world of birth and rebirth is not activity per se but "fruititive activity," that is, activity done with a desire for certain outcomes. Of course, every action has its result, but only an action done *with a result in mind* taints your soul and traps you in this world of birth and rebirth. This is just how the universe works: it is the natural law. However, actions performed by you without attachment to a particular outcome are "empty" actions and so attract no karmic effects. As a result, you can be freed from this world and so return to Brahman.

But what exactly are the appropriate actions which I must perform with no mind to the results? Further "remembered" writings (smriti) emerged in Hinduism to answer that question. These are known as *dharmasutras* ("threads of duty"). Among the most famous of these are *The Laws of Manu* (first century BCE) and the *Law Book of Yajnavalkya* (fourth century CE). They outline in great detail the duties of the various castes of Indian society.

Duties of the Married Man according to Law Book of Yajnavalkya

A married man should daily perform ritual action prescribed in texts of secondary authority (*karma smāram*) in the fire [set at the time] of the marriage or inherited at the time of the distribution [of

---

1 *Bhagavad-Gita* 3.19.

the family's wealth]. The ritual action prescribed in Vedic scripture (*śrautam*) [he should perform only] in the sacred Vedic fires. When he has dealt with bodily considerations and done what is prescribed for his cleanliness, a twice born man should attend to the rite prescribed at the morning junction after cleaning his teeth. After making obligations into the fires he should with focused mind, recite mantras dedicated to the sun. And [then] he should study the meaning of the Vedas and diverse treatises . . . He should not cook food [just] for himself. After feeding children, married woman living in their father's household, the elderly, pregnant woman, the sick, girls, guests, and servants, the husband and wife should eat what remains.

Law Book of Yajnavalkya 97–106 (Goodall).

PATH OF KNOWLEDGE (JNANA-YOGA)

Krishna explains to Arjuna another path of liberation open to the faithful Hindu. This one had already featured prominently in the Upanishads. It is the Path of Knowledge.

As we have already seen, the Upanishads teach that your atman (life principle or soul) is made of the same or similar stuff, so to speak, as Brahman. The problem is, the atman is trapped by karma in the cycle of birth and rebirth (samsara) and is unable to unite with Brahman. The teachers of the Upanishads insisted that contemplation, combined with rigorous self-denial, could lead to the mental realisation of your soul's oneness with Brahman. This is the Hindu ascetic path, and Krishna in the

Bhagavad-Gita endorses it, while also pointing out that it is very, very difficult to achieve.

The Bhagavad-Gita on the Path of Knowledge (Jnana-Yoga)

Yoga (*jnana-yoga*) must be performed with firm resolve and with a state of mind free from despondency. This should be done whilst giving up all the desires that arise from material inclinations and restraining the entire group of senses by means of the mind alone. One should undertake this withdrawal little by little, using the resolutely focused intellect. Fixing the mind in conjunction with the atman, one should not think of any other object. One must withdraw the wavering, unsteady mind from wherever it wanders and bring it back under control, fixed on the atman alone. The highest joy comes to that yogin whose mind is tranquil, whose passions are quieted, who exists as Brahman, and who has no blemish. Engaging himself constantly in this pursuit, the yogin who is free of blemish easily makes contact with Brahman and acquires endless joy.

Bhagavad-Gita 6.23–30 (Sutton).

The Path of Knowledge is different from the Path of Duties. Instead of trying to act with detachment, this jnana-yoga tries to avoid action altogether. Bodily comforts are denied, the ancient scriptures are recited, and mystical states of mind are attained (through yoga exercises and meditation). Through these practices, ascetics are able to rise above the karmic effects which tie them to this world, and so they unite with Brahman directly. They are released.

PATH OF DEVOTION (BHAKTI-YOGA)

The third path to salvation is one without much precedent in the earlier writings of Hinduism. Krishna in the Bhagavad-gita reveals to Prince Arjuna a "shortcut" (although a Hindu would not use that term) out of the trap of existence–and–re-existence and into the reality of Brahman. Faithful Hindus, says Krishna, can escape entrapment by devoting themselves utterly to one of the great manifestations of divinity (preferably to Krishna).

The Bhagavad-Gita on the Superiority of the Path of Devotion (Bhakti-Yoga)

The Lord (Krishna) said: In My opinion, those who fix their minds on me, who constantly engage in serving me and who possess absolute faith are engaged in the best way possible (bhakti-yoga). But those who (following jnana-yoga) dedicate themselves to the non-deteriorating, indeterminate, non-manifest feature, which is present everywhere, is unknowable, and is situated in the transcendent realm, unmoving and constant, Who control their senses and who are equal-minded in all ways, also attain me, delighting as they do in the welfare of all beings. But there is greater difficulty involved for those whose thoughts adhere to the non-manifest feature. For embodied beings, the way to the non-manifest feature is one of suffering. But for those who are devoted to me (bhakti-yoga), who surrender all their actions to me, who worship me and meditate on me through single-pointed yoga,

I become without delay the deliverer from the ocean of death and rebirth, Partha, for their consciousness is absorbed in me.

Bhagavad-Gita 12.1–7 (Sutton).

If you perform all your actions in this world with absolute devotion to Krishna (or some other avatar) he will deliver you from the effects of karma, and you will be free.

Prince Arjuna liked the idea of the Path of Devotion. Having heard the teaching and witnessed a vision of the glory of Krishna (as the embodiment of Lord Vishnu), Arjuna humbly devoted himself to Krishna.

What forms can this "devotion" take? For some, devotion is thought of in deeply *personal* and *emotional* terms: you are to feel intense love and affection for your "favourite god" (your *istadevata*) in all your daily affairs. For others, devotion can take a more *ritualistic* form: paying homage to your god in an act of temple worship, such as offering food or money to the deity. Shrines are often set up in the home for this purpose.

The Path of Devotion, or bhakti, is probably the dominant form of Hinduism in India today, and two gods stand head and shoulders above the rest in terms of sheer numbers of devotees. These are Vishnu and Siva (and their various avatars). From these gods derive the names of the two great "schools" or "denominations" of modern Hinduism. After a brief explanation of these two traditions, we can bring our exploration of Hinduism to a close.

DEVOTION TO VISHNU (VAISHNAVISM)

Vaishnavism is the term used to describe the many different groups in India that are devoted to the god Vishnu and his various avatars (such as Krishna). Worshippers tend to take what they like from the epics of his incarnations (such as the Mahabharata, mentioned earlier) and blend these stories with local customs to produce elaborate practices of worship.

Traditionally, Vishnu is said to have had ten "descents" or avatars, sometimes appearing in animal form, sometimes in human form. The two most popular avatars—and, therefore, objects of devotion—are Rama (of Romance of Rama fame) and Krishna (of Bhagavad-Gita fame).

Vishnu is thought to embody the preserving qualities of Brahman. He and his avatars are thus worshipped as the deities who are active in society for good. Through devotion to Vishnu, the faithful hope eventually to escape birth-and-rebirth and experience release.

DEVOTION TO SIVA (SAIVISM)

Saivism is the term used to describe the many groups in India that devote themselves to the god Siva and his various incarnations. Again, in the great epics of the remembered writings (smriti), worshippers find ample reasons to praise and revere Siva.

Siva is quite different from Vishnu, even though both shine forth from ultimate Brahman. Whereas Vishnu is the friend and preserver of humanity, Siva is the multifaceted master over nature and human beings. He is not responsible to anyone or anything, and he is capable of unpredictable acts of domination. In stories, he can be both a mystical ascetic and an erotic lover. He can strike down, and he can spare. It is no wonder, despite his unpredictable character, that Siva has enjoyed a huge following for over two millennia. As a personal digression, before I became convinced about the claims of Jesus Christ, I learnt martial arts from a group of devout Hindus in my native Sydney. During those years, I myself offered prayers and acts of worship to Siva.

As another Trivial Pursuit™ aside, teachers from a branch of Saivism during the 1200s CE developed a particular form of yoga (*hatha-yoga*) involving difficult breathing and body exercises. This was thought to bring spiritual oneness with the divine. Various forms and adaptations of this hatha-yoga have become immensely popular in the yoga of the West.

Although too brief to give you a detailed picture of the immense tradition we call Hinduism, these few chapters have tried to give you a taste of the flavoursome, three-part cocktail Indians call the Eternal Religion.

HINDUISM ON A PAGE

Hinduism's key question: How can my soul escape the cycle of birth-death-and-rebirth in this material world?

1500–500 BCE: Aryans (or "noble ones") begin to formalise their vedic religion

- The four Vedas, or books of "Wisdom" are composed.
- Many devas or divine beings (fire, storm, etc.).
- Rituals and sacrifice to keep the devas in favour.

1000–300 BCE: Indian gurus begin to unpack the meaning of the Vedas

- Most important writings in this period are the Upanishads.
- Brahman: the One force, or "Flame" of the universe.
- Atman: the soul as a spark from Brahman.
- The Advaita philosophical school: Brahman is everything, and thus the atman is Brahman in the final analysis.
- The Visist-advaita philosophical school: Brahman and the atman are not wholly identical but relate to each other in unity.
- Samsara: the trap of earthly existence and re-existence because of karma.
- Moksha: escape back into Brahman.

300 BCE–300 CE: The composition of many so-called remembered (smriti) writings

- Most important writing in this period is the Bhagavad-gita, or "Song of the Lord."
- Four castes of society
    - *Priests*
    - *Warrior-kings*
    - *Common people*
    - *Servants*
- Three paths to salvation
    - *Do the duty of your caste*
    - *Attain knowledge of your oneness with Brahman*
    - *Devote yourself to a "favourite god"*
- Two major "schools" of Hinduism
    - *Vaishnavism (devotion to Vishnu)*
    - *Saivism (devotion to Siva)*

Facts and Figures on Hinduism Today

- Hinduism is the third largest religion in the world, with 1.1 billion believers according to World Religion Database, Boston University.
- Hindus make up about 14 percent of the world's population.
- Hinduism is found in 114 countries in the world.
- Sanskrit, the language of the Hindu scriptures, is one of the oldest and most well-connected languages on earth, relating to Eastern languages like Hittite, as well as Western languages like Latin and Greek (and therefore English).

- There are an estimated 300 million different devas worshipped in India today.
- In the USA, there are 1.6 million Hindus, or 0.5 percent of the population. In the UK, there are 745,000 Hindus, or 1.11 percent of the population. In Australia, there are 470,000 Hindus, or 1.85 percent of the population.

Famous Hindus

Mahatma Gandhi

> Considered by some the father of the Indian nation, Gandhi was famous for his policy of nonviolent resistance, crucial in the fight for Indian independence. He was assassinated in 1948. It must also be stated that Gandhi is scorned by many in India today for what are perceived to be his numerous compromises in both politics and the Hindu religion.

Julia Roberts

> A famous Hollywood actress, Julia Roberts has won awards for her roles in *Erin Brockovich*, *Pretty Woman*, and *Steel Magnolias*. It was while shooting the movie *Eat, Pray, Love* in India that Julia decided to accept Hinduism as her religion.

Sri Chinmoy

> Indian spiritual leader, athlete, and humanitarian Sri Chinmoy moved to New York in 1964. He founded the "Peace Run" to raise awareness of the need for peace. The motto of the Peace Run is "Peace begins with me." Peace Runs are now run in many countries around the world.

George Harrison

> Beatles guitarist and songwriter Harrison began his search for God in his mid-twenties. It led him to delve deeply into the mystical world of eastern religions, especially Hinduism, Indian philosophy, culture, and music.

Sachin Tendulkar

> An Indian cricketer regarded as one of the greatest batsmen in the world. Up to July 2004, he scored 9470 runs at an average of 57.39 with 37 centuries and a highest score of 241.

Good Books and Sites on Hinduism

bbc.co.uk/religion/religions/hinduism/ (a reliable introductory site from the BBC)

learnreligions.com/hinduism-4684846 (a well-researched and written resource for Hindu beliefs and history)

https://www.pewresearch.org/topics/hindus-and-hinduism/ (a site introducing contemporary statistics about Hinduism around the world)

Beckerlege, G., ed. *World Religions Reader*. 2nd edition. London: Routledge, 2001 (Part Four: Hinduism, 201–320).

Biardeau, M. *Hinduism: the Anthropology of a Civilization*. Oxford: Oxford University Press, 1994.

Brockington, J. L. *The Sacred Thread: Hinduism in its Continuity and Diversity*. Edinburgh: Edinburgh University Press, 1981.

Feuerstein, G. A. *Introduction to the Bhagavad-Gita: its Philosophy and Cultural Setting*. London: Rider and Company, 1974.

Sutton, N. *The Bhagavad Gita: A New Translation and Study*

Guide. Oxford Centre for Hindu Studies. San Rafael, Mandala Publishing, 2020.

Hardy, F. "The Classical Religions of India." *The World's Religions.* Edited by S. Sutherland, et al. London: Routledge, 1988. See pages 569–645.

Johnson, W. J. *Oxford Dictionary of Hinduism.* Oxford University Press, 2009.

Knott, K. *Hinduism: A Very Short Introduction.* Oxford University Press, 2000.

Smart, N., and Hecht, R., eds. "Hinduism." *Sacred Texts of the World: A Universal Anthology.* New York: Crossroad, 2002. See pages 179–230.

Smart, N. *The World's Religions.* 2nd edition. Cambridge: Cambridge University Press, 2003. See pages 43–102.

Zaehner, R. C. *Hinduism.* Oxford: Oxford University Press, 1966.

PART 3
BUDDHISM, THE WAY OF ENLIGHTENMENT
IN A NUTSHELL

Buddhism is a practical philosophy first taught by Prince Siddhartha Gautama, otherwise known as the Buddha, or "enlightened one." At its heart, Buddhism teaches that the suffering of the world, which is all-pervasive, is a direct result of human desire: desire for wealth, desire for comfort, desire for self-recognition, and so on. By removing such desire—through practising the Buddha's teachings—men and women can escape the pain of the world, and so experience the tranquillity of enlightenment.

7

ORIGINS OF BUDDHISM

THE WORLD'S MOST LOVABLE RELIGION

Buddhism may take the prize today for World's Most Lovable Religion. The number of times I hear people say, "Oh, I love the Buddhist philosophy," is quite amazing.

And let's face it, there is a lot to like! Think of the Buddhist Orlando Bloom, the handsome, socially-concerned Hollywood star. Then there's the head of Tibetan Buddhism, the Dalai Lama. He's a very likeable guy. He is always happy, always serene, and always filling venues for lectures on his faith (including in Sydney, where I live). Then, of course, there's the Buddha himself, recognisable to most Westerners as that smiling, contented fellow in the great statues of Asia.

Buddhism is also famously a religion of peace. Everyone knows Buddhists wouldn't hurt a fly (literally), let alone fellow human beings. Given the bloody trail of religious history throughout Europe and the Middle East, it is no wonder Buddhism wins the vote for Nicest Guy on the religious block.

Another attraction of Buddhism is its perceived simplicity. I once overheard a group of (quite obviously) non-religious twentysome-things discussing things spiritual. They were guests at a rather loud dinner party on the balcony next door; and short of leaving the balcony I was on, it was difficult not to eavesdrop. In the course of conversation, one of the guests offered a personal evaluation, contrasting Western religion with Eastern religion. "Western religion," he said with confidence, "is too full of commandments for me. I prefer the Buddhist system," he added, "it doesn't have any of those onerous rules."

As he sipped his Chardonnay, unaware of the Buddha's command *not* to drink alcohol, the others "Hmmm-ed" in agreement. Buddhism, they decided, is the no-stress, no-strings-attached religion.

The attraction of Buddhism is clear. And it is true that the removal of what we call "stress" is a key goal of the Buddhist path. But it would be a mistake to assume that the teaching of the Buddha himself was uncomplicated and undemanding. In fact, after years of studying the various religions, I regard Buddhism as the most intellectually complex of the great faiths and also the one requiring the highest level of discipline from its adherents.

THE PRINCE WHO FELT PAIN

The founder of Buddhism was raised in the sanatana dharma, or what we call Hinduism. His name was Siddhartha Gautama (sometimes spelt Sidhattha Gottama), and he was an Indian prince of the warrior-king caste of Indian society. Historical records about his life—of the kind demanded by Western historians—are not plentiful. We do not have biographies or passing mentions in "secular" sources from the period. What we have are hundreds of illustrative stories about him, preserved initially in oral tradition (verbal rehearsing out-loud of key stories and teachings) and written down two or three centuries later. Some of those sacred writings give the dates of his life as 566–486 BCE (the dates preferred by many traditional Buddhists), and others give 448–368 BCE. Interestingly, archaeological work in 2011–12 led by Professor Robin Coningham of Durham University may favour the earlier, traditional date.[1]

The young prince's parents ruled the Indian kingdom of the Sakyas in northeast India (where Nepal is today). It wasn't unusual in those days for a prince—or anyone, for that matter—to be married quite young, and Gautama was no exception. At sixteen years of age he married the beautiful Yasodhara, also sixteen years old, after he impressed her with his skills in archery and other "manly" activities.

Palace life for the prince would have been pleasant and safe, well protected from the poverty and sickness experienced by many on the other side of the walls. He had lily ponds to play in, female musicians to entertain him, and three palaces to enjoy at different times of the year.

All of this was to change, however, when around twenty-nine years of age, Gautama ventured beyond the palace to inspect his kingdom. On either one day or over several days (traditions differ), Siddhartha saw the "four signs" which spurred him on to his road of discovery. On one occasion, he observed a frail old man, "broken-toothed, gray-haired, crooked and bent of body" (Jataka I.58,81). On another occasion, he witnessed a desperately ill man and, finally, a corpse. We are told that the prince returned home "agitated in heart." The next day, Siddhartha saw a fourth man,

---

1 R. Coningham, K. Acharya, K. Strickland, C. Davis, M. Manuel, I. Simpson, D. Sanderson, "The earliest Buddhist Shrine: Excavating the Birthplace of the Buddha, Lumbini (Nepal)," *Antiquity* 87, no. 338 (2013): 1104–23.

the fourth "sign," quite different from the others. This was a sight that would change his life forever. The fourth man was a Hindu ascetic—a guru who had chosen the "Path of Knowledge" discussed in chapter 6. So impressed was Gautama by the peaceful look on the teacher's face that the prince decided immediately to give up his life of luxury and set out to discover for himself the secret of serenity in a world of pain.

And so, before his thirtieth birthday, Siddhartha Gautama left his privileged life, his beautiful wife, and his newborn child to search for an answer to the troubling dilemma of suffering. This is the key question of the Buddhist philosophy: How does one find peace in a world of sadness and decay?

The first path the ex-prince pursued was, naturally enough, the way of asceticism, denying all earthly comforts and striving for meditative states of mystic consciousness. For six long years, say the records, Gautama wandered the region of the Ganges River in northeast India studying the ancient Hindu traditions and submitting himself to the demands of the famous gurus he met along the way. He became a master of these practices. But nothing satisfied. Suffering and evil were still as potent and troubling to Siddhartha as before.

THE MOMENT OF ENLIGHTENMENT

Having experienced the path of luxury most of his life, and then the path of denial for six long years, Siddhartha was convinced that neither extreme provided the answer he was looking for. The key to the removal of suffering, he thought, must lie somewhere else. With this in mind, he committed himself to pondering the dilemma night and day until he found the solution.

One night in May, while sitting under a tree, the answer came to him in a moment of pure insight. This was the moment of *enlightenment* for Siddhartha. From that time on, he would be known to his disciples as the "Buddha," which means "enlightened one." I will adopt this conventional title of respect throughout these chapters.

Description of the Buddha's Moment of Enlightenment by the Second-Century CE Convert Asvaghosa

Then, as the third watch of that night drew on, the supreme master of trance turned his meditation to the real and essential nature of this world: "Alas, living beings wear themselves out in vain! Over and over again they are born, they age, die, pass on to a new life, and are reborn! What is more, greed and dark delusion obscure their sight, and they are blind from birth. Greatly apprehensive, they yet do not know how to get out of this great mass of ill.' He then surveyed the twelve lines of conditioned co-production [a complex Buddhist doctrine mentioned in the next chapter], and saw that, beginning with ignorance, they lead to old age and death, and, beginning with the cessation of ignorance, they lead to the cessation of birth, old age, death and all kinds of ill. When the great seer had comprehended that where there is no ignorance whatever, there also the karma-formations are stopped—then he had achieved a correct knowledge of all there is to be known, and he stood out in the world as a Buddha.

Buddhacarita, 35–66, Discourse on
the Acts of Buddha (Takakusa).

I should note another title regularly used by Buddhists to refer to the Buddha. He is frequently called Tathagata (Pali and Sanskrit) which either means "one who is thus gone," in the sense of "one who is emancipated," or "one who understands things as they are." The etymology, or word origin, is debated, even in the Buddhist texts. In any case, the traditions say that this was the title the Buddha himself preferred to use.

Buddha or Tathagata had been raised as royalty with the duty of ruling over the people of northeast India, but for the next forty-five years (the texts agree he lived to be eighty), he would devote himself exclusively to teaching his insights to all who would listen.

He began with a small group of just five disciples, to whom he preached his first sermon immediately after his enlightenment (recorded in a scripture called *Setting in Motion the Wheel of Truth* (Dhammacakkappavattana Sutta). One of them, Annakondanna, became enlightened immediately. These five disciples were the beginning of the *sangha*, or Buddhist community. Buddha won many more converts over the next forty or so years.

After Gautama's death, his teachings were preserved in spoken form through a process of memorisation and proclamation (conducted mainly in monasteries) known as *oral tradition*. The material was eventually written down sometime in the first century BCE. Despite this three-hundred-year gap between the Buddha's life and the first Buddhist writings, oral tradition was such a powerful ancient method of preservation (in a period when few people could read or write) that we can be confident the intellectual sophistication and uniqueness of the Buddha still shines through these sacred pages.

8
BUDDHA'S CRITIQUE OF HINDUISM

Some of the Buddha's insights under that tree (known as the Bodhi Tree, or "tree of wisdom") were what you might call *innovations* in religious thinking: new religious ideas. Some of them, however, involved simple rejections of the religion he grew up with. Before we look at what Siddhartha proposed, it might be helpful to explore what he threw out.

THE "MIDDLE PATH"

Siddhartha Gautama had experienced both pleasure and deprivation. In his view, neither of these extremes led to true insight. Both were paths of ignorance, he insisted. In his Indian context, this amounted to a rejection of the two extremes (as he saw it) of Hindu religion. What Siddhartha proposed in their place was called the "Middle Path" (*Majjhima Patipada*). It got this name not because it was a happy balance between the two extremes—a little bit of pleasure and a little bit of pain—but because it dismissed both paths altogether. Attachment to delight and attachment to asceticism are both delusions that keep one from enlightenment.

"Avoiding both these extremes," the Buddha said in his first sermon, "the Tathagata [Buddha] has realised the Middle Path: it gives vision, it gives knowledge, and it leads to calm, to insight, to enlightenment, to Nibbana [Nirvana]" (*Setting in Motion the Wheel of Truth*, Samyutta Nikaya 56.11 [Rahula]).

THE CASTE SYSTEM

Another aspect of Hinduism that Siddhartha rejected was the belief in the four castes. Although born into the privileged Indian caste of the warrior-king, Prince Gautama refused to make any distinction between members of the human race. He mixed with all, taught all, and was adamant that everyone—including lowly servants, or sudras—could reach the highest goal of his teaching. The ethical life, not caste, is the important quality for Buddha.[1]

THE ROLE OF THE BRAHMANS

Related to this "egalitarian" view of society was Siddhartha's insistence that the Brahmans (Hindu priests), with their rituals and speculative philosophy, were as ignorant about the truth as anyone else. Some of the most scathing criticisms in Siddhartha's teachings are reserved for this particular class of Indian society. On one occasion, the Buddha led a brahman youth through a series of questions which arrive at the conclusion that brahman religion (Vedic Hinduism) is blind: "The words of the brahmans turn out

---

1 See the Discourse with Esukari (Esukarisutta), Majjhima-Nikaya 96, from the Sutta Pitaka (Horner).

to resemble a string of blind men: neither does the foremost one see, nor does the middle one see, nor does the hindmost one see" (Discourse with Canki (Cankisutta), Majjhima-Nikaya 95, from the Sutta Pitaka [Horner]).

GOD, THE SOUL, AND THE SELF

Earlier in the book, we discussed the Hindu belief that each living being, including humans, possesses an atman, the soul or "real you," behind the simple everyday consciousness. This atman is a "spark," says Hinduism, from the eternal "flame" which is Brahman, the ultimate reality behind the universe.

Siddhartha Gautama rejected these fundamental Hindu ideas. He regarded teachings about God (or ultimate reality) and the soul as pure guesswork and completely irrelevant to the path of wisdom. He did not come out and say, "Friends, there is no God in the universe." So, it might not be accurate to describe him as an atheist (one who believes that God does not exist). He simply dismissed such questions outright. In his view, they were ignorant and foolish matters. He was, if you like, a practical atheist if not a theoretical one.

Things get more complex. Not only did Siddhartha think there was no eternal soul worth worrying about—whether a human soul or a divine one—but he believed there was no actual *you* to think about, either. You might want to pause here and let this thought occupy your mind for a moment. A key doctrine of Buddhism is *anatman* ("not self"), the belief that YOU (as well as John Dickson) do not ultimately exist.

The Buddhist argument here is difficult to follow and a little counterintuitive, but it is brilliant. The Buddha said that the thing you call *you* is really just a combination of ever-changing physical and mental activities going on in the same location (your body and brain). These activities are the result, he said, of physical and mental activities that occurred a moment earlier. These, in turn, are the result of ones that occurred a moment before that, and so on.

There is no *you* arising from this chain of cause-and-effect. There is just the chain of cause-and-effect itself—just physical and mental activities causing further physical and mental activities. The thing you think of as *you* is just a fantasy, taught Gautama, born of ignorance. It is an illusion.

The Doctrine of No-Self Expounded by the Revered Founding Monk Nagasena in Answer to a Disciple's Question

[Disciple] "Bhante Nāgasena, if there is no Ego to be found, who is it then furnishes you priests with the priestly requisites,—robes, food, bedding, and medicine, the reliance of the sick? Who is it makes use of the same? who is it keeps the precepts? who is it applies himself to meditation? . . . When you say, 'My fellow-priests, your majesty, address me as Nāgasena,' what then is this Nāgsena?"

[Nāgasena] "Pray, bhante, is the hair of the head Nāgasena?"

[Disciple] "Nay, verily, your majesty."

[Nāgasena] "Is the hair of the body Nāgasena?"

[Disciple] "Nay, verily, your majesty."

[Nāgasena] "Are nails . . . teeth . . . skin . . . flesh . . . sinews . . . bones . . . marrow of the bones . . . kidneys . . . brain of the head Nāgasena?"

[Disciple] "Nay, verily, your majesty."

[Nāgasena] "Are, then, bhante, form, sensation, perception, the predispositions, and consciousness unitedly Nāgasena?"
[Disciple] "Nay, verily, your majesty."
[Nāgasena] "Bhante, although I question you very closely, I fail to discover any Nāgasena. Verily, now, bhante, Nāgasena is a mere empty sound. What Nāgasena is there here? Bhante, you speak a falsehood, a lie: there is no Nāgasena."

There is no Ego (Self), Milindapanha 25, Khuddaka Nikaya, from the Sutta Pitaka (Warren).

For Buddhism, this is not just a brain teaser designed to mystify students of religion; it is a key to the Buddhist life. The goal of Buddhism is to help people realise that they do not ultimately exist. Once we realise this fact and live accordingly, we will have become enlightened. But more about that later.

THE FIVE AGGREGATES OF ATTACHMENT

For now I need to unpack a related and complex Buddhist teaching known officially as the "Five Aggregates of Attachment" (Skanhas), that is, the five ways in which people attach themselves to the world at large and to the idea of the self.

The idea behind the "Five Aggregates of Attachment" is that there are five basic factors in the human person, all of which are constantly changing, none of which can be called a continuing *you*, and all of which go to make up the illusion of the human self. Here are the five factors:

1. Matter (*rupa*). The first and most obvious factor in the thing you think of as your self is the material factor—physical matter, sights, odours, sounds, etc. Included here are the four traditional Buddhist elements of earth, air, fire, and water. This physical existence, along with some brain functions, make up part of the illusion you call *you*.

2. Sensation (*vedana*). When material elements in the world bump into other material elements in the human body, sensations arise. For instance, an odour up my nose might result in the sensation of smell. Again, a sound in my ear might result in the sensation of sound. Sensations of happiness and sadness are also included in this category, since they, too, are often just the effects of material causes.

3. Perception (*samjna*). Perception, said Gautama, is the recognition of physical or mental functions. For example, I might recognise a certain smell to be the smell of my body odour. Again, I might recognise a certain sound as the sound of music. I have no control over my perceptions. They are just reflex realisations resulting from matter and sensations.

4. Mental Formations (*samskara*). Whenever I direct my mind towards a particular thought or action, I am experiencing a mental formation, said the Buddha. For example, upon perceiving my own body odour, I might decide to have a bath. Upon perceiving the sound of music, I might decide to turn up the volume. These decisions, or acts of the will, are mental formations. Mental formations also include things like concentration, forcing your mind to think about one thing for a time (you might be finding that particular mental formation quite difficult right now). Mental formations also

include decisions of the will such as desire, hate, jealousy, and so on. It's important to appreciate, however, that in Gautama's view, there is no *you* directing these mental formations; there are just the formations themselves.

5. Consciousness (*vijnana*). At first, this aggregate is difficult to differentiate from perception (the third aggregate), but there is a difference. *Perception* recognises things as particular things (odour, sound, etc.). *Consciousness* is simply an "awareness" of the presence and characteristics of a thing (whether physical or mental). To continue the examples we've been using: consciousness is the awareness of a smell which is unpleasant, whereas perception identifies the smell as, say, my body odour. Again, consciousness is the awareness of a sound with certain tones and volumes, whereas perception identifies that sound as the sound of music.

The details of the Skandhas or Five Aggregates might seem complex, but the important thing to realise about this teaching is its purpose. Siddhartha is taking the thing we usually think of as the *self* and breaking it down into its component parts. By doing this, he demonstrates that there is no self, after all. There is just a chain of cause-and-effect operating within these five aspects of the human being. There is no enduring you (or me), just the illusion caused by these five ever-changing, arising, and disappearing factors of human experience. Put another way, the sum of the parts does not make up a greater whole called the self. All that exists are the parts. It is only because people are ignorant of the Buddha's fivefold breakdown of human experience that they experience the illusion of self-existence and the pain that goes with foolishly believing you really exist. There is another complex Buddhist doctrine that explains the process by which this illusion of self-existence emerges within us. It is called "Conditioned Arising or Co-production" (*patityasamutpada*). See more advanced texts on Buddhism for the details. For our purposes, it is simply worth noting that the first part of the process is "ignorance," that is, ignorance of the Buddha's truths.

For now, it is probably helpful to put the point crudely, but no less accurately. According to the teaching of the Five Aggregates of Attachment and Conditioned Arising, there is no thinker, there are just thoughts; there is no smeller, there are just acts of smelling; there is no listener, there are just acts of listening. In short, there is no *you* at all.

Please note: throughout his teaching, Buddha still used pronouns like *I, you, she, oneself,* and so on. This is not a contradiction of his No-Self (anatman) doctrine. Pronouns were still required, believed the Buddha, in order to refer to those entities which (the Buddhist knows) in reality possess no enduring self. They are shorthand, if you like, for talking about that collection of matter, sensations, perceptions, mental formations, and consciousness which people (wrongly) think of as themselves.

Why is it so important in Buddhism to remove the notion of the self? Because in Buddha's view, the idea of the self is the root of all suffering. It is your (and my) desire for self-existence, self-satisfaction, self-harm, and self-improvement that creates the experience of pain. Remove the self, realise there never was such a thing in the first place, and your suffering will evaporate. This is the heart of Buddhism, and we are going to say a lot more about it later.

REBIRTH VERSUS REINCARNATION

If there is no *soul* or *you*, then clearly there can be no reincarnation, at least, not in the full Hindu sense of a continuing self re-existing after death in another body. Although Buddhism and Hinduism are often lumped together in their views of the afterlife, they are, in fact, quite different.

The Buddha taught an idea known simply as *rebirth*. Rebirth does not involve getting a new body for an old soul; it is just the continuation of the five factors of existence (the Five Aggregates) in a long chain of cause-and-effect. Since every human sensation, perception, and mental formation is determined by prior sensations, perceptions, and mental formations, Gautama argued that rebirth must also work like this. The final sensation, perception, and mental formation of this life determines the first sensation, perception, and mental formation of the next life. For the Buddha, existence is just one long chain of cause-and-effect, and death does not end that chain, even if there is never any real *you* at any point along the chain.

Why Buddhist "Rebirth" Is Not Hindu Reincarnation, According to the Great Nagasena in Answer to an Enquiring King

Said the king: "Bhante Nāgasena, does rebirth take place without anything transmigrating [passing over]?"

"Yes, your majesty. Rebirth takes place without anything transmigrating."

"How, bhante Nāgasena, does rebirth take place without anything transmigrating? Give an illustration."

"Suppose, your majesty, a man were to light a light from another light; pray, would the one light have passed over [transmigrated] to the other light?"

"Nay, verily, bhante."

"In exactly the same way, your majesty, does rebirth take place without anything transmigrating."

"Give another illustration."

"Do you remember, your majesty, having learnt, when you were a boy, some verse or other from your professor of poetry?'

"Yes, bhante."

"Pray, your majesty, did the verse pass over [transmigrate] to you from your teacher?"

"Nay, verily, bhante."

"In exactly the same way, your majesty, does rebirth take place without anything transmigrating."

"Bhante Nāgasena," said the king, . . . "If it is not this same name and form that is born into the next existence, is one not freed from one's evil deeds? . . . Give an illustration."

"Your majesty, it is as if a man were to take away another man's mangoes, and the owner of the mangoes were to seize him, and show him to the king, and say, 'Sire, this man hath taken away my mangoes;' and the other were to say, 'Sire, I did not take away this man's mangoes. The mangoes which this man planted were different mangoes from those which I took away. I am not liable to punishment.' Pray, your majesty, would the man be liable to punishment?"

"Assuredly, bhante, would he be liable to punishment."

"For what reason?"

"Because, in spite of what he might say, he would be liable to punishment for the reason that the last mangoes derived from the first mangoes."

"In exactly the same way, your majesty, with the name and form one does a deed - it may be good, or it may be wicked—and by reason of this deed another name and form is born into the next existence. Therefore is one not freed from one's evil deeds."

> Rebirth is not Transmigration, Milindapanha 71 and 46, Khuddaka Nikaya, from the Sutta Pitaka (Warren).

So far, we have been exploring what the Buddha *rejected* from his Hindu heritage—the caste system, God, the idea of the self, the doctrine of reincarnation, and so on. More significant by far, however, is what he discovered in his enlightenment and then proclaimed for the next forty-five years. That is the subject of the next two chapters.

9

THE FOUR NOBLE TRUTHS

Almost everything Siddhartha Gautama taught in his long career was an exposition of four basic beliefs and eight disciplined habits. This makes memorising the Buddhist system (which is not the same as understanding it, of course!) relatively easy. The four beliefs are known as the Four Noble Truths. The eight habits are known as the Eightfold Path. Let's now unpack these (4 + 8 =) 12 essentials of Buddhism.

We've already seen that Siddhartha Gautama was motivated from the start by a search for peace in a world of suffering. The Four Noble Truths are all about experiencing this tranquillity.

THE FIRST NOBLE TRUTH: SUFFERING EXISTS

The First Noble Truth is easy to understand. It involves simply acknowledging the existence and nature of suffering.

The word used by the Buddha to summarise the First Noble Truth is *dukkha*. Dukkha has a broader meaning than the English word *suffering*. One major book on Buddhism I read (published by Oxford University Press) even avoids translating dukkha. Throughout the book, this scholar writes: "Dukkha this" and

"Dukkha that." It gets pretty confusing. In my opinion, as long as we keep in mind that suffering in Buddhist thought is a bigger concept than we are used to, the English word will do just fine.

For the Buddha, dukkha refers to just about everything in life, not only to pain and hardship but also to the fleeting nature of existence. Everything is momentary, here-today-gone-tomorrow. In this sense, the Buddha can even describe positive experiences as suffering because they tend to evaporate shortly after they appear. Anyone who has experienced an emotional high only to come down to a great low will know what the Buddha meant.

According to Gautama, the Five Aggregates of Attachment are also suffering. What he means by this is not difficult to see. If everything you think of as *you* is simply a series of effects produced by prior causes (which themselves are the product of earlier causes) then unenlightened existence itself, by its very nature, is tragic. It is dukkah. In the Buddha's own words from his first sermon: "The Noble Truth of Suffering (dukkha), monks, is this: Birth is suffering, aging is suffering, sickness is suffering, death is suffering, association with the unpleasant is suffering, dissociation from the pleasant is suffering, not to receive what one desires is suffering; in brief the five aggregates subject to grasping are suffering" (*Setting in Motion the Wheel of Truth*, Samyutta Nikaya 56.11 [Bodhi]).

The First Noble Truth, then, is simply the recognition that suffering exists in all these forms.

THE SECOND NOBLE TRUTH: THE ORIGIN OF SUFFERING

The Second Noble Truth tries to explain the origin of suffering. Siddhartha's logic is powerful. Suffering, says the Buddha, arises in your life because of desire or craving. At its most basic level, the logic goes like this. If you crave riches, then poverty will feel painful to you. If you desire comfort, then discomfort will trouble you. Think about it for a moment; it is difficult to argue with! The Buddha stated it simply: "Now this, bhikkhus, is the noble truth of the origin of suffering: it is this craving which leads to renewed existence, accompanied by delight and lust, seeking delight here and there; that is, craving for sensual pleasures, craving for existence, craving for extermination" (*Setting in Motion the Wheel of Truth,* Samyutta Nikaya 56.11 [Bodhi]).

For the Buddha, craving comes in several forms. First, there is desire for sensual pleasures. This includes craving wealth, comfort, physical gratification, and so on. Second, there is the desire for existence. When people are ignorant of the teaching about the Five Aggregates, they live under the false impression that they possess a continuing self. They nurse this self and strive to prolong its experience. They long for re-existence. Such craving for existence, thought Gautama, is the cause of much suffering.

The third type of desire is the craving for "extermination" or non-existence. This may seem illogical at first. If craving for existence is wrong why would craving for the opposite be wrong as well? Basically, because *craving* is the problem, not the thing craved for. Craving, even if it is craving for the end of yourself, still assumes the existence of a *you* who is passionately wishing for something. That is ignorance.

Karma and the Second Noble Truth

Before we move on to the Third Noble Truth, I have to pause and say something about the Buddhist understanding of karma, which is similar but not identical to the Hindu idea of karma.

Within Buddhism, karma usually refers to wilful action, or actions which grow out of your desires/cravings. There is such a thing as non-wilful action, which we will look at in a moment.

A morally good action will produce a good effect, and a morally bad action will produce a bad effect. In both cases, an action produces an onward effect. That is in the nature of karma; it is just how the universe works, said the Buddha.

It would be a mistake, however, to think that the goal of Buddhism is simply to do good deeds in an effort to produce good effects. According to Buddhism, even good actions producing good effects are part of the sad chain of cause-and-effect. Why? Because even the best things in life are fleeting. Beauty fades, pleasure dissipates, and joy passes. And when this happens, regret and sadness emerge, proving that life is just a long line of arising-disappearing-arising-disappearing. For Buddha, then, even relatively "good karma" producing relatively "good outcomes" is ultimately tragic (dukkha).

The greatest tragedy in all this is that the effects of wilful action (of karma) do not cease at death. Karma produces rebirth. Rebirth brings yet more of the fleeting and painful aspects of life. You are trapped, and it is all the fault of karma, of acting out of craving.

The perfected Buddhist, however, is free from the idea of self, and so is able to live in the world without any craving whatsoever. Without craving, action accumulates no karma. Without karma, there is no rebirth. Problem solved. The Buddhist who achieves this perfected level is called an *arhat* or "worthy one." More about that in a moment.

The Second Noble Truth (of the origin of suffering) describes the relationship between craving, karma, and suffering. This is the "bad news" of Buddhism. The good news is contained in the Third Noble Truth.

THE THIRD NOBLE TRUTH: THE END OF SUFFERING

Once you have understood the existence of suffering (the First Noble Truth) and have understood its root cause (the Second Noble Truth), the removal of suffering follows naturally, if not easily. Suffering disappears when you get rid of desire. As the Buddha said, "The Noble Truth of the Cessation of suffering is this: It is the complete cessation of that very thirst, giving it up, renouncing it, emancipating oneself from it, detaching oneself from it" (*Setting in Motion the Wheel of Truth*, Samyutta Nikaya 56.11 [Rahula]).

The Third Noble Truth is simply the realisation that peace in the midst of suffering comes through the elimination of human craving, detachment from desire.

Nirvana and the Third Noble Truth

At this point, I should introduce the Buddhist idea of *nirvana*, a word which means "blowing out" or "extinction." Nirvana is not a heavenly place, or a blissful state of mind. It is the extinguishment of all desire—whether the desire for pleasure, for existence, or for non-existence. Put another way, nirvana is the realisation that the self does not really exist, and that human desire is therefore empty. A person who has come to this realisation is able to act in this world with complete detachment, that is, without desire. His or her actions are without karma. The person who attains the state of nirvana has escaped the world of cause-and-effect and is free from the cycle of birth and rebirth.

Is nirvana a negative idea? Within a Buddhist framework, not at all. How could the realisation of reality—of the way things really are—be considered negative? Only an unenlightened person would consider the extinction of the false idea of self and the eradication of craving as negative. Nirvana is neither positive nor negative. It is just the truth, said Buddha.

Will the realisation of nirvana be a happy experience? Yes, says the Buddhist, but not in the normal Western sense of the word *happy*. If by *happy* we mean a "sensation" or "feeling" of joy then, no, nirvana is not a happy experience. Remember, emotional sensations are always dependent upon something else; they are part of this arising-disappearing world. The happiness of nirvana is the true joy of having realised the ultimate truth. It is the blessed state of escaping the endless chain of cause-and-effect.

Nirvana is fully realised at death, when the physical body of the enlightened person ceases functioning. This is termed *parinirvana* (or *parinibbana*), "total unbinding." However, nirvana can also be experienced before death. There are four stages in the Buddhist life, each with its own increasing realisation of nirvana:

1. The "Stream-entrant," or novice, only catches a glimpse of nirvana in the teaching of the Buddha.
2. The "Once-Returner," as the name suggests, is destined to be reborn in this physical world just one more time before experiencing full nirvana.
3. The "Never-Returner" has an even deeper knowledge of nirvana and is assured that he or she will not be reborn.

4. The "Worthy-One" (arhat) is totally pure and completely free from desire. Such a person has experienced nirvana here and now, and will know it fully at death, when all matter, sensations, perceptions, mental formations, and consciousness will disappear forever.

I should also make clear that the arhat ideal is not accepted by all Buddhists. In the tradition known as *Mahayana* ("Great Vehicle") Buddhism, discussed in a moment, the arhat stage is considered inferior to the Buddhist who has achieved enlightenment and the ability never to return but who makes a decision to remain in the cycle of rebirths in order to assist others to attain enlightenment. This type of Buddhist makes a vow to help others before entering full nirvana. He is known as the *bodhisattva*, "one whose essence is bodhi ('enlightenment')" or "Buddha-to-be." More about that later.

The Third Noble Truth is simply this: if you eradicate your craving for all things (pleasure, existence, and non-existence) suffering evaporates.

It is easy to see how this might work in theory. If you live with detachment from the delights and pains of the world, and even from the idea of self, almost by definition you will feel unaffected by the changing fortunes of life. Hardship will not trouble you since you have no desire for comfort. Poverty will not disappoint you, for you do not crave wealth. Personal insults will not hurt, because you are detached from the very idea of the self. This is the logic behind the tranquillity Westerners often associate with Buddhism. The Buddha put it plainly: "A learned and noble disciple, who sees (things) thus, becomes dispassionate with regard to the eye, becomes dispassionate with regard to . . . odours . . . flavours . . . the body . . . mental impression . . . Being dispassionate, he becomes detached; through detachment he is liberated. When liberated there is knowledge that he is liberated. And he knows: Birth (i.e., rebirth) is exhausted, the holy life has been lived, what has to be done is done, there is no more left to be done on this account" (The Fire Sermon, Samyutta Nikaya 35 [Rahula]).

This notion of detachment as the path to the end of suffering is taken so seriously by Buddhists that the story of the Buddha's own death is told to illustrate the point. The disciples who witnessed the Buddha's serene passing suddenly burst into tears at the devastating knowledge that they will never see their Tathagata again. "Too soon!" they cry, "Too soon!" Then they realise that they are disobeying the Buddha's own teaching by being attached to the Buddha and letting their emotions get the better of them. Suddenly, they wipe away their tears, focus on the Third Noble Truth, and return to the equilibrium expected of the true Buddhist.

The Account of the Death, or Total Unbinding, of the Buddha

When the Blessed One was totally unbound [i.e., when he died], some of the monks present who were not without passion wept, uplifting their arms. They fell down and rolled back and forth, crying, "All too soon is the Blessed One totally unbound! All too soon, is the One with Eyes disappeared from the world!" But the Venerable Anuruddha addressed the monks: "Enough, friends. Don't grieve. Don't lament.

Hasn't the Blessed One already taught the state of growing different with regard to all things dear and appealing, the state of becoming separate, the state of becoming otherwise? What else is there to expect? It is impossible that one could forbid anything born, existent, fabricated, and subject to disintegration from disintegrating." . . . Then Venerable Anuruddha and Venerable Ananda spent the remainder of the night in Dhamma talk.

Maha-parinibbana Sutta: The Great Discourse on
the Total Unbinding, Digha Nikaya 16 (Thanissaro).

During his life, Siddhartha Gautama warned that the removal of desire and the attainment of tranquillity are not easy goals. People do not just hear the first three Noble Truths and suddenly realise nirvana (well, some people do; most don't). People need a path, a method for cultivating the thoughts and actions conducive to this realisation. That is what the Fourth Noble Truth is all about.

THE FOURTH NOBLE TRUTH: THE PATH TO THE END OF SUFFERING

Although Buddhism is highly intellectual, it is also very practical. Buddhist writers sometimes criticise Western writers on Buddhism (like me) for wrongly emphasising the philosophical over the practical. The path of the Buddha, Buddhists themselves insist, is a practical way of living in the world, just as much as it is a comprehensive way of thinking about the world. The Fourth Noble Truth bears this out.

Earlier in the chapter, I said that almost everything the Buddha taught can be understood as an exposition of four basic beliefs (the Four Noble Truths) and eight basic habits (the Eightfold Path). However, it turns out that the Fourth Noble Truth *is itself* the teaching about the eight basic habits. In the Buddha's words: "The Noble Truth of the Path Leading to the Cessation of Suffering is this: It is the Noble Eightfold Path, and nothing else, namely: right understanding, right aim/thought, right speech, right action, right livelihood, right effort, right mindfulness and right concentration (*Setting in Motion the Wheel of Truth*, Samyutta Nikaya 56.11 [Rahula]).

The eight basic habits are known collectively as the Eightfold Path. They are not, however, just eight random rules for gaining enlightenment. They are expressions of the three essential categories of the Buddhist way of life:

1. Wisdom. Two of the habits in the Eightfold Path (Right Understanding and Right Aim/Thought) fall into the category of wisdom. These habits are designed to enhance your appreciation of the truths of Buddhism, truths such as the Five Aggregates, Karma, the Four Noble Truths, and so on.

2. Ethical Conduct. Three of the eight habits (Right Speech, Right Action, Right Livelihood) promote the lifestyle Buddha said was necessary for removing desire and experiencing nirvana. These habits are all ethical in nature. That is, they have to do with morality.

3. Mental Discipline. The final three habits (Right Effort, Right Mindfulness, Right Concentration) are thinking

exercises or what are called *mental disciplines*, which are designed to cultivate the thought life required for attaining nirvana.

With these three categories of the Buddhist life in mind, in the next chapter I will unpack the Eightfold Path, the path to the full realisation of nirvana.

10

THE EIGHTFOLD PATH

The first three of the Four Noble Truths contain the heart of the Buddhist philosophy: suffering exists, suffering is produced by our desires, suffering is overcome by detaching ourselves from all desire. The fourth of the Four Noble Truths discloses the path to full detachment. It is an Eightfold Path.

The Eightfold Path contains the habits of life that are necessary for seeing things as they really are. By practising this path, the Buddhist is able to remove all craving and so bring an end to all karma formations. Such a person is free from the need to be reborn.

In the category of wisdom are two habits.

THE FIRST HABIT: RIGHT UNDERSTANDING

A Buddhist is required to cultivate a correct understanding of Siddhartha Gautama's teaching. In its most basic form, this aspect of the Eightfold Path involves gaining a thorough knowledge of the Four Noble Truths, the Five Aggregates of Attachment, and the Twelve Steps of Conditioned Arising. Since these concepts are found in the Buddhist scriptures themselves, study of the sacred Buddhist texts is essential for this "right understanding." You cannot gain "right understanding," as the Buddha conceived of it, just by reading about Buddhism in a book like this. Sorry.

THE SECOND HABIT: RIGHT AIM

A Buddhist must not let thoughts arise and disappear at random. This would be a sign that one was still trapped in the fleeting nature of existence. Instead, the faithful are to aspire to Buddhist ideals. This is "right aim," and it involves directing your mind towards detachment from the world, compassion toward other creatures, and so on.

The next three parts of the Eightfold Path have to do with ethical conduct.

THE THIRD HABIT: RIGHT SPEECH

Buddhists are to speak in a way consistent with the removal of desire and the eradication of the idea of self. They are to refrain from lying, slandering, and being rude. To do otherwise would be to act with desire—with a commitment to one's own self.

THE FOURTH HABIT: RIGHT ACTION

The followers of Gautama are also to *act*—not just speak—in a way consistent with the negation of desire. Buddhists are therefore to reject dishonest dealings and steer clear of all illegitimate sexual contact. Buddhists must not kill or injure other living creatures, and they are to avoid all consumption of alcohol. Buddhists are also to seek to help others lead honourable lives. Again, to do otherwise would be inconsistent with the ideal of detachment which is so important to the Buddhist outlook.

THE FIFTH HABIT: RIGHT LIVELIHOOD

The fifth aspect of the path has to do with the kinds of employment Buddhists are allowed to pursue. A Buddhist must find a profession which does no harm to other creatures. This rules out jobs involving the trade of weapons, engagement in warfare, the promotion of alcohol, and the killing of animals. Such jobs arise from and foster human craving and the false notion of self.

Concrete expression of Right Speech, Right Action, and Right Livelihood, the three ethical components of the Eightfold Path, is found in the so-called Five Precepts (*Panca-sila*). These are the Buddhist equivalent of the famous Ten Commandments in the Bible. These precepts provide the bare minimum required of the Buddhist. They are:

1. to abstain from taking life;
2. to refrain from stealing;
3. to avoid sexual immorality;
4. to refrain from lying;
5. to abstain from all intoxicants (alcohol, drugs).

When someone becomes a Buddhist in what is called the *Sarana* ("refuge") ceremony, they usually take a vow to obey these five rules in the form of, "I undertake the training rule to abstain from taking life," etc. Following the five Panca-Sila is good for karma and a necessary precondition for engaging in any of the more rigorous aspects the Eightfold Path, such as those belonging to the category of mental discipline.

The three remaining habits of the Eightfold Path fall into the category of mental discipline.

THE SIXTH HABIT: RIGHT EFFORT

Buddhists are meant to engage daily in an energetic decision to put an end to false thoughts and unwholesome states of mind (including the thought of self), and they are to make every effort to promote healthy states of mind. You cannot just drift along in the Buddhist life; you must be diligent. Without Right Effort, no progress will be made in the journey toward enlightenment. Right Effort is not desire or craving. It is a disciplined intellectual decision to think and act appropriately.

THE SEVENTH HABIT: RIGHT MINDFULNESS

For Westerners, this aspect of the Buddhist path may seem unusual and introspective. Buddhists are to strive to be fully aware of everything that goes on around them and within them—every sound, bodily sensation, fleeting thought, emotion, and so on. More than that, the Buddhist must try to be aware of how such sensations and emotions arise and disappear. By noticing this arising-and-disappearing, the Buddhist enhances his or her appreciation of the Buddha's teaching about the Five Aggregates of Attachment. The Buddhist begins to realise that the thing we call the *self* is really just a passing illusion of interacting bodies, sensations, mental formations, and so on. It is just one long chain of cause-and-effect, with no enduring *me* ever truly existing.

THE EIGHTH HABIT: RIGHT CONCENTRATION

Meditation is an essential aspect of Buddhist life. By *meditation*, however, Buddhists do not just mean the "transcendental" kind that we find in the Hindu tradition (Siddhartha had tried this form of meditation and found it to be inadequate for enlightenment, he said). The meditation taught by Gautama basically involves deep concentration.

There are two types of meditation in Buddhist tradition. First, there is in-and-out breathing meditation. This involves sitting upright with legs crossed and attempting to become fully aware of your own breathing. It is designed to enhance your powers of concentration.

On first hearing, the second type of meditation does not sound much like meditation at all. It involves a concentrated awareness of all daily conduct. Think of it as an intense version of "right mindfulness."

When running, for example, you are to concentrate on the movement of your legs, the pattern of your breathing, and any other related sensations. You must not think in terms of *you* running. Rather, you are to focus only on the act of running itself, with all its connected sensations. The same type of meditation, or concentration, can be practised while washing up, doing homework, making coffee, walking in the rain, or even while going to the toilet (this last example was suggested by Gautama himself).

In all of this, the critical aspect of Right Concentration is thinking about all sensations and thoughts in terms of their fleeting character—the way they arise and disappear. Once you have lost the sense of self in this analysis (leaving only an awareness of the actions themselves) you are well on your way to nirvana. All of these daily routines create opportunities to take notice of how every sensation and thought comes and goes. Everything is passing. Everything is dependent on something else. Nothing is enduringly real. Nothing deserves our attachment.

The Zen Buddhist tradition, popular in Japan and in the West, is an extension of this meditative dimension of the Buddha's teaching. *Zen* means "meditation," and this tradition emphasises the power of certain meditative techniques to bring full enlightenment.

The Buddha's Description of the Four Meditative Stages or States Which Are the Goal of Right Concentration

Herein a monk, aloof from sense desires, aloof from unwholesome thoughts, (1) attains to and abides in the first meditative state (jhana) which is detachment-born and accompanied by applied thought, sustained thought, joy, and bliss. (2) By allaying applied and sustained thought he attains to, and abides in the second meditative state which is inner tranquillity, which is unification (of the mind), devoid of applied and sustained thought, and which has joy and bliss. (3) By detachment from joy he dwells in equanimity, mindful, and with clear comprehension and enjoys bliss in body, and attains to and abides in the third meditative state which the noble ones call: "Dwelling in equanimity, mindfulness, and bliss." (4) By giving up of bliss and suffering, by the disappearance already of joy and sorrow, he attains to, and abides in the fourth meditative state, which is neither suffering nor bliss, and which is the purity of equanimity-mindfulness. This is called right concentration.

An Analysis of the Truths, Saccavibhanga
Sutta, Majjhima Nikaya 141 (Thanissaro).

You will notice that the Eightfold Path has little to do with prayer, worship of a god, and religious ceremonies. For this reason, some Buddhists avoid calling their way of life a "religion" at all. The Eightfold Path is all about attaining a realisation of "the way things are" (as Buddhism presents it). Through these mental and moral practices, the Buddhist aims to remove craving and so escape the world of suffering and the need for rebirth.

11

TYPES OF BUDDHISM

The Four Noble Truths and the Eightfold Path are agreed upon by all Buddhists—after all, these were the core of Siddhartha Gautama's message. Nevertheless, in the period after Gautama's death, Buddhist groups, many living in monasteries, began to disagree over various points of belief and practice. Some groups, for instance, attempted to reinstate the idea of a self; others argued over the exact nature of karma; still others differed simply over which texts should be regarded as sacred.

Two main schools of Buddhism eventually emerged out of these ancient Buddhist debates. These are the dominant Buddhisms of today, and each has its own way of interpreting and applying the great man's teaching.

THERAVADA BUDDHISM

The *Theravada* ("School or Way of the Elders") tradition is often described as "classical Buddhism," the form of Buddhism which is most ancient and aligned with the historical teachings of Siddhartha Gautama. This description is not without warrant. So far as historians can tell, the Theravada tradition emphasises what appear to be the earliest and most authentic teachings of Gautama and his first disciples. That said, non-Theravadin Buddhists would dispute this description. They have ways of arguing that their form of Buddhism is the most authentic, precisely because it is an advancement, even a perfection.

Theravada Buddhism is found mainly in Sri Lanka, Burma, Laos, Cambodia, and Thailand. At least four things distinguish this school from other types of Buddhism.

Small Collection of Scriptures (Canon)

First, the group of texts which Theravadins regard as true scripture (their "canon" or agreed-upon collection) is relatively small compared with other forms of Buddhism. The Theravadin canon is preserved in the Pali language and is known as the "The Three Baskets" (*Tripitaka*; also *Tipitaka*). Three types of texts are included here (hence, the name): (1) rules about living in a Buddhist monastery, (2) sayings and sermons attributed to Siddhartha himself, and (3) philosophical reflections on Buddhist teachings.

Do other Buddhists recognise the Theravada scriptures? Yes and no. Non-Theravadins regard Theravadin texts as sacred but incomplete. They also insist that the texts should be read in the Sanskrit translation, not the Pali translation of the Theravadins.

No Gods or Worship

Second, Theravada Buddhists tend to adopt the atheistic viewpoint of Siddhartha Gautama himself. Whereas some Buddhist traditions revere all manner of spiritual beings—some even worship the Buddha himself—Theravadins regard such practices as misguided. They revere Gautama as a perfect man, but not as a divine being.

Self-Effort

Related to the second point, Theravada Buddhism is confident that nirvana is experienced solely through individual human effort. There is no outside help from any god or mystical power in this form of Buddhism; "salvation" comes from within your own moral and mental powers.

The Dhammapada, a Favourite Theravadin Text, Sums Up the Importance of Self-Effort

Oneself indeed is patron of oneself.
Who else indeed could be one's patron?
With oneself well restrained,
one gets a patron hard to get . . .
By oneself is wrong done, by oneself is one defiled.
By oneself wrong is not done. By oneself, surely, one is cleansed.
One cannot purify another;
Purity and impurity are in oneself alone.
Dhammapada 160–66, Khuddaka Nikaya (Carter).

Monks and Laymen

Theravada Buddhism tends to emphasise a distinction between the ordained Buddhist monk and the ordinary Buddhist man or woman (the layperson). Many in this tradition believe that only monks can (in the course of this life) fully attain the detachment from craving which is necessary in order to achieve nirvana. In his *Buddha* (in the Oxford *Very Short Introduction* series), Michael Carrithers of Durham University explains the link in Buddhism between merit through self-effort and the hope of the layperson one day to become a monk:

What the Buddha's teaching had to offer the laity was certain spiritual goods: one was "merit," an immaterial reward garnered by a laymen simply by feeding a monk and listening to his sermon. Merit could be laid up to secure a better rebirth. The more merit in the spiritual account, the better the rebirth. Hence, as there was a high spiritual purpose appropriate to the monk, namely liberation, so there was a lower one appropriate to the layman: better rebirth and the hope that one would eventually be reborn in circumstances allowing one to become a monk and achieve liberation.[1]

MAHAYANA BUDDHISM

Mahayana ("Great Vehicle") Buddhism is the name given to a variety of Buddhist groups with certain beliefs and practices in common. This form of Buddhism is dominant in Tibet, China, Japan, and Korea, and appears to have developed sometime between 100 BCE—100 CE, that is, 400–500 years after Gautama's death. Mahayana Buddhism is distinguished by at least three elements.

Large Collection of Scriptures (Canon)

First, Mahayana Buddhism has a vast collection of sacred texts. Key here are certain additions to the original discourses of the

---

1 Michael Carrithers, *Buddha: A Very Short Introduction* (Oxford University Press, 2013).

Buddha. Whereas Theravadin Buddhism was mainly concerned to preserve statements of the historical Gautama (and those of his immediate circle of disciples), the Mahayana tradition believes that the teaching of the Buddha was ongoing. During meditation or dreams, certain monks could receive revelations from the Buddha disclosing truths not previously comprehended. These were believed to be just as valid as the words of the earthly Gautama himself.

When asked why the historical Buddha did not teach the Mahayana doctrines during his life, Mahayana Buddhists explain that people in his day were not capable of appreciating the deeper truths of Buddhism. The most profound teachings had to be delayed until the world was ready for them. These teachings are called the Great Vehicle, a not-so-subtle critique of the lesser Theravada interpretation.

A Classic Mahayana Explanation of Its Superiority over Theravada

Today the World-honoured One (Buddha) has caused us to ponder over and remove the dirt of all diverting discussions of inferior things. In these we have hitherto being diligent to make progress and have got, as it were, a day's pay for our effort to reach nirvana. Obtaining this, we greatly rejoiced and were contented, saying to ourselves: for our diligence and progress in the Buddha law what we have received is ample. But the World-honoured One, knowing beforehand that our minds were attached to low desires and took delight in inferior things, let us go our own way . . . The Buddha, knowing that our minds delighted in inferior things, by his tactfulness taught according to our capacity, but still we did not perceive that we were really Buddha-sons. Now we have just realised that the World-honoured One does not grudge even the Buddha-wisdom. Wherefore? From of old we are really sons of Buddha, but have only taken pleasure in minor matters; if we had had a mind to take pleasure in the Great, the Buddha would have preached the Great Vehicle Law (Mahayana) to us.

Lotus Sutra, Saddharmapundarika Sutra 4 (Smart).

A Celestial Buddha

Mahayana Buddhism goes beyond the Theravada tradition in teaching that the man Siddhartha Gautama was more than a mortal—he was the incarnation of a celestial, heavenly Buddha who exists throughout time. Mahayana Buddhists serve the Buddha as a divine figure able to assist the faithful in their pursuit of enlightenment. Images of the Buddha, such as those found throughout Asia, are regarded as true objects of veneration. Buddhists bring offerings to them and bow down before them. Doing so achieves great spiritual merit, according to the Mahayana tradition.

The Lotus Sutra, One of the Most popular Mahayana scriptures, Describes in Rapturous Detail the Heavenly Glory of the Buddha

At one time the Buddha was staying at Rajagriha on Holy Eagle Peak with a large group of great monks, twelve thousand in all. Eighty thousand bodhisattva great ones were also there. There were gods, dragons, satyrs, centaurs, asuras, griffins, chimeras, and pythons, in

> addition to all the monks and nuns, laymen and laywomen . . . [and so on]. They placed heavenly banners, flags, canopies, and musical instruments everywhere, pleased the Buddha with heavenly music, then knelt with hands together before him and in one voice wholeheartedly praised him in verse, saying: "He is great, the great awakened one, The great holy Lord, In him there is no defilement, No contamination, no attachment. Trainer of gods and men, elephants and horses, The breeze of his way And the fragrance of his virtue Permeate all. Quiet is his wisdom, Calm his emotion, Serene and firm his reasoning. His will has departed. His self-consciousness has been abolished, Making him serene."
>
> Lotus Sutra, Saddharmapundarika, Sutra 1 (Reeves).

From the point of view of the history of religion, it is fascinating that the world's only atheistic faith (early Theravada Buddhism) was transformed over time into the full-blown theistic spirituality that is Mahayana Buddhism. Such is the longing of the human heart, it seems, to revere someone greater than ourselves.

Mahayana Buddhism also accepts the existence of many divine beings in addition to Buddha himself. Traditions of magic, astrology, and divination have also found a place in the Mahayana spirituality.

Delaying Nirvana: The Bodhisattva Path

I explained earlier that the highest goal of Buddhism is nirvana, the extinction of all desire and escape from rebirth. This is not entirely true for Mahayanists. Even better than attaining nirvana immediately is the life of the bodhisattva (buddha-to-be).

A Bodhisattva is a person who, although qualified to escape rebirth, decides to put off the attainment of nirvana in order to be reborn in this world for the sake of others. The logic is simple. The world is largely ignorant of the Buddha's message and is thus trapped in the sphere of suffering (dukkha). What the world needs, therefore, are people who are willing to delay their own glory, remain in the world, and lead others to liberation. Mahayanists regard this course as the ultimate expression of compassion.

The Buddhist who chooses the Bodhisattva path begins his journey with a vow. The vow includes the three pledges every Buddhist must make: to the Buddha, to the Dharma (or Buddhist teachings), and to the Sangha (Buddhist community). These are called the Three Jewels, and once you have sincerely declared your devotion to these, you have "taken refuge," or (as we might say) become a Buddhist. The Bodhisattva, however, goes beyond this threefold vow, promising—in addition to these three things—to strive for nirvana via the longer, more compassionate route of the Bodhisattva path, helping others gain enlightenment.

Mahayana Buddhism teaches that, after assisting others toward enlightenment and living a life of wisdom and compassion, Bodhisattvas will ultimately arrive at "Buddhahood" themselves. They can "win the sphere of power of a Buddha." Siddhartha Gautama was a Bodhisattva, so Mahayana teaches, who eventually became an all-knowing Buddha. In the same way, all who follow his path and win sufficient spiritual merit can look forward to the glories of full Buddha existence. Once the Bodhisattva has entered Buddhahood, his power to assist unenlightened beings will be greatly magnified.

The Ideals of This Path Are Described Well in a Text Called *The Great Story*

They are Bodhisattvas who live on from life to life (through rebirths) in the possession of manifold good qualities. They are Bodhisattvas who have won the master over karma, and made their deeds renowned through their accumulation of merit . . . They are devoted to the highest good. They win converts by the means of sympathetic appeal . . . They are endowed here in this world with the profound attributes of a Buddha. In their progress towards their goal they are undefiled in acts of body, speech and thought. Through the uprightness of their lives in former existences they are untarnished and pure in conduct possessing perfect knowledge they are men of undimmed understanding. They are eager to win the sphere of power of a Buddha.

The Great Story, Mahavastu 133–134 (Jones).

As another Trivial Pursuit™ aside, the spiritual and political leader of Tibet, the Dalai Lama (whose title means "ocean of wisdom"), is considered to be a shining example of the Bodhisattva tradition. The current Dalai Lama, Tenzin Gyatso, is said to be the thirteenth rebirth (and so the fourteenth Dalai Lama) of the original leader of this Tibetan Buddhist order. He has continued to be reborn not because of the effects of his karma, but because of his decision to continue sharing the truths of the Buddha with the world.

The Dalai Lama illustrates another feature of Mahayana Buddhism just mentioned. Tibetan Buddhism has come to regard the Dalai Lama not only as a repeatedly reborn man, but as a recurring manifestation of one of Mahayana Buddhism's most beloved deities, Avalokitesvara. This deity—and therefore also the Dalai Lama—is believed to be a supreme example of compassion. The Nobel Peace Prize, won by Tenzin Gyatso in 1989, would be considered by Buddhists as testament to this fact.

Theravada ("School or Way of the Elders") and Mahayana ("Great Vehicle") are the two major forms of Buddhism in the world today. However, I should probably point out that many, many more denominations (or subgroups) exist within and beyond these traditions, each with its own perspective and emphasis on the significance of the Buddha's teaching. The so-called Pure Land Buddhism, for example, is a set of traditions within a broad Mahayana outlook which teaches that one can be reborn in alternative planes of existence (pure lands) beyond this corrupt physical earth. There in those planes, one has the opportunity to receive specialist training from glorious Buddhas so as to attain the heights of Buddhahood for oneself or return to earthly planes with greater powers to assist others in their journey toward enlightenment.

Despite the many variations in Buddhist thought and practice, all Buddhists agree on the essentials of Buddhism outlined in chapters 7–10. The Four Noble Truths and the Eightfold Path (as well as the Five Aggregates of Attachment and the Twelve Aspects of Conditioned Arising) remain the unshakable core of all Buddhist belief and activity. Through a commitment to these ideas and habits, the Buddhist aims to extinguish craving and so enjoy the tranquillity of an existence untouched by the sufferings of the world.

BUDDHISM ON A PAGE

Buddhism's key question: Where is peace to be found in this transitory world of pain?

The Founder of Buddhism

- Siddhartha Gautama was an Indian prince born around 500 BCE.
- Siddhartha rejects his native Hindu religion and his life of luxury to discover the solution to the world's suffering.
- Enlightenment came one night in May under a Bodhi Tree.

The Four Noble Truths: The Heart of Gautama's Teaching

- Suffering: existence is marred by suffering.
- The Origin of Suffering: suffering arises from desire.
- The End of Suffering: eradicating desire will release you from suffering and bring the realisation of nirvana.
- The Path to the End of Suffering: the way to end desire, and therefore to eradicate suffering, is to practise the eight habits of the Buddhist life.

The Eightfold Path: The Way to the End of Suffering

- Right Understanding: knowing the truths of Buddhism.
- Right Aim: directing the mind to aspire for the ideals of Buddhism.

- Right Speech: speaking without desire—truthfully, kindly, helpfully.
- Right Action: acting without desire—non-violently, generously, etc.
- Right Livelihood: finding a job fitting to the Buddhist life.
- Right Effort: energetic daily decision to promote good and true thoughts.
- Right Mindfulness: diligent awareness of all sensations of body and mind.
- Right Concentration: practice of Buddhist forms of meditation.

Types of Buddhism: The Two Main Schools

Theravada ("school of the elders"): Often dubbed "classical Buddhism" this school emphasises the historical man Gautama and tends to shun mystical speculation.

Mahayana (the "great vehicle"): With a larger canon of scripture, this school encourages devotion to the Buddha as a saviour-figure. It also emphasises the need to postpone nirvana in order to save others from suffering before eventually becoming a Buddha yourself.

Facts and Figures on Buddhism Today

- Buddhism is the fourth largest religion in the world, with 546 million believers.
- Buddhists make up about 7 percent of the world's population.
- Buddhism is found in 150 countries in the world.
- Buddhism has had a profound impact on religious and cultural life from China, Korea, and Japan in the east to

Afghanistan in the west. It has found a firm footing in southeast Asia, and forms an important part of the religious makeup of Europe and North America.

Famous Buddhists

The Dalai Lama

Tenzin Gyatso was named the fourteenth Dalai Lama in 1937. After the Chinese takeover of Tibet, he was forced into exile. He has spent subsequent years teaching, writing, and speaking out for freedom for Tibet, while advocating non-violent resistance. He was granted the Nobel Peace Prize in 1989.

Leonard Cohen

Leonard Cohen was a Jewish-born Canadian singer, songwriter, and poet. A lifetime of depression, sex, drugs, and rock-n-roll led Cohen to Buddhism. He was ordained as a Monk in 1996, retiring to a Buddhist Centre in Los Angeles. "So Long Marianne," "First We Take Manhattan," "Hallelujah," and "Everybody Knows (I'm Your Man)" are amongst his greatest songs.

Tiger Woods

American professional golfer Tiger Woods is one of the best-known athletes of all time. His 107 worldwide wins include 82 PGA Tour victories. Woods captained the Presidents Cup Team, leading them to a 16–14 victory against the International Team.

Aung San Suu Kyi

A noted campaigner for democracy and human rights in Myanmar (formerly known as Burma), Aung San Suu Kyi was awarded the Nobel Peace Prize in 1991 for her campaign for peaceful democratic reforms. She has become increasingly controversial in the West for her seeming unwillingness to speak openly about her nation's poor treatment of the Rohingya minority.

Good Books and Sites on Buddhism

bbc.co.uk/religion/religions/buddhism/ (a reliable introductory site from the BBC)

www.buddhanet.net (a site seeking to serve all Buddhist traditions)

http://www.dharmanet.org (a site representing the Mahayana tradition)

https://archive.org/details/buddhismintrans03warrgoog/page/n6/mode/2up (an extraordinary collection of Buddhist texts in English translation made a century ago: Warren, H. C. *Buddhism in Translations*. Harvard Oriental Studies, vol.3. Harvard University Press, 1922.

Buswell, R. E., ed. *The Princeton Dictionary of Buddhism*. Princeton University Press, 2014.

Carter, J. R. and Palihawadana, M., trans. *The Dhammapada*. Oxford: Oxford University Press, 2000.

Carrithers, M. *Buddha: A Very Short Introduction*. Oxford University Press, 2013.

Gyatso, K. G. *Introduction to Buddhism: An Explanation of the Buddhist Way of Life*. Cumbria: Tharpa Publications, 2002. (Strongly representing the Mahayana tradition)

Hardy, F. "The Classical Religions of India." *The World's Religions*. Edited by S. Sutherland, et al. London: Routledge,

1988. See pages 569–645, especially "Buddhism," pages 591–603.

Harvey, P. *An Introduction to Buddhism: Teachings, History and Practices.* Cambridge: Cambridge University Press, 1990.

Keown, D. *Buddhism: A Very Short Introduction.* Oxford University Press, 2000.

Rahula, W. *What the Buddha Taught.* Revised edition with illustrative texts translated from the original Pali. New York: Grove Press, 1974. (Representing the Theravada tradition)

Smart, N., and Hecht, R., eds. "Buddhism." *Sacred Texts of the World: A Universal Anthology.* New York: Crossroad, 2002. See pages 231–75.

Smart, N. *The World's Religions.* 2nd edition. Cambridge: Cambridge University Press, 2003. See pages 75–165.

PART 4
JUDAISM, THE WAY OF THE TORAH
IN A NUTSHELL

Judaism is the way of life for God's chosen people, Israel, otherwise known as the Jews. All important for the Jewish believer is the Torah, God's instruction, recorded in the Jewish sacred books known as the Tanakh (what Christians call the Old Testament), Mishnah, and the Talmud. For the Jew, this divine instruction determines everything—the way you work and rest, how you study and what you pray for, what you eat and how you celebrate, and the way you understand Israel's unique place among the other nations (the gentiles).

12

MANY JUDAISMS

Between 1939 and 1945, one-third of all the world's Jews were murdered—that's six million men, women, and children brutally killed in just six years. The program was called *die Endlösung*— The Final Solution. The chancellor of Germany, Adolf Hitler, sought to rid Europe of all people of Jewish descent (including even German Christians with Jewish ancestry). The Holocaust, or *Shoah* as it is known by Hebrew-speakers, represents arguably the vilest moment in human history, and marks out the Jews as a unique people, unmatched in both the depth of their suffering and their will to survive.

As we will soon see, this sense of uniqueness has been part of the Jewish consciousness from the very beginning, ever since God said to Abraham, the founding father of Judaism (1800 BCE), "I will make you into a great nation . . . and all peoples on earth will be blessed through you" (Bereshit [or Genesis] 12:1–3).

Before we explore the unique sufferings and glories of the children of Abraham, I need to clear up some confusion over our modern use of terms like *Jew* and *Israel*.

WHEN IS A JEW A JEW?

The word *Jew* is used nowadays in two quite different ways. *Jew* can be simply an ethnic or cultural term, referring to someone whose ancestry connects them—often centuries ago—with the Hebrew-speaking people of the ancient land of Israel. *Jew*, in this sense, is just like referring to someone as Anglo-Saxon. You will therefore meet people today who insist they are Jews but have little or no interest in the religion we call Judaism.

The word also has a more spiritual usage. *Jew*, in this sense, means someone who follows the religion known as Judaism—they are devoted to the God of Israel. In this sense, people with no cultural or biological lineage to the ancient Israelites may convert to Judaism and be a Jew.

WHICH ISRAEL?

This introduces another problem—the word *Israel*. Today, *Israel* usually means the State of Israel, that country founded in 1948 and which is situated between Lebanon, Jordan, Egypt, and the Mediterranean Sea. A similar political and geographical use of the term was popular in ancient times (say, 1000–100 BCE), when the land of Israel was ruled by Jewish monarchs such as King David (of David and Goliath fame) and others.

Between the ancient land of Israel and the founding of the modern State of Israel, the term *Israel* meant far more than a piece of land in the Middle East. Israel was a collective reference to members of God's chosen people, the Jews, wherever they happened to live. Just as Christians speak of the universal *church* and Muslims speak of the worldwide *umma* (Islamic community) so Jews, for most of their history, have referred to themselves as *Israel*.

The term *Israel* throughout this section will usually be used in this collective spiritual sense. When I want to refer to the political or geographical Israel, I will use phrases like "the (ancient) land of Israel" or "the (modern) State of Israel."

THE FOUR JUDAISMS OF HISTORY

It gets more complicated. We're talking about religion, after all! Our portrait of Judaism in the following chapters moves in four stages, roughly corresponding to four major periods in the history of Israel, and the last of these stages produced three different versions of Judaism:

1. Foundational Judaism (2000–500 BCE): when many of the fundamentals of the faith developed.
2. Interim Judaisms (500 BCE–100 CE): when various factions among the Jewish people all competed for prominence.
3. Classical Judaism (100–1800 CE): when one form of Judaism emerged triumphant and set the course for the bulk of Jewish history.
4. Modern Judaisms (1800–present): when Classical Judaism evolved into the three versions of Jewish faith you might come across today, Orthodox Judaism, Reformed Judaism, and Conservative Judaism.

We begin in the next chapter with Foundational Judaism.

13
FOUNDATIONAL JUDAISM

We begin with an overview of the origins of Israel as portrayed in the oldest Jewish scriptures. As the Holocaust would illustrate for the twentieth century, the story of the Jews is a tale of great drama and endurance.

CIRCUMCISION AND THE FAMILY OF ABRAHAM

I said earlier that Hinduism pips Judaism at the post by about three centuries. This is because it is normal to speak about the religion of Judaism as beginning to take shape with the ancient figure of Moses (of Ten Commandments fame) in the 1200s BCE (or maybe a century or so earlier). Many Jews would prefer to trace their origins 500 years earlier to the so-called patriarchs.

According to the Jewish scriptures, sometime around 1800 BCE, a man named Abram (later called Abraham), from a region in southern Iraq, was approached by the Creator and told to leave his country, his family, his culture, and his pagan gods. In return, God would transform Abraham's descendants into a "great nation" through which all nations in the world would be blessed (Bereshit or Genesis 12:1–3, quoted earlier). Abraham did the sensible thing and placed his destiny in the hands of the Almighty. In time, his family would indeed begin to grow.

At this point, the biblical narrative introduces the rite of circumcision, the removal of the penis foreskin (or *prepuce*, for the technically-minded). Abraham is told that every male in his family from that time on is to be circumcised as the sign of belonging to the chosen family. This "mark" on the male reproductive organ was a perpetual reminder to the Jewish people that, whatever forces may work against them, God's people would multiply until they had reached their destiny.

To this day, the ritual of circumcision (*brit milah*) marks the beginning of Jewish (male) life. On the eighth day of a Jewish boy's life, in the presence of at least ten Jewish men, a *mohel* (circumciser) performs the rite on the child with precision and expertise. Traditional blessings and prayers are said during the ceremony as the infant is welcomed into the promise of God and the world of Judaism.

Abraham's family began to grow. In fact, his grandson, Jacob, had twelve sons. This Jacob was later also named Israel, which means "God strives"—God strives on behalf of his chosen people. The twelve sons of Jacob/Israel headed the twelve family clans, or tribes, of the Jewish people. The famous stage show *Joseph and the Amazing Technicolor Dream Coat* narrates the story of one of Jacob's sons, Joseph, who, after being sold into slavery by his brothers, ended up becoming a chief administrator in Egypt. This turned out rather well for the family of Israel, since it meant they could move to the safety of Egypt and avoid a famine which struck their own land. The family now numbered seventy people—not quite a "nation," but a healthy-sized family, nonetheless.

EXODUS AND THE PASSOVER

Things were looking good for the original family of seventy living in Egypt in the eighteenth century BCE. God's promise to Abraham seemed well on track. But then tragedy struck the family of Israel—the first of many in the course of their long history.

The Jewish scriptures explain that the descendants of Abraham began to increase exponentially, so much so that after a few hundred years, the "family" of Israel numbered many thousands. Now they were a mini nation within a nation. Naturally, the Egyptians were not entirely happy with the expanding Israelite presence in their midst. Just as three millennia later, Adolf Hitler would put Jews into slave camps, the pharaohs of Egypt began to mistreat the descendants of Jacob, using them as a slave nation to work on the massive building programs of northern Egypt in the mid-1200s BCE (others place this a century or more earlier).

Enter Moses. Moses was a Jew with an Egyptian education and upbringing. His loyalty to the God of Israel, however, drove him passionately to seek the deliverance of his people, whom he daily witnessed being abused and even slaughtered. "Let my people go," was Moses's daring demand to Ramses II, the pharaoh in charge of the world's No. 1 superpower. Not surprisingly, Ramses was unmoved. (Again, some date these things to the time of an earlier pharaoh.)

At this point, the Jewish account describes a series of unspeakable disasters that fell upon Pharaoh and his kingdom: locust plagues, hailstorms, and eventually, the mysterious death of Egyptian children. This last tragedy convinces a reluctant Pharaoh to let Israel go. The day is commemorated in one of the most important festivals of the Jewish calendar, the Passover (more about that later). On that fateful evening, God's judgment fell on the tyrannical Egyptians, but "passed over" the Jews. Moses had instructed all the Israelites to kill, cook, and eat a lamb that night, and to paint some of the blood of the animal on the outside doorframes of their homes. In the words of Shemot or Exodus 12:13: "And the blood on the houses where you are staying shall be a sign for you: when I see the blood I will pass over you, so that no plague will destroy you when I strike the land of Egypt."

The people of Israel escaped Egypt, and eventually journeyed to their promised land in the north (the land of Israel). Today, Jews recall this exodus event as a microcosm of their entire history and as a symbol of their future: whatever troubles come upon Israel, the Lord of the universe will restore his chosen people to their rightful glory. God will strive for Israel.

THE TORAH AND JEWISH LIFE

The next dramatic and important event in this potted account of traditional Jewish history is the provision of a national constitution, that is, laws by which the newly liberated people of God could be governed as they settle in the promised land (the land of Israel).

To cut a long story short, a couple of months after leaving Egypt, Moses was called by God to go up a mountain somewhere in the Sinai Peninsula where he received, among other things, the famous Ten Commandments. These ten pieces of instruction are, in a sense, a microcosm of the rest of the Jewish legal material found in three whole books of the Jewish scriptures (Shemot = Exodus; Wayiqra = Leviticus; Devarim = Deuteronomy). This was something close to Israel's "constitution" as determined by God. Social welfare, criminal law, religious rituals, even environmental policy all feature in the vast set of laws Jews call *Torah*.

The first principle of this constitution is monotheism, the belief that there is only one Creator and Lord of the universe. Everything about Jewish piety flowed from this idea. The refusal to have images of the deity (idolatry), the sense of national mission and exceptionalism, and the universal ethic of justice toward every man and woman—all these things flow from monotheism. This is why the first of the famous Ten Commandments demands loyalty to just one God.

The Ten Commandments

I the LORD am your God who brought you out of the land of Egypt, the house of bondage:

You shall have no other gods beside Me.

You shall not make for yourself a sculptured image, any likeness of what is in the heavens above, or on the earth below, or in the waters below the earth. You shall not bow down to them or serve them . . .

You shall not swear falsely by the name of the LORD your God; for the LORD will not clear one who swears falsely by His name.

Observe the sabbath day and keep it holy, as the LORD your God has commanded you. Six days you shall labor and do all your work, but the seventh day is a sabbath of the LORD your God; you shall not do any work . . .

Honor your father and your mother, as the LORD your God has commanded you, that you may long endure, and that you may fare well, in the land that the LORD your God is assigning to you.

You shall not murder.

You shall not commit adultery.

You shall not steal.

You shall not bear false witness against your neighbor.

You shall not covet your neighbor's wife. You shall not crave your neighbor's house, or his field, or his male or female slave, or his ox, or his ass, or anything that is your neighbor's.

Devarim or Deuteronomy 5:6–18 (Tanakh)

Torah is an important word in Judaism, so it requires an explanation. The word derives from the Hebrew for "instruction" and, in the first instance, refers to God's instruction of the Israelites (at Sinai) in these legal, environmental, religious, and social matters. From this usage, the word *Torah* came to refer specifically to the first five books of the Jewish Bible where these laws are narrated. The other two sections of the Jewish Bible are called *Nevi'im* (Prophets) and *Ketuvim* (Writings). The whole Jewish Bible, then, is often given the acronym *TaNaKh* (Torah, Nevi'im, Ketuvim; or Law, Prophets, Writings). From this point on, I will frequently refer to the Jewish Bible (or what Christians call the Old Testament) as the Tanakh.

Getting back to the word *Torah*: because the second and third parts of the Tanakh (the Prophets and the Writings) are heavily influenced by the first section (the Torah, or Law), the word *Torah* came also to be used as a catch-all term for the whole "instruction of God" revealed in all three sections of the Jewish Bible.

For now, it is worth simply remembering that Torah is a central concept in Judaism. It refers to the instruction of God revealed to Israel first through Moses and then through the entire sacred tradition of the Jews. What the Four Noble Truths are to Buddhism, Torah is to Judaism: pretty much everything. The purpose of the Torah was to establish Israel as a divinely blessed people through whom all other nations (*goyim* or "gentiles") would be blessed.

KING DAVID AND THE FUTURE MESSIAH

After the Exodus from Egypt, the revelation of the Torah, and some time wandering around the desert, the newly freed people of Israel entered the promised land, where they encountered stiff resistance from the people who then occupied the land— the Canaanites. From about 1200 BCE to around 1000 BCE (again, the dates are disputed), the nation of Israel was really a loose confederation of twelve not-very-peaceful family clans, each with its own patch of the land. What was needed, thought the Israelites, was leadership.

Enter King David (of David and Goliath fame). David was actually the second king of Israel, but the first, Saul, was such a disaster that we can skip over him with just a mention.

What do we know of King David? Well, for one thing, we know he was a frail human being like the rest of us. Two chapters of the Tanakh describe a rather unflattering affair between David and the wife of one of his loyal military officers. The fact that the Tanakh records this sin is extraordinary, given the tendency of ancient cultures to describe their favourite leaders in glowing terms.

David was also a great musician who wrote many religious songs; he was (and still is) known among Jews as the "Sweet Singer of Israel." The book of Tehillim (Psalms), part of the third section of the Tanakh (the Writings), contains many hymns attributed to David. One of them is introduced as the song of confession written after David's aforementioned affair. It begins: "Have mercy upon me, O God, as befits Your faithfulness; in keeping with Your abundant compassion, blot out my transgressions" (Psalm or Tehillim 51). These songs of David are regularly used in Jewish prayers to this day.

More important than David's humanity and musical accomplishments is what he represented for Israel. This was the man who overthrew the pagan enemies of God, extended the borders of the land of Israel, and captured the Holy City of Jerusalem. These events won David a central place in the hopes and dreams of traditional Jews from 1000 BCE right up to today. According to a prophet of the time named Nathan, God had chosen David as the founder of a kingdom and a dynasty that would last forever: "Your house and your kingship shall ever be secure before you; your throne shall be established forever" (2 Samuel 7:16, Tanakh). The interesting thing here is that this divine promise extends far beyond the time of David (tenth century BCE): the throne of David described here would be "established forever."

The importance of the figure of King David for Judaism is difficult to overstate. The promise that David's kingdom would be "established forever" is the basis for the enduring Jewish belief in a future Messiah. The word *Messiah* (*Christ* is the Greek equivalent) is Hebrew for "anointed one," a reference to the anointing ceremony (or coronation) in which oil was poured over the king as a symbol of divine power and blessing. David was anointed in just this way. According to numerous prophecies in the Tanakh, a future son of David would be the Anointed One in an ultimate sense.

One traditional prayer, said by Jews after each weekday meal, reveals the fervent longing for the promised descendant of King David: "Have mercy Lord, our God, on Israel Your people; on Jerusalem, Your city, on Zion [the hill on which Jerusalem was built], the resting place of Your Glory; on the monarchy of the house of David, your Messiah" (Rahem, Third Blessing After Meals [Siddur]).

The memory of King David, and his rule on God's behalf, established forever in Jewish thought the hope of an eternal king (the Messiah) by whose reign Israel would achieve its purpose.

TEMPLE, FORGIVENESS, AND WORSHIP

David's successor and son, King Solomon, built one of the most important features of Israel's religion, a feature comparable in importance to the Torah and the king. I am speaking about the great temple of God in the Holy City of Jerusalem.

The temple built by Solomon was not an enormous structure—about the size of a large church building today—but its significance in Jewish life was immense. The temple represented the throne room of God, a kind of palace for the universal King. Jews knew that God was located everywhere in the universe, but they also believed men and women could approach the omnipresent King in a tangible way in the Jerusalem temple, just as earthly subjects might humbly approach a king in his royal court.

A huge number of priests was employed to run the temple

functions. Key among their tasks was offering sacrifices to God. Some of these were animal sacrifices, offered to God on huge burning altars in the heart of the temple. The priests often ate the cooked portions of these animals as part of their stipend in lieu of possessing land. Other daily sacrifices included simple offerings of grain and bread. Much of this was also consumed by the priests.

Perhaps the most important temple sacrifice took place just once a year, on the Day of Atonement, or Yom Kippur. It was a festival celebrating the mercy of God toward the whole of Israel. Two goats were presented to the high priest. One was slaughtered and its blood sprinkled on the central altar in the Most Holy Place in the temple. The picture here was of God's judgment falling on the animal instead of the people of Israel. The other goat had a more pleasant fate and provided a wonderful picture of divine forgiveness. The priest would lay both hands on the live goat's head while confessing to God the many sins of Israel. Then, in the company of someone appointed for the task, the goat would be led out into the wilderness of southern Israel and released. This was a potent symbol of Israel's sins being removed from God's presence never to be thought of again. We get the expression *scapegoat* (someone who takes the blame for another) from this ancient Yom Kippur ceremony.

One cannot overstate the central place of the Jerusalem temple in ancient Jewish life—and in modern Jewish imagination—but a mere three centuries after the reign of King Solomon, that glorious structure lay in ruins. Here we arrive at the second great disaster in foundational Jewish history.

DESTRUCTION OF THE FIRST TEMPLE (586 BCE)

The Tanakh is strange in its honesty about God's people. It narrates how, in the period after King Solomon, the Jews did not obey the Torah. Justice was perverted, other gods were worshipped, and violence abounded, even among the kings and priests of Israel whose task it was to keep the rest of Israel on track.

God sent prophets during these centuries, says the Tanakh, many of whose writings are now contained in the second portion of the Jewish scriptures (the Nevi'im, or Prophets). These charismatic leaders, such as Isaiah, Hosea, and Ezekiel, pleaded with kings and commoners alike to return to the Torah, to obey the God who had rescued them from Egypt. The people often rejected the prophets and, in some cases, killed them.

But the warnings of the prophets proved true—which is probably partly why their writings were revered and preserved. These divine heralds predicted that if Israel did not turn back to the way of the Torah, God would allow foreign nations to invade the land, destroy the temple, and expel the Jews into foreign lands where they would again, as in Egypt centuries before, become a slave nation.

Sure enough, in the mid-to-late 700s BCE, the kingdom of Assyria, under kings with such fancy names as Tiglath-pileser III, Shalmaneser V, and Sargon II, conquered the northern part of the land of Israel. Then, 150 years later, King Nebuchadrezzar II (sometimes spelt Nebuchadnezzar) of Babylon, roughly modern Iraq, moved his armies into the southern part of the land of Israel and in 586 BCE did exactly as the prophets had warned: he destroyed the temple and carried off into exile (in Babylon) many of the wealthiest and best-educated members of Jewish society. Israel was now a ghost of what it had once been.

True to form, the prophets of this period also predicted a brighter future for Israel. After a time of judgment, they insisted, God would again restore the fortunes of his people. The temple would be rebuilt, the exiles would return to the land, and Israel would finally become a "great nation" through which all nations would be "blessed."

A Prophecy from 700 BCE of Israel's (and the World's) Recovery

The word that Isaiah son of Amoz prophesied concerning Judah and
    Jerusalem.
In the days to come,
The Mount of the Lord's House [i.e., temple]
Shall stand firm above the mountains
And tower above the hills;
And all the nations
Shall gaze on it with joy.
And the many peoples shall go and say:
"Come, let us go up to the Mount of the Lord,
To the House of the God of Jacob;
That He may instruct us in His ways,
And that we may walk in His paths."
For instruction shall come forth from Zion,
The word of the Lord from Jerusalem.
Thus He will judge among the nations
And arbitrate for the many peoples,

And they shall beat their swords into plowshares
And their spears into pruning hooks:
Nation shall not take up
Sword against nation;
They shall never again know war.

Isaiah 2:1–5 (Tanakh)

Less than fifty years after the sacking of Jerusalem, there was a new superpower on the block, Cyrus II of Persia (modern-day Iran) who, after defeating Babylon, issued a decree in 538 BCE that the Jews should return to their land and rebuild their temple. That is exactly what many Jews did and, less than twenty-five years later, the temple, with its sacred rituals and public worship of God, was back in use. The prophets' predictions had come true—sort of.

14

INTERIM JUDAISMS

S o far, we have been discussing what I have called "foundational Judaism." Much of what first emerged in that era still determines Jewish belief and practice. The importance of belonging to Abraham's family, circumcision, obedience to the laws of the Torah, veneration of the Tanakh as God's Word, celebration of the festivals of Passover and the Day of Atonement, the hope for an eternal messianic kingdom, and so on—all of these are found in various forms of Judaism today.

But significant changes took place in Judaism after this foundational period. The dramas of the Jewish people would go from bad to worse, and Jews would respond to these events in several different, somewhat contradictory, ways. These different responses are what I am calling "interim" Judaisms, that is, the versions of Judaism that existed temporarily before Classical Judaism (discussed in the next chapter) emerged victorious in the second century CE.

THE DRAMAS OF THE SECOND TEMPLE

The Second Temple (referred to earlier) received numerous renovations in the centuries after it was built. In the late first century

BCE, the temple area was expanded to roughly the size of a modern football stadium. It became a cause of great cultural pride for the Jews.

After the Persians (sixth to fourth centuries BCE) came the Hellenistic (or Greek) Empire, under Alexander the Great and his successors (fourth to second centuries BCE). These Hellenistic kings ruled the Jews with a leadership style ranging from indifferent to outright tyrannical. One of the worst was Antiochus IV Epiphanes, who slaughtered thousands of Jews and, in 167 BCE, had the audacity to set up in the Jewish temple an idol to the pagan god Zeus Olympios. Nothing could have been more heartbreaking and offensive to monotheistic Jews.

These events sparked a Jewish rebellion which, amazingly, resulted in a victory for the Jews under the leadership of one Judas Maccabeus, a brilliant army general from a priestly family. Judas quickly restored Jewish worship and rededicated the temple to the one true God (164 BCE). This event is still celebrated today in the Jewish Hanukkah ("dedication") festival, which occurs around Christmas (more about this later).

Just as importantly, Judas Maccabeus founded a decades-long dynasty of Jewish priest-kings who ruled Jerusalem and its environs as a free and autonomous state. Was this the beginning of the glorious future predicted by the prophets? Unfortunately, it was not.

The Hasmonean Dynasty (as the Maccabean kings were called) came to an end in 63 BCE. The Romans had arrived, and most things gave way when the Romans came to town! The entry of the Romans into Palestine (the later Roman name for the land of Israel) marked the end of a free Jewish state. Not until 1948, two thousand years later, would the Jews have any real jurisdiction over the "promised land."

Heavy taxes were imposed by the Romans, and a strong military presence was felt throughout the region. Numerous Jewish uprisings were of little consequence, and, when the Jews started an all-out war against their occupiers (66–70 CE), Rome responded with devastating force. The people of Jerusalem were massacred, and the temple of God was brought to the ground a second time (August, 70 CE). What was once the centre of Jewish religious life was now a mound of rubble.

All that remains of the Second Temple today is a 100-metre section of the western wall, known as the Wailing Wall, where modern Jews cry out to God for the restoration of his temple. Standing where the temple once stood is the Dome of the Rock, the oldest Islamic monument in the world (built around 690 CE). It is the world's most hotly disputed piece of real estate!

Yet, hope remained. In the hotbed of drama that was ancient Judea and Galilee (the southern and northern regions of ancient Israel) it is not surprising that Jews responded to the crises and victories and further crises by proposing different visions of what Israel could and should be. These are the *interim* Judaisms, four of which I will discuss in the remainder of this chapter (and the fifth in the next chapter).

SADDUCEES: ARISTOCRATS AND PRIESTS

The first faction of Judaism in this period was the Sadducees, a group of conservative Jews who rejected innovations in the faith, especially those that might diminish the role of priest and temple. Sadducees appear to have dominated the priesthood and formed a kind of religious aristocracy in Jerusalem.

When the Romans came to power in Palestine (63 BCE), those who remained loyal to Rome were able to keep their positions in Jewish society. The Sadducees largely cooperated with the invaders, and were thus able to assert their influence in the Holy City and bolster their temple-focused vision of Judaism. Of course, things changed after the destruction of the Second Temple.

ESSENES: APOCALYPTIC HOLY MEN

Not everyone was happy with the power and wealth of the Jerusalem elite. The second faction in this period was the Essenes. You may have heard of the so-called Dead Sea Scrolls, a huge collection of writings found over several years beginning in 1947 in caves around Qumran on the northwestern shore of the Dead Sea (southern Israel).

The scrolls are believed by most scholars to have been produced by the Essenes, a group of ultra-devout Jews who avoided the impure cities of Israel and lived in self-sufficient communities where they shared their possessions, studied the Torah, and engaged in meticulous bathing and eating rituals. They believed that God would soon wipe out the Romans and the corrupt Jewish authorities currently controlling the temple, and then the Lord would place them in leadership over the people of God. This did not pan out.

ZEALOTS: FIGHTERS AND PATRIOTS

Another vision of Israel was promoted by a third faction, the Zealots. As you might work out from their name, the Zealots were fiercely loyal to the traditions of Judaism and violently opposed to the Roman presence in the Holy Land. Whereas the Sadducees opted for cooperation with the imperial powers, and the Essenes chose to remove themselves from public life, the Zealots decided to fight. They staged various uprisings, climaxing in a reign of terror around 65–70 CE, in which they resorted to assassinating key Jewish leaders, whom they believed were collaborating with Rome. It was the actions of the Zealots, and those swept up in their vision for a new Israel, that led to the war with Rome and the eventual downfall (in 70 CE) of Jerusalem and its temple.

FOLLOWERS OF YESHUA: HERETICS OF A FALSE MESSIAH

A fourth faction of first-century Judaism was launched by a man named Yeshua ben Yosef, or the more anglicised Jesus son of Joseph. A simple peasant from Galilee in the north, Yeshua explicitly rejected the aims of the Zealots. He demanded that his fellow Jews "turn the other cheek" and "love your enemies" (even the Romans).

Many hailed Yeshua as a great teacher, healer, and prophet. Others denounced him as a deceiver. The Sadducees were deeply troubled by him. Not only was it rumoured that he presumed to hand out God's forgiveness (a core business of the temple), but some began to suppose this man might be the long-awaited Son of David, the Messiah. This threatened to upset the good relations the Sadducees had fostered with the Romans.

Yeshua was removed, crucified outside Jerusalem during a Passover festival in the early 30s CE. His followers, however, preserved his memory and promoted his teachings, first in the land of Israel, then throughout all the lands of the Roman Empire and beyond. This movement came to be known as Christianity.

Within a century or more, it was viewed as a separate religion entirely from Judaism.

There was a fifth type of Judaism in this period, and it would set the course of Israel for the next two millennia. It began with a faction called the Pharisees, and it developed into what is known as Classical Judaism.

15

CLASSICAL JUDAISM

In discussing the rise of Classical Judaism, I do not want to give the impression that this form of the faith was a radical break with what went before. It was not. All of the aspects discussed earlier in our study of Judaism—the sense of family, circumcision, the importance of the exodus, the laws of the Torah, the religious festivals, the hope of the prophets, and so on—featured prominently in Classical Judaism.

Classical Judaism began with a group known as the Pharisees.

THE PHARISEES, THE TEMPLE, AND THE SYNAGOGUES

In the period of the priest-kings of Israel (164–63 BCE), a group arose in Israel that stressed the need for personal purity in the affairs of ordinary life. The group consisted of both scholars and ordinary believers (and included some priests as well). It was more a reform movement than a political party. Members of the movement came to be called *Pharisees*, perhaps from the Hebrew word *parush*, meaning "separated," that is, separated from impure things.

In emphasising individual purity, the Pharisees developed

intricate rules concerning the affairs of daily existence—how you ate, how you washed, how and when you worked, with whom you could associate, how much of your possessions to give to God, and so on. These laws were known as the *traditions of the elders* because they had been passed down from generation to generation. They were sacred and designed to promote total obedience to the Torah revealed to Moses at Sinai.

While the temple was still standing, the Pharisees were simply a parallel movement in Jewish life, sometimes prominent, sometimes peripheral. However, when the Second Temple was destroyed in 70 CE, never to be rebuilt, conditions were perfect for pharisaic teachers, called rabbis, to capture the public imagination.

These rabbis had always said that what counted most in life was personal devotion to the Torah (and the traditions of the elders). With the temple gone, this emphasis seemed the most sensible option. Whereas the followers of Yeshua (later called Christians) argued that the destruction of the temple was a sign that their vision of Judaism was correct—with Yeshua himself as the ultimate atoning sacrifice—the Pharisees insisted that atonement for sins could be found in obedience to the Torah, study, and prayer.

The success of the Pharisees was assisted by the emergence of the synagogue sometime between 500–100 BCE. We might think of a synagogue—a word that means "gathering"—as the Jewish equivalent of a Christian church (an odd way to put things, given that the church emerged from the synagogue). In any case, the synagogue was an official gathering of Jews who met together, usually in a purposefully built space, to pray, to hear the Torah, to sing, and to study. It provided a context in which Jews could express their faith in an organised way outside of the Jerusalem temple. Also, if you lived a long way from the Holy City, this was a "godsend."

For the Pharisees, then, the synagogue was the perfect venue from which to teach the masses the importance of the traditions of the elders. When the temple in Jerusalem was destroyed, and the role of the priests was thereby diminished, the synagogues became indispensable and the role of the Pharisees pivotal.

The result of all this, early in the second century CE, was the triumph of the Judaism of the Pharisees, sometimes also called *Rabbinic Judaism*. All Judaisms, from that time on, owe their existence to this classical form of the faith.

THE RISE OF THE DUAL-TORAH

Let me now try to describe something of the comprehensive vision of (post-temple) Jewish life that was offered by the Pharisees and which was crystallised in Classical Judaism. We begin with perhaps the most significant aspect of that vision, the insistence that the Torah given to Moses was twofold.

After the destruction of the temple in Jerusalem, many rabbis fled the Holy City to establish communities devoted to the study of the Torah and the traditions of the elders. The most famous of these was at Jamnia (near the south coast of what the Romans called Palestine). There rabbis were required to learn and memorise not only the written Tanakh but also the insights and rulings of their rabbinic predecessors. In fact, these ever-growing traditions of the elders were regarded by Rabbinic Judaism as part of the Torah itself, part of the instruction of God revealed to Moses.

How the Oral Torah Was Passed Down

Moses received Torah at Sinai and handed it on to Joshua, Joshua to elders, and elders to prophets, And prophets handed it on to the men of the great assembly. They said three things: (1) "Be prudent in judgment. (2) "Raise up many disciples. (3) "Make a fence for the Torah." Simeon the Righteous was one of the last survivors of the great assembly . . . Antigonos of Sokho received [the Torah] from Simeon the Righteous . . . Yohanan of Jerusalem received [it] from them. Yose b. Yoezer says, (1) "Let your house be a gathering place for sages. (2) "And wallow in the dust of their feet. (3) "And drink in their words with gusto." Yose b. Yohanan of Jerusalem says, (1) "Let your house be wide open. (2) "And seat the poor at your table ["make . . . members of your household"]. (3) "And don't talk too much with women." . . . Hillel and Shammai received [it] from them. Hillel says, (1) "Be disciples of Aaron, "loving peace and pursuing peace, loving people and drawing them near to the Torah."

Mishnah, Avot 1:1–12 (Neusner).

Here is a critical point in the development of Judaism: these rabbis said that the Torah is twofold. When God spoke to Moses at Sinai in the 1200s BCE, only part of that revelation was written down. The other part was passed on orally, that is, by word of mouth, first to Joshua (Moses' assistant), then on to the subsequent generations, right up to the Pharisees of the post-temple period. The traditions of the elders, therefore, are not simply manmade rules as some claimed (Yeshua ben Yosef, or Jesus, for instance); they are the very instruction of God. At this point, then, we must meet the second holy book of Classical Judaism, the Mishnah.

THE MISHNAH

Somewhere around 200 CE, the leader of the Jews of Palestine, Rabbi Judah ha-Nasi, decided to bring into one volume all of the traditions of the elders as they were preserved in the memories of his fellow rabbis. The result was the holy book known as the Mishnah. The word *Mishnah* means "repetition"—repetition, of course, was the principal means of memorising and passing on the traditions.

The Mishnah records the sayings and legal opinions of about 150 rabbis from the first and second centuries CE. Their statements, however, are believed to preserve the instruction given to Moses 1300 years before.

The Mishnah has sixty-three chapters (usually called *tractates*) in six topical divisions: (1) agricultural rules; (2) laws about "appointed times," that is, religious festivals and the like; (3) commands relating to women (marriage and divorce); (4) rulings about legal damages; (5) regulations about the Jerusalem temple; and (6) decrees on purity (food laws, bathing rituals, handling of animals, and so on). My copy of the Mishnah runs over 1,100 pages.

Prohibited Forms of Work on the Sabbath (Day of Rest), According to the Mishnah

The generative categories of acts of labor [prohibited on the Sabbath] are forty less one: (1) he who sows, (2) ploughs, (3) reaps, (4) binds sheaves, (5) threshes, (6) winnows, (7) selects [fit from unfit produce or crops], (8) grinds, (9) sifts, (10) kneads, (11) bakes; (12) he who shears wool, (13) washes it, (14) beats it, (15) dyes it; (16) spins, (17) weaves, (18) makes two loops, (19) weaves two threads, (20) separates two threads; (21) ties, (22) unties, (23) sews two stitches, (24) tears in order to sew two stitches; (25) he who traps a deer, (26) slaughters it, (27) flays it, (28) salts it, (29) cures its hide, (30) scrapes it, and (31) cuts it up; (32) he who writes two letters, (33) erases two letters in order to write two letters; (34) he who builds, (35) tears down; (36) he who puts out a fire, (37) kindles a fire; (38) he who hits with a hammer; (39) he who transports an object from one domain to another—lo, these are the forty generative acts of labor less one.

Mishnah, Shabbat 7:2 (Neusner).

In Classical Judaism, the Mishnah is a holy book on par with the Tanakh. Both documents record God's instruction to his people, Israel. Hence, the Tanakh and the Mishnah, together, are sometimes called the *dual-Torah*, or even simply the *Torah*.

Two other sets of holy books exist in Classical Judaism, and they are still revered today.

MIDRASH AND THE TALMUD

The first set of documents is called *Midrash*, from the Hebrew word for "investigation." Midrash is a vast body of works devoted to interpreting sections of the Tanakh. Very ancient biblical texts are thus recast to have contemporary significance.

Just as Midrash interprets the Tanakh, so another set of books interprets the Mishnah. This is called the *Talmud*, meaning "study" or "learning," and there are two volumes. One Talmud was compiled in the Holy Land around 400 CE and is called the Palestinian Talmud. The other was compiled in Babylon around 600 CE and is called, not surprisingly, the Babylonian Talmud.

The Talmud's Exposition of the Sabbath Rules from the Mishnah

GEMARA (completion of interpretation) . . . "Ploughing." Ploughing, digging, furrowing, are one and the same kind of labor. R. Shesheth said: One who removes a knoll of earth in a house becomes liable for building, and if in a field he is liable for ploughing. Rabha said: Filling up a hole in the house makes one liable for building, and in the field for ploughing . . .

"Binding into sheaves." Rabha said: One who gathers salt from salt works is guilty of the act of binding into sheaves. Abayi, however, said that binding into sheaves applies only to produce of the soil . . .

"Grinding." Said R. Papa: To chop beets is the same as to grind.

> Splitting wood for kindling is the same as grinding. Said R. Ashi:
> Splitting leather is the same class of work as cutting by measure . . .
>
> Babylonian Talmud, Shabbat 7:2 (Rodkinson).

The Judaism of the dual-Torah (written and oral) set the course of the Jewish faith for centuries (and, for many, even today). Let me now unpack some of the most important features of Classical Judaism.

FIVE ANNUAL FESTIVALS OF CLASSICAL JUDAISM

One of the most enduring legacies of Classical Judaism is the fixed Jewish calendar with its festivals of joy and sorrow. Although festivals had always been a part of Judaism, the rabbis of the Mishnah and Talmud set down in detail many of the guidelines for how these celebrations should be conducted.

There are five main festivals on the Jewish calendar, each designed to recall some aspect of the Jewish vision of God and the world.

New Year (Rosh Hashanah)

The Jewish New Year begins with the appearance of the new moon in the month of Tishri (September–October). Far from being an occasion of excitement and joy (as are New Year's celebrations in Western culture), Rosh Hashanah is a sombre day. Israel is reminded by this festival of its important duties as the people of God. The synagogue service for the Rosh Hashanah festival features the sounding of the ram's horn, the *shofar*, as a call to spiritual awakening.

Day of Atonement (Yom Kippur).

Ten days after New Year, the period of self-examination climaxes on the Day of the Atonement, or Yom Kippur (tenth of Tishri). In the chapter on foundational Judaism, we saw that this day symbolises God's forgiveness of his people.

While sacrifices are no longer made on Yom Kippur—because these were only ever to be offered in the Jerusalem temple—the day still commemorates God's mercy. It is marked by prayer; confession of sin; abstaining from food, drink, and sex; and a synagogue service that goes from morning until evening, just as the rabbis of the Mishnah and Talmud instructed.

Feast of Tabernacles (Sukkot)

Five days after Yom Kippur comes the Feast of Tabernacles (Tishri is quite a month), which commemorates the period when Israel wandered in the wilderness of Sinai (just after receiving the Torah) and lived in makeshift tents or tabernacles.

Lasting for eight days, the most striking part of the festivities is the construction of frail huts (recalling the ancient tabernacles). The faithful sit in these to eat their meals.

Passover (Pesach)

Several months after the Feast of Tabernacles comes the great Passover festival. On the evening of the fourteenth of Nisan (around March–April), Jews begin a week-long celebration of God's rescue of his people from Egypt. The meal on the eve of the festival (which is often repeated the next night) is called the *seder*. It is quite an elaborate affair. Following a special service at the synagogue, families gather to eat special foods, each with its own spiritual significance: lamb to recall the sacrifice of the first Passover animal; bitter herbs to remember the suffering of Egypt; bread without leaven in imitation of the first Israelites, who fled Egypt without time to bake leavened bread; and wine to mark the freedom and joy of God's deliverance. Various traditional prayers and blessings are said during the meal. The Passover festival is also called the Feast of Unleavened Bread.

Feast of Weeks (Shavuot)

Fifty days after Passover, the Feast of Weeks (falling in May or June) celebrates the giving of the Law at Sinai. It is also called Pentecost (Greek for "fiftieth day"), and it is marked by special synagogue services at which portions of the Tanakh are read. In addition, many Jews spend the whole night reading and studying the Torah, reminding themselves of the great gift of God's instruction. Jewish schools and colleges sometimes hold their graduations on this day.

OTHER HOLY DAYS

Sabbath (Shabbat)

Just as the five major festivals mark the cycle of the year, so the Sabbath marks the cycle of the week. The fourth commandment of the well-known Ten Commandments mandates the Sabbath as a day of rest. The Mishnah and Talmud further explain what that rest does and doesn't consist of.

The Sabbath officially commences at sunset on Friday evening and concludes at sunset on Saturday evening. The classical rabbis declared that the Sabbath finishes when at least three stars are visible in the Saturday night sky. There are more exact ways to determine the Sabbath times in the modern world, and there are phone apps to indicate the beginning and end of the Sabbath wherever you happen to be in the world. For example, today's Sabbath in Sydney (I happen to be typing these words on Friday, July 2, 2021) commences this afternoon with the lighting of a candle at precisely 4:40 p.m.

No work is conducted by Jews on the Sabbath, and, again, the ancient rabbis stipulated with great care what constitutes "work." But Sabbath is far more than a simple "day off." It is a time for Jews to attend the synagogue with other believers (up to three times in twenty-four hours), to eat meals with family members, to say prayers, to light candles, and, of course, to study the Torah.

Bar/Bat Mitzvah

The Torah is honoured in another ceremony which marks a teenager's transition into Jewish adulthood.

The rabbis of the classical period declared that thirteen was the age at which Jewish boys could understand and obey the dual-Torah. Based on this ruling, a ceremony was devised to celebrate the moment. The *bar mitzvah* ("son of commandment") is a simple ritual. The boy (usually aged thirteen) is called to the front of the synagogue where the Tanakh is found. He then reads aloud two set passages, one from the Law, the other from the Prophets. Prayers are said, wine is shared, and a family meal is usually enjoyed.

A female version of the bar mitzvah is also practised in many synagogues today. It is called the *bat mitzvah* ("daughter of commandment").

Hanukkah

The final festival to be mentioned here is Hanukkah. The word itself means "dedication," and the Hanukkah festival commemorates the rededication of the temple by Judas Maccabeus (164 BCE) after the Hellenistic ruler Antiochus IV Epiphanes had desecrated it by placing a pagan idol inside. Candles are lit for eight days during the modern festival because, according to the rabbis of the Talmud, when Judas Maccabeus relit the sacred oil of the temple lamps, a single day's oil miraculously lasted eight days. Though very ancient, the Hanukkah festival has only risen to prominence in the Jewish community in recent times, partly perhaps as a Jewish alternative to Christmas (both fall in December).

PRAYERS OF CLASSICAL JUDAISM

Any presentation of Classical Judaism would be incomplete without some discussion of the prayers set down by the rabbis of the post-temple period. These sages were not simply legislators of legal and ritual matters; they were deeply religious men with a particular vision of the nature and destiny of Israel. The prayers they devised, which are now found in the *Siddur*, the Jewish prayer book, continue to exert enormous influence over synagogues and individuals today.

The Shema

Nothing is more basic to Jewish prayer than a simple, three-line statement called the Shema (which means "hear"). It originally comes from Deuteronomy or Devarim 6:4. Traditionally, every Jew is obliged to say the Shema in the morning and in the evening. So important is this brief affirmation that the Mishnah treats the Shema as its first topic, setting out in detail when and how the prayer should be performed. With full concentration on the majesty of God, the faithful declare: "Hear (*shema*), O Israel: Hashem [the 'name'] is our God, Hashem, the One and Only."[1] The word *Hashem*, literally "the Name," is used instead of the sacred name of God found in scripture: *Yahweh*, usually rendered in English as "Lord" in small capitals. Avoiding saying the name of God is a sign of respect.

Following the Shema, the faithful proclaim the words of Deuteronomy or Devarim 6:5–7: "You shall love the Lord, your God, with all your heart, with all your soul and with all your resources. Let these matters that I command you today be upon your heart. Teach them thoroughly to your children and speak of them while you sit in your home, while you walk on the way, when you retire and when you arise."[2] The idea is simple: the one true God has set his affection on Israel, and so Israel responds in love for God.

The Eighteen Prayers (Shemoneh Esrei or Amidah)

A generation after the fall of Jerusalem (in 70 CE) the great rabbinical "university" at Jamnia produced a leader whose contribution to the prayer life of the Jews is made clear every day of the Jewish year. Rabbi Gamaliel II (second century CE) brought great unity to the Jews by collecting and revising a set of eighteen fixed prayers

---

1 *The Complete Artscroll Siddur*, 91.
2 *The Complete Artscroll Siddur*, 93.

(Shemoneh Esrei = "Eighteen"). These, like the Shema, are meant to be said by every Jew every day—though, on the Sabbath only about half are said. A nineteenth prayer was added (as No. 12) by Gamaliel or some other rabbi to denounce the *minim*, or "heretics." Among the heretics were almost certainly the Sadducees and the followers of Yeshua (or Jewish Christians). The Shemoneh Esrei is also known as the Amidah ("standing") because of the position in which the prayers are to be said. The Amidah (with the Shema) is of central importance. It is to Jews what the Lord's Prayer (or Our Father) is to Christians: the pinnacle of human communication with the Almighty.

Some Prayers of the Shemonah Esrei or Amidah

1. Patriarchs. Blessed are you, HASHEM, our God and the God of our forefathers, God of Abraham, God of Isaac, and the God of Jacob; the great, mighty, and awesome God, the supreme God, Who bestows beneficial kindnesses and creates everything, Who recalls the kindnesses of the Patriarchs and brings a Redeemer to their children's children, for His Name's sake, with love. O King, Helper, Savior, and Shield. Blessed are You, HASHEM, Shield of Abraham.
2. God's Might. You are eternally mighty, my Lord, the Resuscitator of the dead are You; abundantly able to save, Who sustains the living with kindness, resuscitates the dead with abundant mercy, supports the fallen, heals the sick releases the confined, and maintains His faith to those asleep in the dust . . .
6. Forgiveness. Forgive us, our Father, for we have erred; pardon

us, our King, for we have willfully sinned; for You pardon and forgive. Blessed are You, HASHEM, the gracious One Who pardons abundantly . . .

12. Against Heretics. And for slanderers let there be no hope; and may all wickedness perish in an instant; and may all Your enemies be cut down speedily. May You speedily uproot, smash, cast down, and humble the wanton sinners–speedily in our days . . .

14. Rebuilding Jerusalem. And to Jerusalem, Your city, may You return in compassion, and may You rest within it, as You have spoken. May You rebuild it soon in our days as an eternal structure and may You speedily establish the throne of David within it. Blessed are You, HASHEM, the Builder of Jerusalem.

15. Davidic Reign. The offspring of Your servant David may You speedily cause to flourish, and enhance his pride through Your salvation, for we hope for Your salvation all day long. Blessed are You, HASHEM, Who causes the pride of salvation to flourish . . .

17. Temple Service. Be favorable, HASHEM, our God, toward Your people Israel and their prayer and restore the service to the Holy of Holies of Your Temple. The fire-offerings of Israel and their prayer accept with love and favor, and may the service of Your people Israel always be favorable to You . . .

19. Peace. Establish peace, goodness, blessing, graciousness, kindness, and compassion upon us and upon all of Your people Israel. Bless us, our Father, all of us as one, with the light of Your countenance, for with the light of Your countenance You gave us, HASHEM, our God, the Torah of life, and a love of kindness, righteousness, blessing, compassion, life, and peace. And may it be good in Your

> eyes to bless Your people Israel, in every season and in every hour
> with Your peace. Blessed are You, HASHEM, Who blesses His
> people Israel with peace.
>
> From the *Shemonah Esrei or Amidah* (Siddur).

Although composed nearly 2000 years ago, these Jewish prayers
still exercise enormous power in the life of traditional Jews.

THE THIRTEEN PRINCIPLES OF FAITH

The five major festivals, together with the Shema and the eighteen
(or nineteen) prayers, provide a good summary of Jewish liturgical
(worship) life. What about beliefs? The so-called Thirteen Principles
of Faith were composed in the twelfth century CE by the great
Jewish scholar Moses Maimonides, also known as Rambam. These
thirteen statements take us to the heart of Jewish doctrine. They
are recited by the faithful as part of the weekday synagogue service
even to this day. It is the "creed" of Classical (and contemporary
Orthodox) Judaism.

A Traditional Summary of Jewish Beliefs

1. I believe with complete faith that the Creator, Blessed is His Name,
   creates and guides all creatures, and that He alone made, makes,
   and will make everything.

2. I believe with complete faith that the Creator, Blessed is His Name, is unique, and there is no uniqueness like His in any way, and that He alone is our God, Who was, Who is, and Who always will be.

3. I believe with complete faith that the Creator, Blessed is His Name, is not physical and is not affected by physical phenomena, and that there is no comparison whatsoever to Him.

4. I believe with complete faith that the Creator, Blessed is His Name, is the very first and the very last.

5. I believe with complete faith that the Creator, Blessed is His Name—to Him alone is it proper to pray and it is not proper to pray to any other.

6. I believe with complete faith that all the words of the prophets are true.

7. I believe with complete faith that the prophecy of Moses our teacher, peace upon him, was true, and that he was the father of the prophets—both those who preceded him and those who followed him.

8. I believe with complete faith that the entire Torah now in our hands is the same one that was given to Moses, our teacher, peace be upon him.

9. I believe with complete faith that this Torah will not be exchanged nor will there be another Torah from the Creator, Blessed is His Name.

10. I believe with complete faith that the Creator, Blessed is His Name, knows all the deeds of human beings and their thoughts, as it is said, 'He fashions their hearts all together, He comprehends all their deeds'.

11. I believe with complete faith that the Creator, Blessed is His Name, rewards with good those who observe His commandments, and punish those who violate His commandments.
12. I believe with complete faith in the coming of the Messiah, and even though He may delay, nevertheless I anticipate every day that He will come.
13. I believe with complete faith that there will be a resuscitation of the dead whenever the wish emanates from the Creator, Blessed is His name and exalted is His mention, forever and for all eternity.

> *The Thirteen Principles of Faith,* from Shacharis
> / Weekday Morning Service (Siddur).

16

MODERN JUDAISMS

I have said several times that Classical Judaism reigned supreme in the Jewish faith for most of the last two millennia, from around 100 to 1800 CE. After the complexities of the period of the Interim Judaisms (roughly 200 BCE–100 CE), Classical Judaism was an incredibly stable religious vision. Wherever the Jews lived—and they lived in lots of places—the vision of Israel cast by these ancient classical rabbis dominated the outlook of Jewish existence. This began to change, however, in the eighteenth and nineteenth centuries.

THE "EMANCIPATION" OF THE JEWS

Sadly, for much of the period of Classical Judaism, Jews lived as a tolerated but excluded minority, first under pagan Rome, then under Christian and Islamic rule. In some ways, Classical Judaism coped well with this, since separation from an impure world was a core part of the Jewish mindset in that period. Jews stuck to their own districts, dressed in their own way, ate their own food, managed their own communities, conducted their own rituals, and worked at their own professions and trades. Integration with the wider world just was not on the agenda.

Then came "emancipation," a Europe-wide movement in the late 1700s and early 1800s which sought to bring rights and freedoms to oppressed minorities—to women, to Catholics (in Protestant countries), to slaves, and to Jews.

For the first time in centuries, Israel was invited to enter into wider society. This raised a fundamental question for the Jew: To what extent can I integrate into the non-Jewish world and still be part of God's holy people? Put another way: Can I be both a member of Israel and a good citizen of Germany, France, the United States, or wherever? Jews in the 1800s answered this question—the question of integration—in three divergent ways. These different answers led to the emergence of three distinct Judaisms.

REFORM JUDAISM: THE WAY OF INTEGRATION

In the early 1800s, a German layman named Israel Jacobson (1768–1828) began to propose small changes to the synagogue service. These were mainly designed to make the synagogue more accessible and inviting to his fellow Jews. The prayers and ceremonies were made shorter, choirs were introduced, services were conducted in German instead of Hebrew (which few people understood), and men and women were allowed to sit together in the synagogue. Jacobson's changes were popular and soon spread throughout Europe and the United States.

This interest in changing the form of Jewish ceremonies soon evolved into a desire to change the substance of Jewish belief. Those making the changes had no intention of overthrowing Judaism; rather, they hoped to reform Israel, making it more suitable for the new situation confronting Jews. This movement came to be known as Reform Judaism, complete with its own synagogues and rabbinical training schools.

What was new about Reform belief and practice? First, perhaps the greatest change was the rejection of the oral Torah. Reform Jews regard the Tanakh as God's instruction, but they consider the Mishnah and Talmud to be simply human wisdom that can be discarded—or, at least, reinterpreted—to suit changing times.

Second, Reform Judaism does not look forward to, or pray for, the revived Jerusalem temple, the coming of an individual Messiah, or even the future resurrection of the dead. This means that the bits of the Shemoneh Esrei or Amidah which mention these things—prayers 2, 14, 15, and 17—have been revised in the Reform prayer book.

Third, the intricate food laws and Sabbath rules of Foundational and Classical Judaism are considered by Reform Judaism to be too restrictive in a modern context, and so are declared obsolete. The same applies to some biblical moral laws. Same-sex relationships and marriage, for example, while rejected by Classical Judaism (and its modern manifestation, Orthodox Judaism) are regarded by Reform Judaism as permissible. The spirit of Reform Judaism was codified in a great meeting of Jewish officials in 1885 in the US city of Pittsburgh. This conference produced what's known as the Pittsburgh Platform of Reform Judaism.

Reform is the dominant form of Judaism today, especially in the United States, and is sometimes also called Progressive Judaism.

ORTHODOX JUDAISM: THE WAY OF SEPARATION

Not everyone was happy with the reforms of Reform Judaism. By the middle of the 1800s, many denounced Reform as apostasy, an abandonment of Israel's true faith. This reaction led to the establishment of what is called Orthodox Judaism. The word *orthodox* comes from the Greek "of right opinion," so it is easy to understand how such Jews see themselves. They insist that they are the keepers of the historic (Classical) Jewish faith. They claim that their opinions conform to God's instruction revealed in the dual-Torah. Obviously, then, Orthodox Judaism reveres the Tanakh, the Mishnah, and the Talmud. In this way, Orthodox Judaism and Classical Judaism are almost identical.

Orthodox Jews adhere strictly to the rulings of the ancient rabbis concerning the handling of food, ritual washings, Sabbath keeping, the festivals, and so on. They also conduct synagogue services in Hebrew and prohibit the use of musical instruments in public worship. Deep integration into the politics of society is rejected. Jews are the chosen people and must keep themselves "clean."

There are actually two types of Orthodox Judaism, one which completely rejects integration with society and one which, while living by the dual-Torah, does allow some integration into surrounding gentile culture. This second stream of Orthodox Judaism does not insist, for example, on the wearing of distinctive Jewish clothing. It also permits Jews to conduct business with gentiles and, significantly, to attend non-Jewish schools and universities.

Orthodox Judaism is prominent in South Africa, Australia,

and Europe. It is also the official form of Judaism in the modern State of Israel.

CONSERVATIVE JUDAISM: THE WAY OF COMPROMISE

Disappointed with the integrationist approach of Reform Judaism, yet wary of the separationist approach of the Orthodox, a so-called middle position emerged in Judaism around 1850. It is called Conservative Judaism.

Conservative Jews, like the Orthodox, maintain the food laws, Sabbath rules, all the major festivals, belief in the Messiah, and commit to preserving the Hebrew language. They also revere the Mishnah and Talmud (the oral Torah).

Conservative Jews part company with the Orthodox in believing that the sacred texts of the oral Torah must be subject to historical analysis. This analysis, in their view, reveals which teachings of the ancient rabbis are peripheral (and therefore changeable) and which are central (and therefore unchangeable). Conservative Judaism, for instance, has allowed women to become rabbis for almost twenty years, something not countenanced in the Mishnah or Talmud. Conservatives tend to be less flexible with the teachings of the Tanakh (the written Torah).

Perhaps the best way to think about this middle position in Judaism is to see it as conservative in practice (its rituals and morals) but flexible in its thinking. One Jewish scholar I read recently described the conservative stance as "believe with flexibility but act according to the traditions."

In all this, it must be remembered that, as with the Reform and the Orthodox, there is a spectrum of opinions among Conservative

Jews. Some Conservatives are very similar to Reform Jews, while others are virtually Orthodox (and there's a lot in between, too). Conservative Judaism is the "broad church" of the people of Israel.

During the early twentieth century, Conservative Judaism was the dominant form of Jewish faith. That honour has now fallen to Reform Judaism, as previously mentioned. Nevertheless, the great rabbinical training college of Conservative Judaism, The Jewish Theological Seminary in New York, remains massively influential throughout the United States and beyond.

ZIONISM: THE WAY BACK TO THE HOLY LAND

A final movement within Israel needs to be discussed before drawing our study of Judaism to a close. It is not a "denomination" within Judaism. It is social and political movement of different kinds of Jews (and sometimes Christians). The movement is called Zionism, from the name of the mountain or hill upon which Jerusalem is built. Its key goal was to secure a dedicated Jewish land following centuries of Jewish dispersion.

In the late 1800s, an Austrian journalist named Theodor Herzl (1860–1904) began to argue publicly that Jews should be allowed to found their own state, a political and geographical entity they could govern themselves. The growing anti-Semitism of Germany and elsewhere made this all the more urgent. His idea of Israel as a state was quite different from the Classical Jewish vision of Israel as a spiritual family awaiting the messianic kingdom. Nevertheless, Herzl's program caught on.

In 1897, the World Zionist Organisation was founded. The viewpoint of the organisation was simple: the international community should find a region somewhere in the world to which Jews could emigrate and in which they could establish a self-governing state. The British offered an uninhabited portion (15,000 square km) of Uganda for this purpose; Argentina was another possibility. After some discussion, however, Zionists insisted that only the Holy Land, the historic land of Israel, would do, even though the region had been populated mainly by Muslims ever since the Islamic conquest of Palestine in 637 CE.

Anti-Jewish fever in Europe climaxed, of course, in the horrors of Nazi Germany—prison camps, torture, and attempted extermination. Following the Second World War, as the world learned of the extent of the cruelties against Jews, the United Nations resolved that the surviving Jews of Europe (and elsewhere) should be allowed to move to Palestine, where a small number of Jews (about 100,000) already lived. A section of the Holy Land was determined, new boundaries were drawn, and in May 1948, the modern State of Israel was created. Zionism had triumphed. The Jews had returned home. The World Zionist Organisation still exists to gain international support for the Jewish cause in the State of Israel.

Needless to say, while the international community acted out of a desire to bring justice to post-Holocaust Jews, the effect of this homecoming on the local Palestinian population of the period was devastating. The Arab-Israeli war of 1948–1949 gained more land for the State of Israel and left more than half a million local Palestinians displaced, many of whom were forced across to Jordan in the east and others up into Lebanon in the north. Approximately two million Arabs (mainly Muslim, some Christian) live within the borders of the State of Israel today, making up about 20 percent of the population of the country. Many more Palestinian Arabs (approximately four million) live in the West Bank and Gaza Strip, regions which enjoy varying degrees of autonomy from Israel.

Our world still reaps the consequences of all these events. One suspects that new sufferings as well as glories lie ahead for the ancient people of Israel.

JUDAISM ON A PAGE

Judaism's key question: How should God's people (Israel) live in order to fulfill their divine calling in the world?

Foundational Judaism (2000–500 BCE): The fundamentals of the faith are developed

- God promises Abraham that he will become a great nation and that he will be a blessing to all nations. Circumcision is introduced as the sign of this covenant.
- The Jews living in slavery in Egypt are redeemed by God in a mass exodus (1200s BCE). The Passover festival is introduced to commemorate the event.
- The Torah is given by God to Moses at Mt. Sinai—Israel now has its way of life revealed, developing into the Tanakh, or Bible of Judaism.
- God promises that King David's throne will be eternal—here are the foundations of the Jewish belief in the Messiah.
- The first temple is built in Jerusalem (900s BCE) as a place for atonement and the praise of Israel's God.
- After a long period of disobedience, Israel is invaded by the Babylonians who destroy the temple (586 BCE). The Second Temple is built (512 BCE).

Interim Judaisms (500 BCE–100 CE): Jewish factions compete for prominence

- Sadducees are the aristocrats and priests, Essenes are the apocalyptic holy men, Zealots are the patriots who fight the Romans, and the followers of Yeshua (or first Christians) are deemed heretics of a false Messiah.
- The (second) Jerusalem temple is destroyed by the Romans (70 CE).

Classical Judaism (100–1800 CE): One form of Judaism emerges triumphant and sets the course for the bulk of Jewish history

- The Pharisees rise to prominence (100 CE) and govern Jewish religion.
- The rabbinic teachings are collected and compiled in the Mishnah (200 CE). Further reflection on the Mishnah and Tanakh leads to the production of the Talmud and the Midrash (400–800 CE).

Modern Judaisms (1800 to today): Classical Judaism splits in three

- Reform Judaism: a movement of deep integration with the gentile world.
- Orthodox Judaism: a movement insisting on separation from the gentile world.
- Conservative Judaism: a movement seeking a path between Reform and Orthodox Judaism.

Facts and Figures on Judaism Today

- Judaism is the sixth largest religion in the world, with approximately 15 million people identifying as Jews.
- Jews make up about 0.2 percent of the world's population.
- Judaism is found in 147 countries worldwide.
- Approximately 900,000 Jews live in Jerusalem, making Jerusalem the metro area with the third largest Jewish population in the world, behind New York (two million) and Tel Aviv (3.5 million).
- Of the estimated world population of 15 million Jews, more than 6 million live in Israel, and almost as many (just under 6 million) live in the United States.
- Jews were highly involved in establishing the early Hollywood film studios including Twentieth Century Fox, MGM, and Warner Brothers.

Famous Jews

Anne Frank

Anne recorded her life in a diary when her and her family were forced into hiding to escape Nazi persecution of the Jews during World War II. They were discovered and arrested by the Gestapo. She died in a concentration camp at the age of fifteen.

Barbara Streisand

Movie star, singer, and director Barbara Streisand has won numerous Oscar, Academy, Grammy, and Golden Globe awards. She is considered one of the highest selling female recording artists of all time. Streisand wrote the music for the song "Evergreen" (Love Theme from *A Star is Born*) for which she received an Oscar.

Lord Professor Rabbi Jonathan Sacks

A highly influential philosopher, author, and public intellectual, Sacks was the Chief Rabbi (Orthodox) of Britain. Famed for his ability to integrate spirituality and academic disciplines such as history and science, he won the Templeton Prize in 2006. He passed away in November 2020.

Good Books and Sites on Judaism Today

bbc.co.uk/religion/religions/judaism/ (a reliable introductory site from the BBC)

torah.org (a site dedicated to Jewish readings and rituals)

jewishencyclopedia.com (a comprehensive introduction to Jewish history and belief)

Berlin, A. *The Oxford Dictionary of the Jewish Religion.* Oxford University Press, 2011.

Grabbe, L. L. *An Introduction to First Century Judaism: Jewish Religion and History in the Second Temple Period.* Edinburgh: T & T Clark, 1996.

Jacobs, L. *The Jewish Religion: A Companion.* Oxford: Oxford University Press, 1995.

Neusner J. *The Way of the Torah: An Introduction to Judaism.* Belmont, CA: Wadsworth Publishing, 1997.

Solomon, N. *Judaism: A Very Short Introduction.* Oxford University Press, 2014.

Smart, N., and Hecht, R., eds. "Judaism." *Sacred Texts of the*

World: A Universal Anthology. New York: Crossroad, 2002. See pages 45–89.

Smart, N. *The World's Religions*. 2nd edition. Cambridge: Cambridge University Press, 2003. See pages 246–74.

PART 5
CHRISTIANITY, THE WAY OF THE CHRIST
IN A NUTSHELL

Christianity is the belief and practice of those who revere Jesus Christ as the incarnation of Israel's God. Central to Christ's divine mission was to fulfill the promises of the Old Testament, teach people God's ways, die for the sins of the world, and rise again to establish God's kingdom for all nations, forever.

17

JESUS AND THE SOURCES OF CHRISTIANITY

The word *Christianity* tells you a couple of very important things about the topic of these next few chapters. First, it lets you know that the faith of Christians has a lot to do with a person, Jesus Christ. Just how much it revolves around this man will soon become clear.

The other thing the word *Christianity* tells you is that this faith is intimately related to ancient Judaism. The word *Christ* is an important Jewish term. It is not a surname like Dickson—Jesus' parents were not Mr. and Mrs. Christ. As I said in chapter 13, *Christ* means "anointed one" in Greek. Its Hebrew equivalent is *Messiah*. It is the title given by Jews to the awaited king God will one day send to redeem Israel and all the nations. By naming Jesus *the Christ* and his followers *Christians* (people of the Messiah), Christianity claims to be the fulfilment of the hopes of Judaism. As I noted in chapter 10, the movement we call *Christianity* was, for its first few decades, just one of the interim Judaisms, alongside the Sadducees, Essenes, Zealots, and Pharisees.

NON-BIBLICAL SOURCES ABOUT JESUS

Christianity arrived on the scene at a time of great literary activity: philosophers were writing weighty tomes on the meaning of life, poets and playwrights were composing material to make people laugh and cry, emperors were crafting royal propaganda to ensure they were remembered, and historians were recording for posterity all that they could discover about their cultural heritage. The non-biblical writings of the first few centuries AD (*anno Domini*, "the year of our Lord") would fill many shelves in a modern library.

One lucky outcome of this flurry of literary activity is that a Galilean teacher named Yeshua, or Jesus, managed to rate a mention in Roman, Greek, and Jewish writings of the time. Some of the references are neutral; others are antagonistic, such as my personal favourite from Cornelius Tacitus (AD 56–120), ancient Rome's most famous historian, who described the movement Jesus started as a "pernicious superstition" and a "disease."[1] By a stroke of good luck, we can sketch an outline of Jesus' life without relying on Christian scripture.[2]

CHRISTIAN SOURCES ABOUT JESUS

It is generally acknowledged that our earliest and best sources of information about Jesus come from those closest to the events. The Christian New Testament (the counterpart to the Old Testament, or

---

1 Tacitus, *Annals* 15.44 [Jackson, LCL 322].

2 For an account of these sources, see my book *The Christ Files: How Historians Know What They Know About Jesus* (Grand Rapids, MI: Zondervan, 2010).

Jewish Tanakh) continues to take centre stage in modern research into Jesus and, of course, in the religious life of Christians.

The most important of these New Testament documents, for understanding the mission and message of Jesus and the foundations of Christianity, are the so-called Gospels. The word *gospel* means "grand news," and these biographical accounts of Jesus' life purport to tell the grandest news of all—the arrival of God and his kingdom in the person of Jesus.

We possess only four Gospels that can be confidently dated to the century in which Jesus lived (The much-talked-about "Gnostic Gospels" date from the following century, or even later):

1. The Gospel of Mark. Probably written in the mid-60s AD by a man named Mark, a colleague of an original follower of Jesus called the apostle Peter. *Apostle* means one "sent out" by Christ to proclaim the gospel.

2. The Gospel of Luke. Probably written in the AD 70s by Luke, a colleague of the apostle Paul, who, like Peter, claimed to have seen the resurrected Jesus shortly after his crucifixion. Most scholars believe that Luke used at least three earlier sources in composing his work, in much the same way that other biographies of the same period used various source materials.

3. The Gospel of Matthew. Probably written in the AD 80s by followers of the apostle Matthew, another original follower of Jesus. Traditional Christians (and some scholars) prefer to say that the eyewitness Matthew himself penned this Gospel. Matthew's Gospel, like Luke's, appears to rely heavily on two or three prior sources.

4. The Gospel of John. Written sometime between AD 60–90 (there's lots of debate here) by one of two Johns. Traditionally, the Gospel is attributed to the apostle John, a contemporary and eyewitness of Jesus. Others argue it was composed by another John who was also an eyewitness but not one of the select twelve apostles.

Another set of New Testament writings provides a further historical, as well as theological, source for our knowledge about Jesus. The letters of Paul are a collection of correspondence from the apostle Paul to various Christian groups around the Mediterranean in the first few decades after Jesus—in Galatia (in modern Turkey), Corinth, Rome, and elsewhere. These letters provide the earliest sources about Jesus, being written between AD 48–64. Passing references to Jesus in Paul's letters confirm that things like Jesus' descent from king David, his teaching about love, his "Last Supper," his betrayal, death, resurrection, and appearances were already widely known throughout the Mediterranean years before the four Gospels were published as official biographies. These letters also contain a wealth of ethical reflection, urging Christians to live in the light of the news about Christ.

A Reflection on the Meaning of Jesus in a Letter of Paul to Corinth (from AD 56)

In the following directives I have no praise for you . . . for when you are eating, some of you go ahead with your own private suppers.

As a result, one person remains hungry and another gets drunk. Don't you have homes to eat and drink in? Or do you despise the church of God by humiliating those who have nothing? What shall I say to you? Shall I praise you? Certainly not in this matter! For I received from the Lord what I also passed on to you: The Lord Jesus, on the night he was betrayed, took bread, and when he had given thanks, he broke it and said, "This is my body, which is for you; do this in remembrance of me." In the same way, after supper he took the cup, saying, "This cup is the new covenant in my blood; do this, whenever you drink it, in remembrance of me." For whenever you eat this bread and drink this cup, you proclaim the Lord's death until he comes. So then, whoever eats the bread or drinks the cup of the Lord in an unworthy manner will be guilty of sinning against the body and blood of the Lord. Everyone ought to examine themselves before they eat of the bread and drink from the cup.

1 Corinthians 11:17–28

In chapter 7, we noted that the Buddhist scriptures were first written down 300–400 years after Siddhartha Gautama's death. In chapter 15, we discussed the Jewish Mishnah compiled 150 years after the death of many of the rabbis quoted in the work. As I also pointed out in those chapters, such time gaps do not make these writings unreliable records of the sacred material. In contrast to modern times, ancient men and women preserved the sayings of important teachers by using centuries-old techniques of memorisation and verbal transmission. Only about 10 percent of people could read, so writing things down was actually not the most effective means of passing on a teacher's wisdom. *Oral tradition*, as this process was called, was the preferred method for many in antiquity.

What was true for Buddhists, Jews, and (as we shall see) for Muslims, was equally true for the first Christians: oral tradition was regarded as the most trusted way to safeguard and pass on the sacred teachings. In the case of Christianity, this method was relatively short-lived. The rapid expansion of Christianity beyond the borders of Galilee and Judea meant that written communication emerged relatively early in Christian history. Through writing (whether in the Gospels or the letters), prominent Christian leaders could teach and maintain contact with converts over long distances.

In the next chapter, we will begin to explore the content of these documents and, therefore, the basics of the Christian faith.

18

THE LIFE OF JESUS OF NAZARETH

Jesus was born around 5 BC. How Jesus could have been born "before Christ" is not odd as it sounds. The man who gave us the calendar distinction between BC and AD was an Italian scholar of the sixth century named Dionysius Exiguus ("Denis the Little"). In proposing a new dating system, commencing with the birth of Jesus, Denis sifted through the available historical records to arrive at the most probable date for the first *anno Domini*, "year of the Lord." He missed by just a few years (not bad considering the limited resources he had!). Based on the historical information available today, modern scholars confidently place Jesus' birth between 6–4 BC.

CARPENTER AND KING

Comparatively little is known of Jesus' childhood. All we can say with confidence is that he grew up in the district of Galilee (the northern region of the traditional land of Israel) in a little town called Nazareth where, like most Jewish boys, he would have followed in the trade of his father, Joseph. This meant Jesus was a carpenter, making and fixing furniture, fences, and other household items. By our standards, he was poor. By ancient norms, he was about average.

More important than Jesus' trade was his ancestry. The Gospels of Matthew and Luke, as well as one of Paul's letters, indicate that Jesus was a descendant of king David (1000 BC), the greatest of Israel's kings and the one to whom God had promised an eternal throne (discussed in chapter 13). To be clear, having royal blood did not necessarily make you special. My wife is a direct descendant of Robert the Bruce, first king of Scotland (AD 1274–1329), and sadly, it comes with no perks whatsoever—no castle, no cottage, not even a distillery. Nevertheless, as people began to claim that Jesus was the promised Messiah, his connection with the ancient royal family became vitally important.

PREACHER OF THE "KINGDOM OF GOD"

What Jesus did between his childhood and his adult career is completely unknown. That has not stopped one well-known New Age writer from proposing that Jesus journeyed to India to learn eastern wisdom.[1] Historians offer more boring proposals. Jesus likely did what most Jewish boys of the time did—stayed put and worked with the family. If Jesus' father died early—as many suspect—the "staying put" theory provides the only plausible scenario. Staying

---

1 I did a whole podcast episode on this fun theme: "Teenage Jesus," episode 44, *Undeceptions*, undeceptions.com/podcast/teenage-jesus.

at home to look after his mother (Mary) and the other members of his extended family would have been his duty.

Sometime around AD 28, when he was in his early thirties, Jesus emerged from Galilee as a teacher. It is unlikely Jesus had any formal education, apart from what many Jewish children got in the home and in the local synagogue. But Jesus quickly attracted a great deal of attention.

People today often associate Jesus with words of simple ethical wisdom: "Turn the other cheek," "Do unto others what you would have them do unto you," and so on. But the truly dramatic thing about Jesus' teaching was his daring announcement that the long-awaited "kingdom of God" had arrived, or at least come "near." The opening words of Jesus in the earliest Gospel are, "The time has come . . . The kingdom of God is near. Repent and believe the good news!" (Mark 1:14–15).

It is difficult to convey just how explosive such a message would have been in first-century Palestine. Declaring that "the kingdom of God is near" was equivalent to saying that everything the Jews longed for was finding fulfilment in their midst. It meant that the everlasting throne promised to king David (1000 BC) was being realised, that judgment upon evil was close at hand, and that all nations would finally submit to the one true God.

For many Jews of this period, the phrase *kingdom of God* evoked strong political aspirations: the promised eternal throne was hoped to be an earthly throne, God's judgment upon evil was thought to be aimed at Rome in particular, and the submission of the nations to God was expected to involve the submission of the nations to Israel, as well. Jesus' idea of the kingdom, however, was different.

THE "FRIEND OF SINNERS"

At the heart of Jesus' message about the kingdom was the insistence that it was open to everyone—even to those normally thought to be excluded from God's plans and deserving of his judgment.

One group of outsiders was the tax collectors. Tax collectors were widely criticised by their fellow Jews as traitors for raising revenue on behalf of the Romans (and Roman collaborators) and scoundrels for getting rich in the process. Nevertheless, Jesus regularly sought out these "sinners" and offered them God's mercy.

Perhaps not surprisingly, Jesus began to be criticised in public by his more conservative fellow Jews as "a glutton and a drunkard, a friend of tax collectors and sinners" (Luke 7:34). These tags may sound cool today, but they were intended as a sharp insult.

A Typical Scene from the Ministry of Jesus, According to the Gospels

Once again Jesus went out beside the lake. A large crowd came to him, and he began to teach them. As he walked along, he saw Levi son of Alphaeus sitting at the tax collector's booth. "Follow me," Jesus told him, and Levi got up and followed him. While Jesus was having dinner at Levi's house, many tax collectors and sinners were eating with him and his disciples, for there were many who followed him. When the teachers of the law who were Pharisees saw him eating with the sinners and tax collectors, they asked his disciples: "Why does he eat with tax collectors and sinners?" On hearing this, Jesus said

to them, "It is not the healthy who need a doctor, but the sick. I have
not come to call the righteous, but sinners."

The Gospel of Mark 2:12–17

It is a curious fact that no person in the Bible—Old Testament
or New Testament—spoke more about hell (the place of judgment
in the future kingdom of God) than Jesus. And yet, Jesus is also
the figure most often associated with wining and dining with
"sinners" and handing out God's forgiveness.

FORGIVENESS AND THE TEMPLE

Jesus' offer of forgiveness of sins was one of the most striking
features of his ministry. "Sins" are those things in human conduct
that offend God. So how could Jesus go around forgiving sins?
That was precisely the question the religious leaders asked: "Why
does this fellow speak in this way? It is blasphemy! Who can forgive
sins but God alone?" (Mark 2:7).

As I explained in chapter 13, ancient Jews had highly developed
rituals of forgiveness. These were conducted in the Jerusalem temple.
The role of the priest in the process was merely to conduct the
ceremonies and announce divine forgiveness to the worshippers.
The priest did not actually forgive people's sins himself. That was
God's business, according to Jewish theology.

Jesus seemingly cut right across this centuries-old tradition by
claiming that if you were connected with him—were a member
of the kingdom he talked about—you would be cleansed from all

your sins. This was as good as claiming yourself to be a substitute temple, an alternative locus of God's presence and mercy.

BAFFLING DEEDS

The claim that Jesus performed unexplainable deeds is everywhere in our ancient sources—both Christian and non-Christian sources. Even the most critical specialists today, historians such as John Meier, John Dominic Crossan, Paula Fredriksen, and Ed Sanders (to name just four from the more sceptical end of scholarship) acknowledge that, historically speaking, the evidence indicates that Jesus performed deeds which everyone (including opponents) believed to be "miraculous," especially healings and exorcisms.

According to the Gospels, some in Jesus' day dismissed his wonderworking as a kind of black magic. Jesus said his healings were signs of the kingdom of God, previews of God's mending of all things in the future. As Jesus put it, his deeds were evidence that "the kingdom of God has come among you" (Matthew 12:28).

The widespread belief in Jesus' powers partly explains his great popularity throughout Judea and Galilee—a popularity that culminated in some very dramatic events.

MESSIAH COMES TO TOWN

Toward the end of his three-year career as a preacher, healer, and religious controversialist, Jesus set his sights on Jerusalem, about a hundred miles to the south of his home district of Galilee. Jerusalem, of course, was the city King David had founded; it was the home of the ancient royal palace; and, most importantly, it was where the great temple stood.

When Jesus eventually went public about his messianic claims, he did not do so by declaring, "Friends, I am the long-awaited Son of David, the Messiah." He chose to reveal his identity in a piece of theatre, acting out one of the most famous prophecies in the Old Testament (the Jewish Tanakh) about the coming of God's Christ. In the book of Zechariah (written centuries before), the prophet predicted that the Messiah would arrive in Jerusalem riding on a donkey. According to the Gospels, Jesus arranged to enter Jerusalem during the Passover festival on a donkey. As he commenced his ride over the Mount of Olives and down into the ancient city, a crowd of pilgrims, aware of the significance of this act, began to shout in unison like fans at the football match about the "coming kingdom of our ancestor David!" (Mark 11:9–10).

What did the newly proclaimed king do once he entered the Holy City? He went into the temple courts, a structure about the size of a professional football stadium, and began to denounce the temple priests.

The temple courtyard at this time was filled with worshippers. It was the week leading up to the Passover festival, so Jews from all over the Roman world were making their pilgrimage to the Holy City to take part in this most sacred day of the Jewish calendar. They were there, as discussed in chapter 13, to commemorate Israel's liberation from Egyptian slavery centuries before. A lamb would be sacrificed to recall the original Passover lamb whose blood was placed on the doorframes of Jewish homes. When God came in anger against the Egyptians that fateful night in the thirteenth century BC, he saw the blood of the lamb and preserved the Jewish families. His judgment fell upon Egypt but passed over the Jews.

When Jesus entered the temple courts all those years later, the temple officials were conducting business as usual, part of which included selling sacrificial animals (lambs, doves, etc.) to the visiting pilgrims. A lot of money changed hands at Passover time, and not all of it was honest. Jesus was disgusted, and he overturned the tables and declared God's judgment on the temple.

Jesus' Entry to Jerusalem as the Cause of His Arrest

On reaching Jerusalem, Jesus entered the temple courts and began driving out those who were buying and selling there. He overturned the tables of the money changers and the benches of those selling doves, and would not allow anyone to carry merchandise through the temple courts. And as he taught them, he said, "Is it not written: 'My house will be called a house of prayer for all nations'? But you have made it 'a den of robbers.'" The chief priests and the teachers of the law heard this and began looking for a way to kill him, for they feared him, because the whole crowd was amazed at his teaching.

The Gospel of Mark 11:11–18

Jesus had criticised the religious leaders before, but this was taking dissent to a new level. Clearing out the temple courts was a dramatic, symbolic, public attack on the heart of Israel's leadership. Within days of this defining moment, Jesus would be dead.

THE JEWISH PASSOVER AND THE DEATH OF JESUS

Jesus managed to avoid arrest for most of the coming week. His days were spent speaking to large crowds of pilgrims in the temple courtyard before slipping away at night to a friend's home a few miles east of Jerusalem.

The final night was different. It was the eve of the Passover, and Jesus wanted to celebrate this special occasion with his colleagues in the Holy City itself. When Jesus sat down to celebrate this Passover meal, now known as The Last Supper, things would have proceeded in much the same way as they had for the 1200 years before—cooked lamb, traditional spices, wine, unleavened bread, prayers, songs, and so on. But Jesus added one highly unusual element that evening. He took the bread and wine in his hands and gave them an intriguing new meaning: "Jesus took a loaf of bread, and after blessing it he broke it, gave it to the disciples, and said, 'Take, eat; this is my body.' Then he took a cup, and after giving thanks he gave it to them, saying, 'Drink from it, all of you; for this is my blood of the covenant, which is poured out for many for the forgiveness of sins'" (Matthew 26:26–28).

Jesus took the traditional Passover themes of *blood* and *forgiveness* and related them to what was about to happen to him. Jesus' blood, just like that of the Passover lamb, would be poured out for the forgiveness of God's people. God's judgment would fall upon the "lamb" (Jesus) so that it might pass over "sinners." This, according to Jesus, was his destiny. This was how the undeserving—the sinners, tax collectors, and others—could be welcomed into his kingdom.

Within hours of this Last Supper, Jesus was arrested, put on trial, and found guilty. His crime—from the point of view of the Roman governor Pontius Pilate—was claiming to be king. This was a treasonous challenge to Rome. Pilate executed people for much less during his ten years as prefect of Judea.

Political explanations of Jesus' death are just one way of looking at the event. Christians insist that the truest meaning of the event is found not in politics but in Jesus' own explanation of his death: "[T]his is my blood of the covenant, which is poured out for many for the forgiveness of sins." According to the New Testament, Jesus died as a sacrifice for sins. He was the lamb for a worldwide Passover.

THE RESURRECTION OF CHRIST

If the Gospels had left Jesus in a martyr's tomb, this would have been a perfectly respectable way to conclude a story about a great Jewish teacher. Religious martyrs were widely revered in first-century Palestine. Contrary to all expectations, however, the first Christians insisted that the tomb in which Jesus was laid on Friday afternoon was empty on Sunday morning.

Explanations abound, of course: perhaps Jesus' followers stole the body and kept quiet about it to their deaths; maybe Jesus simply recovered from his injuries and convinced people he had been resurrected. Jesus' followers offered an entirely different explanation, and their claim launched a movement that would utterly transform the world: God, they said, had raised the Messiah from the dead. He appeared to his disciples over a period of forty days, and then ascended into heaven (a doctrine known as the ascension) until he will return to judge the world (a doctrine known as the second coming).

The most significant statement about the resurrection, in the opinion of virtually all historians, is one tucked away in a letter of the apostle Paul to the new Christians in Corinth. The statement is important not simply because Paul claims in it to be an eyewitness but because the account of the resurrection cited here was probably crafted in the early-to-mid-30s AD, within months or a few years of the purported events themselves. In the passage, Paul quotes a creed, a formal summary of Christian belief, that he himself received around the time of his own conversion in AD 31–32. The creed declares: "that Christ died for our sins according to the Scriptures, that he was buried, that he was raised on the third day according to the Scriptures, and that he appeared to Cephas [Peter] and then to the Twelve" (1 Corinthians 15:3–8).

Whatever contemporary readers make of the resurrection of Jesus, it is this claim that launched the early Christian movement. Many people, filled with zeal and conviction that they had seen the risen Jesus, spread out through the Mediterranean world with the message that God's kingdom had broken into human history, and God was now inviting Israel and the nations to enjoy forgiveness of sins and eternal life in the kingdom. The details of this developing mission and message are the focus of the next chapter.

19

FROM CHRIST TO THE NEW TESTAMENT

I have emphasised throughout these chapters that what we call "Christianity" began as a Jewish phenomenon. Jesus was a Jew, all of his first followers were Jews, and many Christians continued to attend their Jewish synagogues (as well as church) right throughout the first and second centuries. Only as pharisaic Judaism, or Classical Judaism, emerged as the dominant form of Judaism did Christianity and Judaism come to be seen as two distinct religions.

FROM JUDAISM TO CHRISTIANITY

One of the striking things about the first Christians is the way they tried to work out how the news about Jesus' life, death, and resurrection (the "gospel message," as they called it) ought to be brought to gentiles (non-Jews). After all, according to the ancient prophecies of the Tanakh or Old Testament, the kingdom of God would be for all nations, not just Israel. The early followers of Jesus had some radical thinking to do.

One big issue was circumcision. The rite of circumcision had long been regarded as the key sign of belonging to God's family Israel. So, the question for the first Christians was: Should gentiles who want to follow Christ also be circumcised? Put another way, should gentiles become fully fledged Jews in order to be real Christians? It may surprise you to know that many of the first Christians answered "yes" to this question. This made conversion to Christianity for adult male Greeks and Romans a very difficult process.

After vigorous debate between conservative Christians and more liberal-minded ones, a decision was made (at a council in Jerusalem in AD 48) that would have huge significance for the religious landscape of the world. It was determined that although circumcision was the sign of membership in Israel, it was not necessarily the sign that you followed Israel's Messiah. Gentiles could henceforth enjoy the benefits of Jesus' kingdom *as gentiles*, without circumcision. As the apostle Paul put it to his churches in Galatia (central Turkey) in the middle of the first century, "For in Christ Jesus neither circumcision nor uncircumcision has any value. The only thing that counts is faith expressing itself through love" (Galatians 5:6).

The effect of this decision cannot be overstated. Suddenly, this small Jewish movement exploded throughout the Roman world. Preachers, such as the apostles Peter and Paul (and hundreds of others), took this news to the farthest reaches of the empire. Wherever they went, they established "churches," small groups of believers who would gather together to pray, sing songs, learn more about Christ, and eat meals in his honour.

The movement spread like wildfire. What started as one of the several interim Judaisms of the first century managed to make itself history's first world religion.

LETTERS TO THE CHURCHES

Many of the New Testament books—the books regarded by Christians as sacred—were simply letters sent by the first Christian leaders to the recently founded churches scattered throughout the Roman world. The book of 1 Corinthians, for example, is one of two letters in our possession written by the apostle Paul to a group of new Christians meeting in Corinth. Some New Testament books were *circulars*, that is, letters intended for distribution among a number of Christian communities. One such book is James, a letter sent by a relative of Jesus, named James, to Christian groups scattered throughout the Mediterranean.

Excerpt from the New Testament Letter of James

My brothers and sisters, believers in our glorious Lord Jesus Christ must not show favoritism. Suppose a man comes into your meeting wearing a gold ring and fine clothes, and a poor man in filthy old clothes also comes in. If you show special attention to the man wearing fine clothes and say, "Here's a good seat for you," but say to the poor man, "You stand there" or "Sit on the floor by my feet," have you not discriminated among yourselves and become judges with evil thoughts? Listen, my dear brothers and sisters: Has not God chosen those who are poor in the eyes of the world to be rich in faith and to inherit the kingdom he promised those who love him? But you have dishonored the poor. Is it not the rich who are exploiting you? Are they not the ones who are dragging you into court? Are they not the ones who are blaspheming the noble name of him to whom you belong?

If you really keep the royal law found in Scripture, "Love your neighbor as yourself," you are doing right. But if you show favoritism, you sin and are convicted by the law as lawbreakers.

James 2:1–9

These early Christian leaders were greatly revered because of their contact with Jesus. As a result, their writings were preserved. Copies of their letters were also made, and these were passed on to other churches so they too could hear what the apostles had to say on such wide-ranging issues as sex, money, marriage, politics, and suffering, as well as subjects like God, death, and the future. These letters, along with the four Gospels, make up what Christians call the New Testament.

WHOSE NEW TESTAMENT?

Because of the popularity of the first-century Christian literature (the Gospels and the letters), groups in the second and third centuries began to produce similar materials and tried to pass them off as original apostolic writings. These include the Gospel of Thomas, the Acts of Paul, the Letter of Barnabas, and many others. Eventually, churches all around the Mediterranean met in a series of councils, climaxing in the councils of Rome (AD 382) and Carthage, North Africa (AD 397). One purpose of these meetings was to determine which documents should be regarded as sacred and authoritative and which should be deemed otherwise.

The church councils embraced as scripture only those documents that had long been recognised throughout the churches as penned by the first generation of Christian leaders, that is, by those whom Jesus appointed (Peter, Paul, James, etc.), or by their immediate colleagues (Mark, Luke, etc.). That left us with just twenty-seven books of the New Testament (the Gospels and the letters). The other writings (Gospel of Thomas, etc.) were published in separate collections and are all readily available in English translations today.

Many thousands of ancient copies of the New Testament still exist today and are on display (inside sealed cabinets) in some of the great libraries of the world—the British Library in London, the Chester Beatty Library in Dublin, the library of the University of Michigan in the United States, and so on. Modern translations of the New Testament are made from these ancient manuscripts.

20

MAJOR TEACHINGS OF CHRISTIANITY

The first-century Gospels and letters make up the New Testament. The New Testament, together with the Old Testament (the Jewish Tanakh), makes up what Christians call the "Bible" (from the Greek word *biblos* or "book"). It remains now to unpack some of the major teachings of the Bible as believed by mainstream Christians throughout the centuries. Then, in the following chapter, we can look at the distinctive teachings of the various "brands" of Christianity.

TRINITY: ONE GOD IN THREE PERSONS

I said earlier that one of the most striking aspects of Jesus' ministry was his insistence that God's forgiveness could be received directly through him, without needing to go to God's official dwelling place, the Jewish temple in Jerusalem. In a first-century Jewish context, this was as good as claiming yourself to be a substitute temple, an alternative locus of God's presence and mercy. The scandalous nature of this claim is seen in the response of the

Jewish leaders: "'It is blasphemy! Who can forgive sins but God alone?'" (Mark 2:7).

It is not an easy thought to ponder, but Jesus implied to his contemporaries that he personified the presence of God on earth. The one true God of Jewish history had entered into first-century life in the person of the Messiah.

What Jesus implied, numerous New Testament writers make explicit: Jesus and God are, in fact, one. The man from Nazareth is not merely the Messiah of Israel; he is God in the flesh. The Gospel of John makes this point by describing Jesus as God's very "Word made flesh": "In the beginning was the Word, and the Word was with God, and the Word was God . . . The Word became flesh [Jesus] and made his dwelling among us" (John 1:1, 14).

Here we have the beginning of the Christian doctrine of the *Trinity*. The word *trinity* means something like "three-in-oneness." It was coined by Christians of the second and third centuries as a way of saying in a single word what the Bible teaches in many words.

According to the Bible, God has revealed himself as the Father, the Son (that's Jesus), and the Holy Spirit. The Father and the Holy Spirit were already known to Jews through statements in their Tanakh (Old Testament). But it was never clear there whether the Holy Spirit was a distinct *person* within God, or just God's own divine power. The New Testament clarifies this issue, describing the Holy Spirit as a fully divine person and yet distinct from God the Father. The first Christians then added to this picture by affirming Jesus also as fully God and yet distinct from both the Father and the Holy Spirit.

Without embarrassment or any hint of contradiction, the Bible teaches that God is three persons sharing one divine nature. This does not mean that God simply appears in three modes, as H2O can appear as either liquid or steam or ice. Nor does it mean that God has three different parts, as a triangle has three sides. As difficult as it is to comprehend—and I still get a headache thinking about it—the biblical doctrine of the Trinity, believed by Christians of all varieties, states that the one true God exists as three equal persons. I suspect the doctrine of the Trinity rivals the Buddhist doctrine of the Five Aggregates of Attachment (discussed in chapter 8) for the Most Difficult Religious Concept Award.

THE "KINGDOM COME": CHRISTIANITY AND THE FUTURE

I said earlier that a central theme in Jesus' own teaching was what he called the "kingdom of God," that is, God's rule (his kingship, if you like) over all things. According to Jesus and the New Testament, God's kingdom is both present and future. It is present in the sense that God's appointed king, the Messiah, has arrived within time and space, offering his mercy and leadership to all who want them. It is future, however, in the sense that this kingdom will be witnessed fully only at the end of history. With this in mind, Jesus urged his disciples to make the hope for the coming kingdom a part of their regular prayers. In the Lord's Prayer (or "Our Father"), he taught his followers to say, "Our Father in heaven, hallowed be your name, Your kingdom come, your will be done, On earth as it is in heaven" (Luke 11:9–10).

Christians throughout the centuries have emphasised several aspects of this future kingdom. First, Christians believe in a so-called second coming of Jesus. In many ways, Jesus' appearance in first-century Galilee and Judea was a foretaste of his ultimate appearance.

There is great debate over the details of the second coming, but all Christians agree that Jesus will return to establish the kingdom forever.

Second, all Christians acknowledge that God's future kingdom will commence with a day of judgment, when God will weigh the conduct of every man and woman. In the Bible, this theme is presented not simply as a scare tactic designed to make us more religious but as a kind of pledge that God sees the injustices of history and will one day console the downtrodden faithful by righting the wrongs of the world.

The third and perhaps strangest aspect of the "kingdom come," as believed by Christians of the last two millennia, has to do with the universe itself. Christianity does not envisage a kingdom of disembodied spirits floating upon heavenly clouds wearing halos and listening to harp music. That is the "heaven" of Hollywood. The future kingdom taught by Jesus, and hoped for by mainstream Christians, is a place in which human beings are resurrected and the creation itself is renewed. What Christianity promises to the faithful is nothing less than "the resurrection of the dead and the life of the world to come," as stated in the Nicene Creed, the official summary of the Christian faith for all three branches of Christianity: Catholic, Orthodox, and Protestant.

The Nicene Creed

I believe in one God,
the Father almighty,
maker of heaven and earth,

of all things visible and invisible.
I believe in one Lord Jesus Christ,
the Only Begotten Son of God,
born of the Father before all ages.
God from God, Light from Light,
true God from true God,
begotten, not made, consubstantial with the Father;
through him all things were made.
For us men and for our salvation
he came down from heaven,
and by the Holy Spirit was incarnate of the Virgin Mary,
and became man.
For our sake he was crucified under Pontius Pilate,
he suffered death and was buried,
and rose again on the third day
in accordance with the Scriptures.
He ascended into heaven
and is seated at the right hand of the Father.
He will come again in glory
to judge the living and the dead
and his kingdom will have no end.
I believe in the Holy Spirit, the Lord, the giver of life,
who proceeds from the Father [and the Son[1]],
who with the Father and the Son is adored and glorified,
who has spoken through the prophets.
I believe in one, holy, catholic and apostolic Church.

---

1 Orthodox Churches do not say the words "and the Son."

I confess one Baptism for the forgiveness of sins
and I look forward to the resurrection of the dead
and the life of the world to come. Amen

> The Nicene Creed, first developed at the Council of
> Nicaea in AD 325 and completed and finally approved
> at the Council of Constantinople in AD 381.

GRACE: SALVATION AS A GIFT

This emphasis on the future should not obscure the fact that Christianity claims also to be a faith of the present. One example of the present benefits of the Christian faith is the New Testament theme of grace. The word *grace* has almost fallen out of usage in modern English, except as a girl's name and perhaps as a way of describing the movement of a ballerina: "She dances with such grace!"

In the New Testament, the word *grace* refers to the unmerited gift of God's pardon. God's mercy can be experienced here and now, not as a reward for religious and moral effort, but as an act of God's favour, his grace.

Many biblical passages treat the theme of grace. The word itself appears over 150 times in the New Testament (more often, in fact, than the word *love*). The impetus for this emphasis on grace came from Jesus himself, who freely handed out God's mercy and gave up his life for the sins of the world.

THE LOVE ETHIC: HOW CHRISTIANS ARE TO LIVE

All Christians agree that believers are to respond to this grace by treating others with the kindness God has shown to them. In other words, Christianity calls on those who follow Christ to live by an ethic of love.

Jesus' command to "love your neighbour" was not new. Jesus derived this teaching from his Jewish Tanakh. What was unusual about Jesus' teaching was his definition of "neighbour" to include everyone, even one's enemies.

It is no exaggeration to say that the success of Christianity in the centuries immediately after Christ can be attributed in large part to the seriousness with which Christians took Jesus' command to love others in the way God had loved them. Huge daily food rosters became commonplace in the early churches. Orphanages were opened, hospitals were established, and visitation programs were implemented in the Roman prisons.

Unfortunately, the Christian church also ended up being party to some spectacular acts of hatred—the European Crusades against the Muslims in the eleventh century, the awful treatment of heretics in the Inquisitions of the fifteenth and sixteenth centuries, and the unforgivable silence at Hitler's treatment of the Jews in the twentieth century, to name a few. I have written a whole book on the evils (and the good) in Christian history, titled *Bullies and Saints*.[2]

---

2 John Dickson, *Bullies and Saints: An Honest Look at the Good and Evil of Christian History* (Grand Rapids: Zondervan, 2021).

BAPTISM: A RITUAL OF CLEANSING

There are a few rituals shared by all forms of Christianity. The first is *baptism*, from the Greek word "to dip." Historians are not entirely sure when baptism emerged, but it seems clear that Jews had been practising the rite for at least a century before Christ.

The central idea in baptism is "cleansing." In its ancient Jewish form, it had to do with purifying yourself after some spiritually polluting activity, such as contact with gentiles (non-Jews). The first Christians inherited this Jewish ritual but changed it in one significant way. Baptism for Christians was a one-off event. When someone decided to follow Christ, taking hold of the grace he offered, that person was considered cleansed from all sin. The new believer (and his or her children) therefore took a kind of "spiritual bath" designed to embody the removal of guilt before God.

In the third century, the question of baptising babies was debated. That dispute continues today, with some Protestant movements (notably the Baptists and many Pentecostals) insisting that baptism should not be performed until a person fully understands the meaning of the ritual. Nevertheless, baptism remains a central rite for all branches of Christianity.

THE LORD'S SUPPER: A RITUAL OF CONNECTION WITH CHRIST

Another ritual going back to Judaism via Jesus is variously known as the Eucharist, Holy Communion, or the Lord's Supper. Whatever you call it, Christians of every variety have celebrated their connection with Christ in this special meal.

The Lord's Supper goes back to Jesus' Last Supper, when he gathered with his disciples to celebrate the Passover, and he instructed them to eat bread and drink wine "in remembrance of me." By the second century, Christians were celebrating this meal each week.[3] It has come to occupy an important place in the practice of Christians ever since. In this Lord's Supper, Christians remember Jesus, they connect with Jesus, and they even feed on him. As they take the bread in their mouths, they realise afresh that Jesus' body was broken for them on the cross. As they sip the wine, they taste, as it were, Jesus' blood given for their sake. As a result, Christians are nourished spiritually.

EASTER: THE CELEBRATION OF CHRIST'S DEATH AND RESURRECTION

From earliest times, the most important annual festival for Christians was Easter. While Christmas has come to have prominence in modern times, especially for the wider community, all denominations of Christianity regard Easter as the central festival.

Easter celebrates the death and resurrection of Jesus for the salvation of the world. Good Friday is usually a solemn day recalling the crucifixion of Jesus. Many Christians fast on this day. Many attend church services with songs and prayers and readings from the Gospels. Two days later is Easter Sunday, the celebration recalling Christ's resurrection. It is marked by great joy and hope, with more songs, prayers, and readings from the Gospels. Christians traditionally greet one another on Easter—in many different

---

3 Justin Martyr, *First Apology*, 67.

languages around the world—with the words: "Christ is risen!" with the response, "He is risen, indeed!"

In recent times, internet memes have suggested that Easter started as a pagan celebration of the northern spring (since it falls in March-April each year), and that Christians co-opted the festival to celebrate the "new life" of the resurrection of Jesus. The confusion seems to have come from a misunderstanding of something said by the medieval English churchman the Venerable Bede (circa AD 673–735). In describing the origin of certain words, Bede wrote that the term "Easter" comes from the name of the old English month in which the Christian festival falls, Eosturmonath. And he adds that this month's name, in turn, derived from an ancient English goddess named Eostre (a bit like the way "Thursday" derives from the Germanic god Thor). Bede does not say that the Easter festival itself has any connection with a pagan god or festival.[4]

The Christian Easter festival derives, of course, from the events of Jesus' death and resurrection during the Jewish Passover festival of the early 30s AD. The point is underlined by the curious fact that the word for Easter in most languages (other than English and German) relates to the Hebrew term *Pesach* or Passover. That's exactly what Hebrew-speaking Christians call Easter: Pesach. In Greek it is known as *Pascha,* in Italian, *Pasqua*, in Turkish *Paskalya*, in Spanish *Pascua,* and so on.

This is not a mere lesson in etymology. It highlights something important about the Christian faith itself: Christianity's central annual celebration of Christ's death and resurrection simultaneously

---

4 The Venerable Bede, *The Reckoning of Time*, 15.

indicates Christianity's Jewish origins. The life, teaching, death, and resurrection of Jesus Christ is, according to all Christians, the fulfillment of God's ancient promises to Israel.

This is not to say that Christians agree on everything. In the following chapter, I will explore some of the ways the major denominations of Christianity have *not* agreed.

21

THREE BRANCHES OF CHRISTIANITY

I have focused above on important aspects of Christian belief and practice common to all mainstream versions of Christianity. In a brief and non-technical way, I want to explore the three major branches of Christianity that exist today—the Roman Catholic Church, the Protestant Church, and the Orthodox Church.

THE ROMAN CATHOLIC CHURCH

The term *Roman Catholic* refers to a worldwide collection of churches that look to the bishop of Rome, known as the pope, as the divinely appointed head of Christianity. *Catholic* comes from the Greek word for "universal." Hence, the Roman Catholic Church is the universal church that takes its lead from Rome. Roman Catholics themselves prefer to go by just "Catholic."

Several features of faith and practice are particular to Catholicism.

1. Authority of the Pope

Roman Catholics regard the bishop of Rome to be the true leader of the worldwide Christian movement. Theologically, this belief is based on Christ's words to the apostle Peter: "And I tell you that you are Peter [Greek *petros* means "rock"], and on this rock I will build my church" (Matthew 16:18). Peter later settled in Rome, where he was probably executed by Emperor Nero (mid-60s AD). The *bishop* (meaning "overseer") who succeeded Peter in Rome inherited Peter's status as the "rock" of the universal church.

Most churches from about AD 100–300 were happy to regard the bishop of Rome, called the *pope* (from the Latin for "father"), as the figurehead of the rapidly growing Christian movement. But it was not until the fourth and fifth centuries that an official doctrine of the pope's universal authority in matters of faith and morality was stringently affirmed. Even then, churches in the eastern part of the Roman Empire—Greece, Turkey, Syria, Palestine, and Egypt—maintained a degree of independence from Rome. These churches preferred to think of the pope as the "elder brother" among church leaders rather than as the "father" of the whole church. These Eastern churches would come to be known as the Orthodox Church—more about that in a moment.

2. Mary, the Mother of Jesus

Catholics venerate Jesus' human mother. The New Testament portrays Mary as a woman blessed and favoured by God. On this basis, Christian leaders between AD 150–350 began to write about Mary in increasingly reverential ways. By the fourth and fifth centuries, Mary was regularly referred to as "Mother of God," a title of immense prestige. Many Catholics pray to Mary. They ask her to approach Jesus for them and secure his favour on their behalf.

They are quick to point out, however, that the veneration given to Mary is never to be thought of as comparable to the worship given to God—the Father, Son, and Holy Spirit.

3. Jesus' Substantial Presence in the Lord's Supper

In Catholic tradition, Jesus is not simply *remembered* in the Eucharist or Communion; he is literally *fed upon* in the bread and the wine. Using a complex philosophical idea known as *transubstantiation* ("change of substance"), Catholicism insists that the bread in this ritual really *becomes* Jesus' sacrificial body and that the wine really *becomes* Jesus' sacrificial blood. Hence, for Catholics, the Lord's Supper has a sacrificial dimension. The priest in the Communion service (called a Mass) re-enacts the offering of Christ on the congregation's behalf. He therefore reclaims God's grace for those taking part in the meal. The Mass is the centre of Catholic church life.

Description of the Mass in the Catholic Catechism, the Official Statement of Catholic Belief

In the Eucharist Christ gives us the very body which he gave up for us on the cross, the very blood which he "poured out for many for the forgiveness of sins."

The Eucharist is thus a sacrifice because it re-presents (makes present) the sacrifice of the cross, because it is its memorial and because it applies its fruit: [Christ], our Lord and God, was once and for all to offer himself to God the Father by his death on the altar of the cross, to accomplish there an everlasting redemption. But because his priesthood was not to end with his death, at the Last Supper "on the night when he was betrayed," [he wanted] to leave to his beloved spouse the Church a visible sacrifice (as the nature of man demands) by which the bloody sacrifice which he was to accomplish once for all on the cross would be re-presented, its memory perpetuated until the end of the world, and its salutary power be applied to the forgiveness of the sins we daily commit.

Catechism of the Catholic Church, §1365–68[1]

4. A Larger Old Testament

The Roman Catholic Church recognises a slightly larger Old Testament than that used by the Protestant and Orthodox churches. The number of books in the Catholic Old Testament was determined by an ancient Greek version of the Jewish Tanakh (known as the Septuagint) which was widely used by the Greek-speaking early church. This Greek version contained about half a dozen small documents not included in the Hebrew version of the Tanakh. It was the Hebrew Tanakh, not the Greek one, that became the authorised scriptures of Judaism. The Protestant and Orthodox churches today follow the official Jewish list of (Old Testament) books, and they call the "additional" documents of the Catholic Old Testament *Apocrypha* (Greek for "hidden away," in the sense of "not for public reading").

---

1 http://www.vatican.va/archive/ENG0015/_P41.HTM.

THE PROTESTANT CHURCH

Protestantism, as the name suggests, was born as a protest movement against the perceived excesses and errors of the sixteenth-century Roman Catholic Church (by the way, many Protestants prefer to call Catholics "*Roman* Catholics," because Protestants usually see themselves as "catholic" in the sense of being a continuation of the *universal* church). Of most concern to these protesters was a practice known as *indulgences*. The medieval church taught that the faithful could avoid some of God's future punishments by making contributions (in the form of money or produce) to the ecclesiastical coffers.

In this context, numerous priests began to hold public debates and publish booklets about church abuses (the printing press had recently been invented). These priests called for reform, particularly in the matter of indulgences. The call was heard by thousands, first in Germany, then throughout Europe. The result was the Protestant Reformation.

It must be remembered that, initially, all of the Reformers were devout Catholics. The movement for reform was internal to the church—no one was suggesting that a new church should be founded, only that the universal church should be transformed by God's truth, as it had been countless times in the centuries between Jesus and the Reformation.

The most vocal man in the early Reformation was a German scholar and monk named Martin Luther (1483–1546). Luther demanded many changes to his beloved church, particularly to the doctrine of indulgences. If salvation was by grace, argued Luther, how could (financial) acts of service to the church atone for our sins before God? The question was potent, and it spread like wildfire throughout Europe.

Martin Luther on the Free Gift of Salvation as the Reason to Do Good Deeds to Others

Lo! my God, without merit on my part, of His pure and free mercy, has given to me, an unworthy, condemned, and contemptible creature, all the riches of justification and salvation in Christ, so that I no longer am in want of anything, except of faith to believe that this is so. For such a Father then, who has overwhelmed me with these inestimable riches of His, why should I not freely, cheerfully, and with my whole heart and from voluntary zeal, do all that I know will be pleasing to Him, and acceptable in His sight? I will therefore give myself, as a sort of Christ, to my neighbor, as Christ has given Himself to me; and will do nothing in this life, except what I see will be needful, advantageous, and wholesome for my neighbor, since by faith I abound in all good things in Christ.

Thus from faith flow forth love and joy in the Lord, and from love a cheerful, willing, free spirit, disposed to serve our neighbor voluntarily.

On the Freedom of the Christian: Letter of Martin Luther to Pope Leo X §126–27 (1520)[2]

---

2 Text from Henry Wace and C. A. Buchheim, *First Principles of the Reformation* (London: John Murray, 1883) https://sourcebooks.fordham.edu/mod/luther-freedomchristian.asp.

Eventually, the major reformers, including Luther, were excommunicated from the church (by papal order), and so was born what is now an independent tradition of the Christian faith known collectively as the Protestant faith. It is made up of numerous independent denominations, including Anglicans (Church of England or Episcopalians), Baptists, Presbyterians, Assemblies of God, Brethren, and many others.

Several features characterise all Protestant churches, and, not surprisingly, most of these are deliberate rejections of Roman Catholic tradition.

1. Authority in the Protestant Church

Protestant churches have no equivalent of the pope. Although various forms of hierarchy exist in most Protestant denominations—Anglicans have archbishops, for instance—none of these structures is viewed as infallible in matters of faith and morality.

For Protestants, the only authority viewed as infallible is the Bible itself. Hence, in Protestant churches, the *sermon*—a talk usually based on a Bible passage—has a central place in the church service.

2. Emphasis on Salvation by Grace

Protestants strongly emphasise the doctrine of grace in a manner that is different from the Catholic Church. While Catholics, too, ultimately believe that salvation is God's unmerited gift or grace to the faithful, Protestant churches underline this fact regularly, pointedly, and often in a way that is set in contrast to the teaching of the Catholic Church. According to the Catholic Catechism (the official statement of Catholic belief) there is a kind of merit in our *response* to God's grace. When we respond to God's mercy by showing love (for God and neighbour), we merit more grace from God, so that in cooperating with God's grace, we journey further into the Christian life and toward our final salvation. Catholics see grace as twofold: (1) the gratuitous gift of initial conversion, and (2) the ongoing gifts of the Spirit enabling us, through our cooperation, to be *sanctified*—that is, to become more holy.[3] Protestants reject any such notion of merit, even merit that might come to us by good deeds produced in us by God.

Love and good deeds, for the Protestant, are only ever *signs* of our faith. They never *merit* any further grace from God. Reformers like the renowned French scholar and theologian John Calvin (1509–64) argued that while our good deeds cannot save us (since there is no merit in them), they are nonetheless vital "evidence" that someone has truly experienced God's grace.

Protestants publish books about grace, compose hymns about it, deliver sermons on it, and embed it in their *liturgies* (their forms of public worship).

Following Protestant criticisms in the sixteenth century, the Catholic Church reformed many aspects of the practice of indulgences (1562). The official Catechism of the Catholic Church, however, still teaches the doctrine of indulgences, in the broad sense of actions of charity, mercy, or prayer that can, by God's grace, remove certain punishments for sin.[4] Protestants insist that further reforms are needed if the Catholic Church is to reflect the doctrine of grace correctly. The debate continues.

---

3 The Catechism of the Catholic Church, §2010.
4 The Catechism of the Catholic Church, §1471–79.

3. Jesus' Spiritual Presence in the Lord's Supper

Protestant churches reject transubstantiation, the idea that the bread and wine of the Lord's Supper become the body and blood of Jesus. Protestants emphasise the words of Jesus, "Do this in *remembrance* of me," and insist that the meal is memorial more than substantial. Anglicans (the Church of England or Episcopalians) do see the bread and wine as "effectual signs of grace,"[5] meaning that the Communion has an effect on those who participate, beyond mere thankful remembrance. Yet even Anglicans agree with other Protestants that the priest or pastor conducting Communion in no sense re-presents the sacrifice of Jesus to God. He or she merely leads the congregation in "feeding" on Christ in a spiritual way.

THE ORTHODOX CHURCH

Unlike Protestantism, the Orthodox Church did not break away from (nor was it excommunicated by) the Roman Catholic Church. In fact, one of the most important features of the Orthodox point of view is the belief that they stand in unbroken connection with the original apostles themselves. As mentioned with reference to Judaism, the word *orthodox* means "of correct opinion," and the churches of the Orthodox tradition literally view themselves as the preservers of the most pure and ancient form of Christianity.

I said earlier that the bishop of Rome (the pope) was widely regarded in the early church as the figurehead of the rapidly

---

5   Article 15 of the Thirty-Nine Articles of Religion, the official statement of Anglican belief.

expanding Christian movement. This was based on the Roman church's connection with the apostle Peter. Churches in the East, however (in Greece, Turkey, Egypt, and elsewhere), did not believe in the Roman pope's special status as the infallible authority in matters of doctrine and morality. They, too, once had apostles in their midst (the apostle John resided in Ephesus, in what is now Turkey).

Disputes between these two geographical giants of Christendom continued. In the fourth century, the churches of the East and West disagreed over the appropriate date for Easter, the most important Christian festival (celebrating Christ's death and resurrection). Over the next few centuries, they disputed over the use of religious icons in worship (largely frowned upon in the Western Catholic Church), the marriage of priests (forbidden in the West), and a complex theological point about the Holy Spirit (Orthodox churches do not say the words "and the Son" in the third stanza of the Nicene Creed quoted earlier). This final dispute triggered what is often called the Great Schism, or separation, between Western and Eastern Christianity (AD 1054). The church of the West would be known as Roman Catholic. The church of the East would be called Eastern Orthodox, made up of the Greek Orthodox, Russian Orthodox, Armenian Orthodox, and other churches.

Keeping in mind that Orthodox churches, along with the Catholic and Protestant churches, share the core of the Christian faith outlined in chapters 17–20, what is *distinctive* about Eastern Orthodoxy?

1. Authority in the Orthodox Church

First, the Orthodox Church is governed not by a central pope but by individual bishops who have authority over their particular region or diocese. The bishops of the various dioceses come together in councils, called *synods*, and, collectively, these form the true "government" of the Orthodox Church. The archbishop of Constantinople (modern-day Istanbul, Turkey) is regarded as the honorary head of worldwide Orthodoxy and is called the ecumenical patriarch. But he does not have the binding authority that Catholics ascribe to the pope.

2. Salvation as Sharing in the Nature of God

A second feature of the Orthodox Church is its emphasis on *deification*, or the believer's sharing in the nature of God.

One New Testament passage declares that God "has given us his very great and precious promises, so that through them you may *participate in the divine nature*, having escaped the corruption in the world caused by evil desires" (2 Peter 1:4). Philosophical reflection on this idea of participation has led to the special Orthodox view of human salvation. Orthodox churches, like Roman Catholic and Protestant churches, believe, of course, that Christ died and rose again for our sins. However, particular emphasis is also given to the *incarnation*—God becoming a man in Jesus. God became a human being, says the Orthodox Church, so that human beings might share in God's nature.

When the Orthodox talk about *deification* (sharing in the divine nature), they are referring to the restoration of human nature back to its original, God-saturated character. According to Orthodox theology, when the first humans, Adam and Eve, disobeyed God, they lost their true nature as people "made in the image of God." From that time on, men and women were less than truly human, less than what the Creator had intended them to be. This situation was reversed when God himself took on human nature—in Jesus Christ—experienced death and resurrection on our behalf, and so renewed humanity's share in the original divine nature. All who now participate in Christ and his church "participate in the divine nature" made possible by Jesus.

The Classic Statement of Deification, Found in the Writings of the Fourth-Century Bishop of Alexandria, Saint Athanasius

[Let us] marvel that through such a paltry thing things divine have been manifested to us, and that through death incorruptibility has come to all, and through the incarnation of the Word the universal providence, and its giver and creator, the very Word of God, have been made known. For he [Christ] was incarnate that we might be made god; and he manifested himself through a body that we might receive an idea of the invisible Father; and he endured the insults of human beings, that we might inherit incorruptibility. He himself was harmed in no way, being impassible and incorruptible and the very Word and God; but he held and preserved in his own impassibility the suffering human beings, on whose account he endured these things. And, in short, the achievements of the Savior, effected by his incarnation, are of such a kind and number that if anyone should wish to expound them he would be like those who gaze at the expanse of the sea and wish to count its waves.

Saint Athanasius, Patriarch of Alexandria,
On the Incarnation §54[6]

---

6 Athanasius, *On the Incarnation*. Popular Patristics Series, Book 44

3. The Use of Images in Worship

The third aspect of the Orthodox faith I wish to mention is the use of icons, or images, in the worship of God. As I just mentioned, Orthodox Christians place special emphasis on the incarnation (God becoming man). Icons are an extension of this idea. God revealed himself in the visible, tangible person of Jesus Christ. Religious paintings of Christ, or Mary, or the apostles, or some other figure, continue this visible mode of engaging with God. Orthodox Christians are quick to explain that they do not *worship* the images. (Catholics and *especially* Protestants are wary of this.) Orthodox believers are well aware that the second of the famous Ten Commandments forbids bowing down to divine images. But within the Orthodox view, icons are tangible windows to the reality of the spiritual realm and, ultimately, to God. The icon's depiction of the holy figure (Mary, for example) helps the believer to contemplate that figure's higher qualities and to imitate their example. This enables the worshipper—so the Orthodox insist—to look beyond the icon to the God from whom all grace and power flow.

(Yonkers, NY: St. Vladimir's Seminary Press, 2011), 167.

Christianity's key question: How can this fallen world (both humanity and the creation) be reconciled and restored to the Creator for eternity?

The Life of Jesus of Nazareth

- Born about 5 BC and raised as a carpenter in Galilee.
- Emerges in AD 28 as a famed healer, "friend of sinners," and preacher of God's Kingdom.
- Is executed during the Passover festival of AD 30 for his claim to be the Messiah.
- Disciples discover an empty tomb and witness Jesus raised from the dead.

From Christ to Christianity

- The followers of Jesus abandon circumcision as the sign for gentiles of belonging to Christ.
- As the gospel is proclaimed far and wide, churches spring up throughout the Roman Empire.
- Christian leaders compose the letters (to churches) and the Gospels (about Jesus) which would form most of the New Testament.

Major Teachings of Christianity

- Trinity: the Father, Son, and Holy Spirit share in one divine nature.
- The "kingdom come": when Jesus returns, people will be resurrected and judged, and the creation will be renewed.
- Grace: God's unmerited gift of salvation.
- The love ethic: Christian life is to be characterised by love of all people, including one's enemies.
- Baptism: a "spiritual bath" celebrating God's forgiveness of sins.
- The Lord's Supper: a "meal" of bread and wine embodying Christ's body and blood given on the cross.
- Easter or Pascha: the central annual festival recalling the death and resurrection of Jesus.

Three Branches of Christianity

- Roman Catholic Church: the worldwide church that looks to the pope, or bishop of Rome, for final authority in matters of doctrine and morality.
- Protestant Church: the worldwide church that sought to reform perceived abuses in the sixteenth century church and so split with Roman Catholicism.
- Orthodox Church: the worldwide church that originated in the eastern Roman Empire and emphasises salvation as sharing in God's own nature.

Facts and Figures on Christianity Today

- Christianity is the largest religion in the world today with approximately 2.5 billion adherents.
- Christians make up 32 percent of the world's population.
- Christianity is found in 234 countries.
- Approximately half of the world's Christians are Catholic (over 1.2 billion). There are close to 1 billion Protestants and approximately 300 million Orthodox.
- The United States has the largest Christian population in the world, followed by Brazil and Mexico.
- The largest cohort of professing Christians in the US is women of colour.[1]
- Roughly equal numbers of Christians today live in Europe (26 percent), Latin America and the Caribbean (24 percent), and sub-Saharan Africa (24 percent).[2]

Famous Christians

William Wilberforce

> British politician who led the fight to end slavery in British colonies.

J. R. R. Tolkien

> Author of *The Hobbit* and *The Lord of the Rings*.

Mother Theresa

---

1 "Racial and Ethnic Composition among Christians (US)," Pew Research Center, 2015, https://www.pewforum.org/religious-landscape-study/christians/christian/racial-and-ethnic-composition/.

2 The Global Religious Landscape," Pew Research Centre, 2012, https://www.pewforum.org/2012/12/18/global-religious-landscape-exec/.

The "Saint of the Gutters," Mother Theresa founded an order of nuns called the Missionaries of Charity in Calcutta, India, who are dedicated to serving the poor. She worked for around 50 years serving the poorest of the poor in Calcutta. She was awarded the Nobel Peace Prize in 1979.

Bono

Irish born rock singer and member of the massively popular band U2, Bono talks openly about Jesus as the Son of God and Jesus as Messiah. He believes in the power of prayer and in miracles. "With or Without You," "Where the Streets Have No Name," and "I Still Haven't Found What I'm Looking For" are amongst the band's most well-known hits.

C. S. Lewis

C. S. Lewis was a Fellow and Tutor at Oxford University until he was elected to the Chair of Medieval and Renaissance Literature at Cambridge University. A prolific writer, he wrote many books on Christian apologetics as well as children's fantasy. *Mere Christianity* and *The Chronicles of Narnia* are still widely read today.

Good Books and Sites on Christianity

bbc.co.uk/religion/religions/christianity/ (a reliable introductory site from the BBC)

christianitytoday.com (leading Protestant website)

vatican.va/content/vatican/en.html (official English language website of the Roman Catholic church) goarch.org (official site of the Greek Orthodox Archdiocese of America, with numerous links to Orthodox topics of interest)

Bauckham, R. *Jesus: A Very Short Introduction.* Oxford University Press, 2011.

McGrath, A. E. *An Introduction to Christianity.* 3rd edition. Oxford: Blackwell, 2015.

Frend, W. H. C. *The Early Church: From the Beginnings to 461.* London: SCM Press, 2003, 1966.

Bockmuehl, M. *The Cambridge Companion to Jesus.* Cambridge: Cambridge University Press, 2001.

Dickson, J. P. *Bullies and Saints: An Honest Look at the Good and Evil of Christian History.* Zondervan, 2021.

Smart, N., and R. Hecht, eds., "Christianity." *Sacred Texts of the World: A Universal Anthology*, 91–124. New York: Crossroad, 2002.

Smart, N. *The World's Religions.* 2nd edition. Cambridge: Cambridge University Press, 2003. On Christianity, see pages 246–84, 326–47.

Woodhead, L. *Christianity: A Very Short Introduction.* Oxford University Press, 2005.

PART 6
ISLAM, THE WAY OF SUBMISSION
IN A NUTSHELL

I slam, from the Arabic word for "submission," is a life of surrender to the ethical and ceremonial will of Allah (God) as revealed in the Quran and modelled in the life of the prophet Muhammad.

22

GETTING BEYOND SEPTEMBER 11

Twenty years ago, talking about Islam got a whole lot trickier. Since 9/11 (September 11, 2001) non-Muslims in the West seem to divide themselves into two passionate camps. On one side are those who criticise Islam as an intrinsically violent religion, a force bent on flying planes into buildings, oppressing women, and shunning the Western ideals of equality and democracy. Partly in response to this group, another large cohort of non-Muslims have risen up to defend Islam. They insist that Muslims are peace-loving "just like us." And those "fundamentalist Muslims" are not *real* Muslims; they are a fraudulent minority with about as much connection to Islam as the Ku Klux Clan has to Christianity.

My emotional sympathies lie with the second group. But I often wonder whether these defenders of Islam know and understand the faith any better than those who criticise it. Critics of Islam tend to "other" Muslims in a manner disconnected from Islamic life and belief. But defenders of Islam frequently engage in a strange westernisation of the religion, transforming it into just another expression of our own values. The logic seems straightforward: We are good; Islam is good; Islam must be just like us. Few stop to wonder whether Islam might be good without being anything like us.

Throughout these chapters, it is important that we all put aside our assumptions about Islam. We must not allow the shadow of 9/11, Osama bin Laden, or the Charlie Hebdo murders to obscure our view of Islam. In a moment, I will talk about the early Islamic wars and Islam's teaching on *jihad*. I would ask you—if you are instinctively critical of Islam—not to take any of this as proof that Islam is inherently violent. I would also ask you—if you are instinctively defensive of Islam—not to interpret my account of Islamic warfare as evidence that the author has a lurking desire to cast Islam in a negative light. The fact of the matter is that war was a feature of early Islamic history and teaching. It would be virtually impossible to narrate the birth of the religion without referring to its early remarkable military successes. This does not, however, mean that violence is a necessary feature of Islamic faith.

We begin by looking at the life of the "founder" of Islam, Muhammad. I put the word *founder* in quotes because Muslims do not see their Prophet as the originator of the faith. He was, rather, the last in a long line of prophets and reformers sent by God to bring the world back to what Muslims call "the straight path."

23

FROM MERCHANT TO MESSENGER OF GOD: THE LIFE OF MUHAMMAD

When we discussed the life of Siddhartha Gautama (the Buddha), we saw that the accounts of his life were written centuries after his death. Even so, most historians believe that it is possible to reconstruct a broadly reliable account of the great man's life. Ancient people, as I have said, were much better than we are at memorising and passing on their central narratives. This point is worth remembering as we ask, What do we know about Muhammad and how?

SOURCES ABOUT MUHAMMAD'S LIFE: SIRA AND HADITHS

Our best knowledge of Muhammad's life comes from two sources. The first is a biography of Muhammad's life, written about 125 years after his death by a Muslim scholar named Ibn Ishaq (704–67 CE). The biography is called the *Sira* ("life"), and, after some further revisions in the following half-century, it came to be regarded as the official account of Muhammad's life. It ranks as one of the truly important books of Islamic faith.

The second source of our knowledge of Muhammad are the *Hadiths* ("reports"). The Hadiths are a vast collection of individual reports about the words and deeds of Muhammad, collected two to three centuries after his death. They are the accounts remembered and passed on by his early followers. All the statements in the Hadiths begin with a reference to the person who reported the deed or saying of the Prophet: "Umar bin Al-Khattab said, 'I heard Allah's Messenger (Muhammad) saying, "The reward of deeds depends upon the intentions and every person will get the reward according to what he has intended" (Sahih al-Bukhari §1 [Khan]).

Because of their relatively late date, there is naturally debate among Western historians—and some Muslim scholars—about the reliability of the Sira and Hadiths. The kinds of questions raised about the first Buddhist, Jewish, and Christian texts also resurface in connection with the Sira and the Hadiths. Traditional Muslims point out, however, that the practice of passing on oral tradition has a long history in Middle Eastern societies. As I have emphasised, before the invention of the printing press in the fifteenth century, this was the principal way cultures preserved their heritage.

What follows is the traditional Islamic account of Muhammad's life, as told in the Sira and Hadiths.

FROM ORPHAN TO PROPHET

Muhammad ibn Abdullah (the son of Abd Allah) was born in 570 CE (or perhaps 571) in the bustling commercial city of Mecca in central western Arabia. Mecca was not only a centre of trade, it was a focus for religious beliefs from all over Arabia. At the heart of the city was a huge box-like building called the Kaaba. In it were housed the 360 idol-gods of Arabia. Prior to Islam, Arabia was mainly polytheistic (many gods) in outlook—except, of course, among the Jewish and Christian communities scattered throughout the region. This Kaaba building would become an important symbol in the story of Islam; it is still there today in the centre of the Great Mosque of Mecca (more about that later).

Tragedy struck early in Muhammad's life. Before he was born, his father died. Then, when he was only six, his mother died, too. After a brief period of living with his grandfather, who died when Muhammad was eight, he was cared for by his uncle, Abu Talib, who was a prominent clan leader in Mecca and a successful international trader. Muhammad's early life was filled with a rich variety of cultural and business experiences.

As he grew, Muhammad displayed a flair for trading. Indeed, while managing the goods of a wealthy Meccan widow named Khadija, Muhammad so impressed the woman that she offered herself to him in marriage. Khadija and Muhammad were married in 595. Muhammad was twenty-five; his bride was forty. Khadija was the first of eleven wives for Muhammad, which was not unusual at the time. She bore him three sons, who died in infancy, and four daughters.

Muhammad was a contemplative man, and he loved to leave the hustle and bustle of the city to go up into the mountains surrounding Mecca to a solitary cave where he could ponder the mysteries of life. Then, one day in 610, during the Arabic month of Ramadan, something unexpected happened, something that would change Muhammad's life—and the course of history—forever.

According to Muslim tradition, the forty-year-old businessman from Mecca heard a heavenly voice repeating the word, "read/recite" (*quran*). Muhammad did not know what to "read/recite" until finally the voice—identified as that of the angel Gabriel—explained to Muhammad that he had been chosen as a "messenger of God" to restore to the world the truth about the Creator.

The Hadith Concerning Muhammad's First Revelation

Narrated by Aisha (the mother of the faithful believers): The commencement of the Divine Inspiration to Allah's Messenger was in the form of good dreams which came true like bright daylight, and then the love of seclusion was bestowed upon him. He used to go in seclusion in the cave of Hira where he used to worship (Allah alone) continuously for many days before his desire to see his family. He used to take with him the journey food for the stay and then come back to (his wife) Khadija to take his food likewise again till suddenly the Truth descended upon him while he was in the cave of Hira. The angel came to him and asked him to read. The Prophet replied, "I do not know how to read." The Prophet added, "The angel caught me (forcefully) and pressed me so hard that I could not bear it any more. He then released me and again asked me to read but again I replied, 'I do not know how to read.' Thereupon he caught me again and pressed me a second time till I could not bear it any more. He then released me and again asked me to read but again I replied, 'I do not know how to read (or what shall I read)?' Thereupon he caught me for the third time and pressed me, and then released me and said, 'Read in the name of your Lord, who has created (all that exists), created man from a clot. Read! And your Lord is the Most Generous." Then Allah's Messenger returned with the Inspiration and with his heart beating severely.

Sahih al-Bukhari §3 (Khan).

From this moment on, Muhammad was referred to by his followers as the "Prophet" or "Messenger." In the remainder of the book, I will follow this conventional way of referring to the founder of Islam, just as I referred to Siddhartha Gautama as the "Buddha" (enlightened one).

Over the next twenty-two years (until his death in 632 CE), the Prophet received frequent revelations. After each encounter, he committed the messages to memory. Others wrote them down on parchment made from sheep or goat skin, on stone, and even on tablets made from the dried shoulder blades of camels. These messages were proclaimed to all who would listen. They were eventually compiled in a book that became the central holy book of Islam, the *Quran* (also spelt *Koran*), meaning "recitation."

For Muslims, the Quran is not a product of Muhammad's creative ability—the traditions insist that he was illiterate. It is rather the record of the actual words of God. When I was given my first Quran years ago by a Muslim leader in Sydney, he asked me to be careful never to put the book on the ground and always to wash my hands before handling it. (I have kept the first rule. I am afraid I have not always kept the second.) The reverence shown by Muslims to this word of God is difficult to overstate.

According to the Sira and the Hadiths, Muhammad was

reluctant at first to accept his role as God's messenger. He thought he might be going insane, or else being tricked by some evil spirit. However, after the encouragement of his wife and his wife's cousin (who was a Christian), Muhammad eventually embraced his new responsibility and began to promote the revelations throughout his home city of Mecca.

These reluctant beginnings stand in stark contrast with the zeal that would soon envelop Muhammad as he began to gather together a small band of committed followers. Among his first converts in Mecca was his son-in-law, Ali. Ali became a towering figure in Islam. He was the fourth leader (*caliph*) of the Muslim community after the death of the Prophet, and for millions of Muslims today (the Shi'ites), he is an object of deep devotion. More about that later.

Physical Description of Muhammad

Narrated Anas: Allah's Messenger was neither very tall nor short, neither absolutely white nor deep brown. His hair was neither curly nor lank. Allah sent him (as an Apostle) when he was forty years old. Afterwards he resided in Mecca for ten years and in Medina for ten more years. When Allah took him unto Him, there was scarcely twenty white hairs in his head and beard.

Narrated Al-Bara: Allah's Messenger was the handsomest of all the people, and had the best appearance. He was neither very tall nor short.

Narrated Qatada: I asked Anas, "Did the Prophet use to dye (his) hair?"
He said, "No, for there were only a few white hairs on his temples."
Narrated Al-Bara: "The Prophet was of moderate height having broad
shoulders (long) hair reaching his ear-lobes. Once I saw him in
a red cloak and I had never seen a more handsome than him."
Narrated Abu 'Is-haq: Al-Bara' was asked, "Was the face of the Prophet
(as bright) as a sword?" He said, "No, but (as bright) as a moon."
Sahih al-Bukhari §1483–87

REJECTION IN MECCA

How did the people of Mecca react to this one-time-businessman-
turned-prophet-of-God? Not very well. At least, not in the
early days.

We will look at the content of Muhammad's revelations in a
later chapter. For now, I want to mention just two aspects of his
message that greatly threatened the governing officials of Mecca.
The first was his insistence that there is *just one God*, Allah. The
word *Allah* had been used by Meccans for centuries to describe the
supreme god who governed the other divinities (all 360 of them).
Muhammad, however, insisted that Allah was not simply the head
god; he was the *sole* God. All the idols of the Meccan Kaaba (that
large box-shaped building) were simply illusions, said the Prophet;
they were false gods. This was like telling the curators of the Louvre
in Paris that all of their works of art were fakes.

Muhammad gave the leaders of Mecca another cause for concern. He said that on the judgment day, Allah would overthrow anyone who had mistreated the poor. Reminiscent of Jesus, and of the Old Testament prophets before that, Muhammad proclaimed a message of justice for all. Given that Mecca was a centre of commerce and trade, you can imagine that ideas such as integrity and charity were not terribly popular.

The Quran on God's Justice Against the Ungodly Rich

The fire of Hell shall drag him down by the scalp, shall claim him who had turned his back and amassed riches and covetously hoarded them. Indeed, man was created impatient. When evil befalls him he is despondent; but, blessed with good fortune, he grows niggardly. Not so the worshippers who are steadfast in prayer; who set aside a due portion of their wealth for the beggar and for the dispossessed; who truly believe in the Day of Reckoning, and dread the punishment of their Lord (for none is secure from the punishment of their Lord); who restrain their carnal desire . . . These shall be laden with honours in fair Gardens.

Quran 70.1–35 (Dawood).

Naturally, Muhammad's message did not go over well with the power brokers of Mecca, and tensions began to boil over. For close to a decade, Meccans resisted Muhammad's preaching as a minor annoyance. Toward the end of that time, however, things got tense and potentially dangerous. Muhammad decided (or was forced) to emigrate to a city north of Mecca called Medina. A new phase of the Prophet's life was about to begin.

ACCEPTANCE IN MEDINA: THE FIRST MUSLIM STATE

Medina was a safe distance from Mecca (over 300 km), and the people of the city were far more receptive of Muhammad's message. This signalled a turning point, and in many ways marked the real beginning of the religion we call Islam.

At Medina, the Prophet was able to establish a community centred on two things: belief in Allah as the one true God and commitment to Muhammad as Allah's messenger. But Muhammad was far more than a guru-figure for this new religious community. At Medina, he was elevated to the position of a civic ruler. Thus was born the Islamic state (the *umma*), a very important concept for Muslims.

So important was this turnaround in the Prophet's career that the year of his move to Medina and founding of the first Islamic state (622 CE) marks the beginning of the Muslim calendar. In the Islamic world, the year in which I am writing this book is not AD 2021 but AH 1442. "AH" stands for the Latin *anno Hegirae*, "the year of the emigration" to Medina. In other words, I am writing 1442 years after Muhammad moved from Mecca to Medina and established the first Islamic government and society.

For the mathematically minded, you may have noticed that 622 CE (the year of Muhammad's move to Medina) plus 1,442 does not add up to 2,021. It makes 2,064. This is because the Muslim year is the shorter *lunar* year, based on the twelve cycles of the moon. There are about 354 days in a lunar year.

Life in Medina was not trouble-free. To begin with, not everyone in the city was happy to accept Muhammad's status as the Prophet. There was a sizeable Jewish community in the city at the time. Although Jews approved of Muhammad's monotheism (belief in one god), they remained sceptical about his claim to speak on God's behalf. Jews, of course, had their own prophets in the Torah—Moses, Isaiah, and the rest.

The initial solution to this problem involved a simple treaty with the Jewish communities. Muhammad would recognise the Jews as a legitimate independent community, as long as they remained politically loyal to the Muslim majority. Stability in the first Islamic state was ensured for the moment.

THE QUEST FOR MECCA

Relations with the city of the Prophet's birth were not so stable. Many Meccans regarded Muhammad as a traitor and a threat to Arabian life. This impression was not helped by a series of raids conducted by Muhammad against Meccan trade convoys. It might be difficult for a Western reader today to envisage the founder of a great religion engaging in battles. We should remember, though, that Muhammad was not simply a prophetic figure; he was also very much a political leader and successful military commander. In seventh-century CE Arabia, there was little separation between religion and politics, between ethics and legislation.

Tensions between the Muslims of Medina and the pagans down south in Mecca reached a high point in 624 CE. Pagan Meccan forces came to a town near Medina called Badr. Muhammad's men were massively outnumbered—about three to one. Despite the odds, Muhammad and his men gained a fantastic victory over the unbelievers. The Battle of Badr is regarded by Muslims as a sign of the supremacy of Allah over the false gods of the world. As the Quran puts it, "You did not slay them, but it was God who slew them. You did not smite them, but it was God who smote them so that He might richly reward the faithful. God hears all and knows all. Even so; God will surely frustrate the designs of the unbelievers" (Quran 8.17–18 [Dawood]).

Many other skirmishes took place during these years. In one of them (625 CE), Muhammad himself was injured. Slowly but surely, however, the forces of the Prophet grew in number and prestige—so much so that the mighty city of Mecca was forced (in 628 CE) to sign a truce with Muhammad. This allowed Muslims in Medina to make pilgrimages to Mecca to visit the birthplace of the Prophet.

In 629 CE, Muhammad accused the Meccans of breaking the terms of the agreement. He marched on the city with ten thousand men. Mecca was powerless. The citizens readily converted to Islam, and Muhammad gladly accepted them. He preferred to offer amnesty rather than to wield a sword against the people of his birthplace.

JIHAD: STRIVING FOR ALLAH

A comment is probably needed at this point about the much-discussed concept of *jihad*, sometimes translated as "holy war." The root of the word *jihad* means "struggle against" or "strive against," and many Muslims stress that in its broadest sense, jihad refers to the struggle to be a good Muslim, including actively opposing injustice. This meaning of jihad is emphasised by a great many Muslims, including those we are likely to meet in Australia, Britain, or the US today.

That said, numerous passages of the Quran call on the faithful to engage in military "struggle" for the cause of Islam.

Important Texts on Military Jihad

It is reported on the authority of Abu Hurayra that the messenger of God said: I have been commanded to fight against people so long as they do not declare that there is no God but God, and he who professed it was guaranteed the protection of his property and life on my behalf.

Sahih Muslim, 1.9.30 (Peters)

Fight those in the way of God who fight you, but do not be aggressive: God does not like aggressors. And fight those wheresoever you find them, and expel them from the place they had turned you out from. Oppression is worse than killing. Do not fight them by the Holy Mosque unless they fight you there. If they do, then slay them: such is the requital for unbelievers. But if they desist, God is forgiving and kind. Fight them until sedition comes to an end, and the law of God prevails. If they desist then cease to be hostile, except against those who oppress.

Quran 2.190–93 (Peters)

Those who barter the life of this world for the next should fight in the way of God. And we shall bestow on the one who fights in the way of God, whether he is killed or is victorious, a glorious reward.

Quran 4.74 (Peters)[1]

---

1 Cited in F. E. Peters, *A Reader on Classical Islam* (Princeton University

Narrated by Abu Musa: a man came to the Prophet and asked, "A man fights for war booty; another fights for fame; and a third fights for showing off; which of them fights in Allah's Cause?" The Prophet said, "He who fights that Allah's Word (i.e., Allah's Religion of Islamic Monotheism) be superior, fights in Allah's Cause."

Sahih Al-Bukhari §1218 (Khan)

In a seventh-century Arabian setting, armed conflict, including raiding other tribes, was a normal part of life. Islamic history reports that Muhammad united the warring tribes of Arabia under the banner of a shared faith. He was magnanimous to all who embraced Islam. For the followers of Muhammad, a key purpose of fighting "in the path of Allah" was to establish an Islamic peace in which everyone was free to embrace Islam. Many Muslims today stress that the "Islamic terrorism" we see in various parts of the world—attacking innocents without warning—contradicts the teaching of the Quran.

I think about early Islamic history a bit like I think about the history of imperial Rome. The ancient emperors felt they had a heavenly mandate to establish a Roman peace on earth, the famous *pax Romana*. This often involved fighting those who resisted Roman order and government, but the emperors strongly preferred welcoming with open arms any city or nation that chose to embrace the privileges and duties of belonging to the greatest empire the world had ever seen. Muhammad and his generals were possessed

Press, 1994), 154–55.

with the same courage to fight, the same sense of righteous cause, and the same preference for peace—a *pax Islamia*—over war. In this mode, Islamic forces swept throughout the Middle East and Africa with astonishing swiftness.

THE EXPANSION OF ISLAM

It is sometimes suggested that Islam "beat" the world into submission to Allah. But Muslims are quick to point out that Muhammad (and later Muslim leaders) customarily gave communities three options when they came into contact with Islamic expansion:

1. Conversion

Communities could convert to Islam and become part of the great Muslim community, or umma. This brought great privileges as well as responsibilities. Many villages, towns, and countries embraced this course.

2. Protection

Some communities could seek the status of "protected peoples" (*dhimmis*). This meant that a community could keep its way of life (under the protection of the Prophet) but was obliged to pay a special protection tax (*jizya*) to the wider Muslim community. The Jews of Medina lived under this agreement until they were accused of treachery and punished. Protected status extended to Jews and Christians, and probably other kinds of monotheists, but not to idol worshippers and polytheists. Islamic countries no longer impose the Jizya on non-Muslims.

3. Battle

The third option available to non-Muslim peoples in the regions of Islamic growth was to take their chances in battle against the might of the Muslim sword, no small task! Only when a community refused to accept the first two options would Muhammad be forced to wield the sword in military jihad.

Muhammad was not bloodthirsty, and numerous passages in the Quran and the Hadiths stress moderation in warfare and a preference for peace. Muhammad was simply convinced that Islam, as the true religion, had to spread throughout the world as a purifying force. Within a few years of Muhammad's death in 632 CE, the Mujahideen—"Those engaged in jihad"—had defeated the eastern Roman/Byzantine army in Syria (636), Palestine and Jerusalem (637), all of Egypt (642), northern Africa and Carthage (698), and some regions of Spain (711). This is without including the many victories in the east beyond Persia (Iran) and into central Asia. Within eighty years, Islam had conquered a land mass equal to that of the Roman Empire at its height. Nothing like it had been seen since the campaigns of Alexander the Great (356–323 BCE) a thousand years before.

In thinking about jihad, it is important to stress that modern Muslims, aware of the military meaning of the term in various passages of the Quran, choose to emphasise the spiritual interpretation of jihad as fighting against sin and injustice. For a large proportion of the Muslims you are likely to meet in the Western world, jihad is simply the "struggle" to do good and has nothing to do with taking up arms in the service of Allah.

THE DEATH OF MUHAMMAD AND THE LEADERSHIP OF ISLAM

By about 630 CE (twenty years after his call to be Prophet), Muhammad was the undisputed leader of all Arabia. He was the commander of the army, the head of state, and the infallible spokesman for Allah. Two years later, at the age of sixty-two, the Prophet made his final pilgrimage to Mecca. While there, he delivered a farewell sermon to his Meccan followers. In the address, he urged them to remain faithful to Allah and loyal to one another as brothers (and sisters) in the worldwide umma (Islamic community). Returning to Medina, Muhammad fell ill and died in June 632. An extraordinary life had come to an end.

After the death of the Prophet, the leadership of Islam fell to Abu Bakr, Muhammad's most trusted advisor and one of his fathers-in-law. Abu Bakr's title was *caliph*, which means "deputy" (as in "deputy" of the Prophet). The term is still used by some Muslims to refer to their preferred leader of the Islamic world. Abu Bakr was not regarded as a "prophet." His authority was mainly legal and military. This first caliph initiated several great conquests in the further expansion of Islam, notably over Iraq, Syria, and Palestine.

In the decades following Muhammad's death, a growing tension arose over how to determine the rightful leader of Islam. No one could replace the Prophet—everyone agreed about that—but the question remained: Who is the appropriate ruler of the Islamic community? Disagreement over this question would eventually split Islam in two.

24

TYPES OF ISLAM

To understand the differences between the major "parties" of Islam, we have to go back to the year of Muhammad's death in 632 CE.

LEADERSHIP TENSIONS IN EARLY ISLAM

When the Prophet died, there was a crisis over who should lead the growing Islamic community (the umma). Muhammad does not appear to have explicitly appointed anyone to take his place. The first three leaders of Islam, called caliphs, were all close companions of the Prophet:

Caliph 1. Abu Bakr was an advisor to Muhammad and the father of one of Muhammad's wives. He led for three years (632–34).

Caliph 2. Next was Umar, who enjoyed a reputation as one of the greatest military leaders of his era. He led for a decade (634–44). Shortly before he died, Umar appointed a selection committee to elect the next caliph once he was gone.

Caliph 3. The selection committee chose a leading man of Mecca named Uthman. He led for about twelve years (644–56). So far so good.

Things appeared to be going well until the fourth caliph was chosen, a man named Ali. Ali was Muhammad's son-in-law, the husband of the Prophet's beloved daughter, Fatima. Ali ruled for about five years (656–61), but his time was marked by great unrest among the faithful. Ali was more than just a companion of Muhammad; he was family, and some in Mecca believed that the leadership of Islam should *remain* in the family forever. Others believed that it definitely should not. Tension was in the air.

Groups loyal to Abu Bakr (caliph 1) and Uthman (caliph 3) rebelled against Ali, launching the first of several Muslim civil wars. The story gets more complicated at this point, but the important thing to note is that one of the relatives of Uthman (caliph 3) emerged from this struggle as the leader of Islam, thus becoming caliph 5. His name was Muawiyah, and he ruled (from Damascus in Syria, not Mecca in Saudi Arabia) for almost twenty years (661–80). He elevated the caliph role to a kind of monarchy.

The next step in the story split Islam in two to this very day. When the fifth caliph, Muawiyah, died, the role of caliph passed to his son, Yazid (caliph 6). Those who thought the leadership of Islam should have remained in the family of the Prophet were outraged. They rallied around a man named Husayn, the son of Ali (caliph 4 and son-in-law of Muhammad), and urged him to start a rebellion to win back the leadership of Islam for Muhammad's own family. He tried but was brutally slain in Karbala (central Iraq) in 680 CE by forces loyal to Yazid (caliph 6). According to the traditional accounts, Husayn's head was sent to Yazid as a trophy.

This event wrenched Islam in two. On one side were those who accepted the leadership of caliph 6 (Yazid and his successors). On the other were those who insisted that after Ali (caliph 4), the leadership of Islam should have remained in the Prophet's family. The first group are the Sunni; the second are Shi'ite. These are the two great traditions within Islam today.

SUNNI: TRADITIONAL ISLAM

Sunnis ("traditionalists") might be regarded as those who follow a more orthodox path—that's certainly how they see themselves. About 85 percent of today's Muslims are Sunni, so they have good reason for thinking of themselves as the mainstream. In line with this, Sunnis pride themselves on not being factional or interested in speculative sidetracks in theology. From their perspective, they just get on with the business of submitting to God's law as they perceive it.

One aspect of Sunni faith that highlights this self-awareness as majority Islam is their view of how Islam should be governed. Sunnis accepted the selection committee's decision about who should be the caliph. In line with this, Sunnis today believe that matters of religious importance should be decided by a similar consensus (*ijma*). This is not exactly "democracy" in the Western sense, since the "consensus" referred to here is that of the *ulama*, or council of scholars. Final authority in Sunni Islam rests on the opinion of a special group of men expertly trained in the law (Sharia) of Islam.

Another tendency in Sunni Islam also goes back to the days of Ali (caliph 4), the son-in-law of Muhammad. When some were calling for the caliph role to remain in the Prophet's family, the majority rejected what they saw as an excessive devotion to mere mortals. Ever since that time, Sunni Muslims have continued to display a similar aversion to (what they see as) "superstition"—the veneration of Islamic "saints," worship at Muslim shrines and tombs, and so on. Sunnis do have their own heroes and holy sites, but the mystical significance of these is less pronounced than in the second branch of Islam, Shi'ite.

SHI'ITE: THE PARTY OF ALI

Shi'ites are the minority group in Islam, making up just 15 percent of today's Muslims (although they are in the majority in countries like Iraq and Iran). The characteristic feature of this form of Islam is a deep passion for the memory of Muhammad, Fatima, Ali, and all the other members of the Prophet's family. Several things emerge from this devotion to the "holy family."

Shi'ites do not acknowledge the authority of the Sunni "consensus of scholars." This, of course, goes right back to the days following the death of Ali (caliph 4). Shi'ites then believed that only a member of the Prophet's family, such as Ali, or Ali's son, Husayn, should rule Islam. When Husayn was slain, they turned to other members of the family to rule their branch of Islam. Each successive leader was called not a caliph (as in Sunni Islam) but an *Imam* ("leader"). Imams were considered faultless in matters of doctrine and law. They were thought to be blessed with unusual closeness to Allah and could therefore even become an object of religious devotion.

There were twelve successive Imams in early Shi'ite history, and all of them are now objects of veneration: their tombs are visited, their births and deaths are commemorated, and so on. The Imams are even thought to be able to intercede with Allah on behalf of the faithful. Whereas Sunni Muslims believe that a person is responsible for his or her own salvation, Shi'ites believe that the religious "credit" of the great Imams can be passed on to the faithful here and now. Various aspects of Shi'ite practice are designed to access some of that credit.

Another interesting feature of Shi'ite faith is the belief that the twelfth Imam, Muhammad al-Mahdi (born 869 CE), who lived and disappeared in the ninth century, will reappear at the end of history. Shi'ites say that when he comes back, he will restore justice to the world and establish Islam (Shi'ite Islam) throughout the world. For now, this Imam is hidden, but Allah will reveal him in due course. He is therefore known as *Mahdi*, the "expected one."

At the heart of Shi'ite Islam is a belief in the glory of martyrdom. This goes back to the brutal slaying of Husayn, son of Ali (caliph 4). Shi'ites view this event as a symbol of the faith. They are the persecuted minority who must fight against the forces of evil, whatever the cost. This point is reinforced each year in the great Shi'ite pilgrimage to Karbala in Iraq, where Husayn was killed. Hundreds of thousands of Muslims travel there to re-enact the bloody events. By doing so, the faithful reaffirm their commitment to the family of the Prophet and rededicate themselves to the path of persecution and martyrdom. Doing so earns spiritual merit with Allah.

Fatima, the daughter of Muhammad (wife of Ali), is also an object of veneration in Shi'ite Islam. Like the Imams, she is regarded as a mediator between God and humankind. She also exemplifies the virtues of womanhood and is a popular focus of devotion among Shi'ite women.

SUFISM: MYSTICAL ISLAM

As Islam emerged as the major religion of Arabia and beyond (eighth to ninth centuries), the Islamic elite became increasingly vulnerable to the criticism of worldliness. Their interest in power and possessions was viewed by some as a departure from true Islam. A tradition emerged in response to this worldliness that would eventually become a mass movement. It is called Sufism, the mystical branch of Islam. It is not a separate "denomination," however, since the vast majority of Sufis belong to the Sunni theological tradition.

The story of Sufism begins with a man named Hasan al-Basri (642–728). As a member of the Sunni council of scholars (the ulama), Hasan was part of the privileged class of Arabian society. He rejected power and wealth, however, preferring a life of discipline and simplicity. Hasan and others were Muslim ascetics, and they believed that the only way to cultivate true faith in God was to deny the false charms of the world. The word *sufi* derives from the Arabic word for "wool"; ascetics at the time were known to wear long woollen robes.

The next stage in the emergence of Sufism involved a woman named Rabia al-Adawiyya (late 700s). Rabia was a woman of extraordinary faith in Allah. She took the asceticism of Hasan and combined it with a more devotional approach to the worship of God. Her faith was not only about discipline and denial but also about affection for the Almighty: "O my Lord, if I worship You from fear of Hell," wrote Rabia, "burn me in hell, and if I worship You in hope of Paradise, exclude me from there, but if I worship You for Your own sake, then withhold not from me Your Eternal Beauty."[1]

---

1   Rabia al-Adawiyya, cited in J. Esposito, *Islam: the Straight Path* (Oxford

This blend of monk-like discipline and emotional spirituality would define the character of Sufism from then on and launch Sufism into a popular movement. By the 900s CE, Sufism was thriving throughout the Islamic world.

The popular appeal of Sufism in the tenth to twelfth centuries could easily have brought its downfall. Sufis tended to bypass the hierarchy of Islam, believing you could create your own contact with God. As you might imagine, this was unacceptable to the traditional scholars of Islam, whose role was to preserve and interpret the teachings of the Prophet without innovation and distortion. Sufis threatened this order and so became objects of persecution from mainstream Islamic leaders.

Sufism may well have been wiped off the face of the earth if it were not for the third person in the Sufi story, Abu Hamid al-Ghazali (1058–1111). Al-Ghazali was a hero of mainstream Islam. He was a scholar, lecturer, and prolific writer. He had been particularly useful in the fight against Islamic heretics. Amongst the scholarly ulama (council) he was very highly regarded.

At the height of his fame, al-Ghazali became strangely ill, losing the ability to speak. He withdrew from public life and found comfort in Sufism. Al-Ghazali did what he did best: he wrote a book. In it, he sought to demonstrate that traditional Islam fitted perfectly with the devotional and ascetic approach of Sufism. The book was a huge success, and it is credited with saving Sufism from possible extinction. From that point on, Sufism was regarded as a credible—if not always completely trusted—branch within mainstream Islam.

University Press, 1998), 102.

Several things characterise Sufism in modern Islam. First, there is a strong tendency amongst the Sufis to deny the pleasures of the world. This, they believe, is the only path to true knowledge of God. Second, related to this is a commitment to poverty as a way of life. Some Sufis belong to monastery-like communities in which they live simply and separately from society.

Third, Sufis are known for their mystic devotion. Believers often spend hours in the study of the Quran (to find its hidden meanings), in prayer, and in the repetition of sacred verses (from the Quran or sacred poetry). This is occasionally accompanied by breathing exercises reminiscent of yoga. Many historians believe Sufism was, in fact, influenced at some point by contact with Indian gurus. Connected with this mystical approach is the Sufi delight in sacred music. Some Sufis believe that singing and dancing (in a rather hypnotic manner) can lift you beyond yourself into an experience of oneness with God (google "Whirling Dervish").

Fourth, like Shi'ites, Sufis venerate certain dead and living "saints" and regard them as mediators between God and humankind. Some Sufi groups have extended their mystical tendencies in fairly extreme ways, advocating drunkenness and even erotic behaviour as a means of experiencing the love and power of God. Needless to say, mainstream Islam looks on such superstition with disdain.

This discussion of the various types of Islam should not obscure the fact that Muslims of all varieties agree on basics of the faith. These Islamic fundamentals are discussed in the next chapter.

25

THE FIVE PILLARS OF ISLAM

THE QURAN AND THE EXAMPLE OF THE PROPHET

Despite the heated disputes over who should rule Islam, Muslims have always agreed on where the ultimate authority lies.

Two things govern Muslim existence, whether in the seventh century or the twenty-first. First and foremost is the Quran, the very Word of God, according to Muslims. Second is the example of the Prophet. The things Muhammad did and said in his life provide the model for Muslim living. This model is called the Sunna of the Prophet.

We saw earlier that the life of Muhammad is recorded in the Hadiths, or "reports" about his words and deeds. Muslims do not regard these Hadiths as "divinely inspired" in the way the Quran is, but the pattern of Muhammad's life contained in them is regarded as inspired, or at least authoritative. What the Prophet did and said, as narrated by the Hadiths, is considered infallible and binding for all believers. Two statements in the Quran itself guarantee the authority of Sunna or example of the Prophet:

> Should you disagree about anything refer it to God and the
> Apostle [Muhammad], if you truly believe in God. (Quran
> 4.59 [Dawood])

> There is a good example [*sunna*] in God's apostle for those
> of you who look to God and the Last Day and remember
> God always. (Quran 33.21 [Dawood])

Daily life for a Muslim is about doing the will of Allah.
Knowledge of that will is found in the Quran and the Sunna. In
the Quran, one hears the words of God; in Muhammad's example
(Sunna), one sees the ways of God lived out in concrete terms.

Let me now unpack the will of Allah and talk about the major
beliefs and practices of Islam as revealed in the Quran and in the
example of the Prophet (according to the Hadiths).

SUBMISSION TO GOD'S LAW: THE HEART OF ISLAM

You may have been wondering for the last couple of chapters what the
word *Islam* means. Unlike the words *Hinduism* and *Judaism*, which
give away little about the religion of India or the Jews, the term *Islam*
takes us to the very heart of the practice of Muslims. Islam means
"submission." It is a reference to surrendering one's life to God. The
related word *Muslim* means, of course, "a person who submits" (to God).

The term *Islam* tells us something essential about the religion
contained in the Quran (and the Sunna). The faith of the Muslim
is a comprehensive way of life more than a wide-ranging set of
beliefs. Muslims will often underline this. To be a Muslim, they

point out, does not require belief in complex ideas, such as the Christian doctrine of the Trinity or Buddhism's Five Aggregates of Attachment. Being a Muslim is simply being someone who submits to the will of Allah. Islam is much simpler than both Christianity and Buddhism, many Muslims will point out. As a Christian, I must admit there is some truth in this. Islam does have its own fixed set of beliefs (or "dogma"), but these are easier to get your head around than some of the Christian ideas.

What Islam lacks in the complexity of its beliefs it more than makes up for in the extent and rigour of its commandments. As any Muslim will tell you, the life of submission to Allah has implications for every area of life: what you eat, what you wear, when you pray, how much money you give away, the places of pilgrimage, and so on.

The central concept of the Muslim life is not "faith" (as in Christianity) or "enlightenment" (as in Buddhism) but submission to God's law as revealed in the Quran and in the example of Muhammad. That law is called *Sharia*, which literally means a "path to a watering hole." It is a lovely image, implying a pathway through the desert to life-giving water. And this is exactly how Muslims see it. Surrendering yourself to God's Sharia leads to eternal paradise. Disobedience to that law leads to destruction on the day of judgment.

All Muslims agree that the heart of the Sharia—this law leading to life—is found in just five simple practices. These are often called the "Five Pillars of Islam," and every Muslim is obliged to obey them. By submitting to these five demands, men and women hope to secure their place in paradise.

THE FIRST PILLAR: DECLARATION OF FAITH (SHAHADA)

At least once in life, every Muslim must confess out loud his or her belief in the twin essentials of Islam: the uniqueness of Allah as the only god, and the status of Muhammad as Allah's final Prophet. This confession is expressed in the words of the *shahada*, or official "declaration" of the Muslim: "There is no god but Allah; Muhammad is the Prophet of Allah."

The declaration is simple, but it has to be made sincerely and with full knowledge of what it implies. This is where it gets a little more detailed.

Obviously, the first part of the declaration affirms monotheism, the belief that there is just one god. In its seventh-century context, this affirmation is set against both pagan polytheism and Christian teachings about Jesus.

The first of these is obvious. Muhammad completely rejected the idol worship and polytheism of his native Mecca. One of his first acts when he took leadership of the city was to cleanse the Kaaba (the box-like building housing the Meccan idols) and claim it for Allah. Actually, the Prophet believed he was *reclaiming* it, since tradition holds that the Kaaba was originally built by Abraham (around 1800 BCE). Abraham is believed to be the first true worshipper of Allah.

The statement "There is no god but Allah" is set against Christian beliefs as much as pagan ones. We have already seen that Christians understood Jesus to be God in human form, which constitutes the doctrine of the incarnation. For Muhammad, this idea involves an unacceptable association of a creature (the man Jesus) with the Creator. God in his greatness, insists Islam, could never become subject to human weakness and mortality. The Christian doctrine of the *incarnation* (literally, "in-flesh") was regarded as absurd. The Quran does not mince words about it.

The Islamic Critique of Christian Theism

They do blaspheme who say: "God is Christ the son of Mary." But said Christ: "O children of Israel! Worship God, my Lord and your Lord." Whoever joins other gods with God,—God will forbid him the Garden, and the Fire will be his abode. There will for the wrongdoers be no one to help. They do blaspheme who say God is one of three in a Trinity: for there is no God except one God. If they desist not from their word of blasphemy, verily a grievous penalty will befall the blasphemers among them. Why turn they not to God, and seek his forgiveness? For God is oft-forgiving, most merciful. Christ the son of Mary was no more than an Apostle; many were the apostles that passed away before him. His mother was a woman of truth. They had both to eat their daily food. See how God doth make his signs clear to them; yet see in what ways they are deluded away from the truth!

Quran 5.75–78 (Ali)

The Quran accuses Christians of believing in three different gods—Allah, the Holy Spirit, and Jesus (in one Quranic passage, Mary is said to be one of the Christian deities). The absurdity of Christian belief is underlined in the statement of Quran 5.78 that Jesus had to "eat . . . daily food." The Muslim picture of God as eternal and majestic completely rules out the notion that he could lower himself to the point of needing food and drink. An Islamic leader once said to me, "Are you saying that God (in Jesus Christ) had to go to the toilet?!" Put like that, the Christian notion of the incarnation is confronting, to say the least.

When Muslims declare the first part of the *shahada*—"There is no god but Allah"—they are self-consciously refuting both pagan and Christian ideas about God.

The second part of the Muslim's declaration of faith has to do with the status of the founder: "Muhammad is the Prophet of Allah." This statement has at least three implications for a Muslim. First, it expresses one's belief in the Quran as the word of God. This is obvious, since the main evidence of Muhammad's prophetic activity was the Quran itself.

For Muslims, the Quran is a miracle and proof of the truth of Islam. Muhammad, they say, was illiterate, yet he was able to produce the finest piece of literature in the history of the world. Nothing approaches the Quran's literary quality, say Muslims. Its rhyme, rhythm, and acoustic beauty are unparalleled. Interestingly, this is not claimed for translations of the Quran (English or otherwise). Muslims believe that a translation of the Quran is not really a Quran at all. The true Quran was revealed to Muhammad in Arabic. It was a perfect copy of an original Arabic Quran stored in heaven. That said, if you cannot bring yourself to learn Arabic, our Muslim friends would still urge us to read a translation of the Quran to learn some of the basic ideas of the religion. The truths of Islam, if not their fully expressed beauty, are obvious in any language, say Muslims.

There is another implication of the declaration that "Muhammad is the Prophet of Allah." Implicit here is a commitment to the example (Sunna) of Muhammad. As we saw earlier, the words and deeds of the Prophet set the agenda of a Muslim's life. How could it be any other way? If Muhammad really was the chosen instrument of Allah, his pattern of life must embody God's ideal. Much of the motivation for a Muslim's daily conduct comes from a desire to emulate the great Prophet. Because of this, the stories of Muhammad's life contained in the Hadiths (reports) are extremely popular throughout the Muslim world.

Third, a Muslim's conviction that "Muhammad is the Prophet of Allah" implies an awareness of Muhammad's place in religious history. In particular, it involves an understanding of his connection with Jesus, Moses, and Abraham, who were also prophets.

Muslims believe that Allah revealed himself to Abraham and Moses, but that the Jewish people twisted the original message into the teachings now contained in the Torah (or Old Testament). Only a dim reflection of the true revelation of Allah is still visible in the Jewish scriptures, say Muslims.

The same applies to Jesus. Muslims believe Jesus was a great prophet sent by Allah to bring guidance to his people. His message, however, was soon distorted into the religion reflected in the New Testament.

The Quran certainly has higher regard for Jews and Christians than for pagans. It calls Jews and Christians "people of the book," a phrase that affirms them as recipients of God's former revelations. However, if one wants to discover the unchanged, reliable account of God's truth, one must turn to the Quran. In one sense, then, the Quran *confirms* the scriptures of the Jews and Christians, endorsing those bits that do not contradict the Quran. In another sense, the Quran stands guard over these scriptures, correcting their perceived errors.

The Islamic View of Jewish and Christian Scriptures

Wrongdoers are those that do not judge according to what God has revealed. In their trail We sent forth Jesus son of Mary, confirming the Torah [Jewish scripture] revealed before him; and We gave him the Gospel [Christian scripture], in which there is guidance and light, corroborating what was revealed before him in the Torah: a guide and an admonition to the righteous. Let those who follow the Gospel judge by what God has revealed in it; ungodly are those that do not judge by what God has revealed. And to you We have revealed the Book with the Truth [the Quran]. It confirms the Book which came before it and supersedes it. Therefore pronounce judgment among them by what God has revealed and do not follow their whims or swerve from the Truth made known to you.

Quran 5.47–48 (Dawood)

The statement "Muhammad is the Prophet of Allah" casts Muhammad as the final and authoritative messenger of God in a long line of messengers whose original teachings have been distorted.

Offering the shahada—the confession of faith—with a careful understanding of what it implies is the first and foundational pillar of Islam. It is the beginning of God's Sharia, the law leading to life.

THE SECOND PILLAR: DAILY PRAYER (*SALAT*)

The second pillar of God's law is the obligation of daily prayer: "Recite your prayers at sunset, at nightfall, and at dawn; the dawn prayer has its witnesses. Pray during the night as well; an additional duty, for the fulfilment of which your Lord may exalt you to an honourable station" (Quran 17.78 [Dawood]).

In Islam, prayer (*salat*) takes a slightly different form from that found in, say, Christianity. Christians tend to pray in an informal manner, bringing their daily needs to God, thanking him for various blessings in their lives, and so on. The prayers Muslims are required to offer are what you might call fixed prayers. This is not to say Muslims do not also engage in informal prayers. Many do. It is simply to point out that Islamic prayer is more fixed and communal than that of many Christians.

Muslim prayers take place on five occasions during the day, reminding the faithful that they are dependent on Allah for all things at all times. The specific hours of prayer and the body movements that go with each prayer are described in the example, or Sunna, of the Prophet. Muhammad prayed (and so now Muslims pray) at dawn, midday, mid-afternoon, sunset, and evening every day of the year. Before each time of prayer, a symbolic washing of the face, hands, and feet also takes place. Sometimes water is used for this, sometimes dust or sand. This cleansing ritual prepares the worshipper to approach God.

During these prayers the worshipper will lie prostrate (with face to the ground) several times. This is always done in the direction of Mecca, the birthplace of the Prophet, and is intended to convey humility before the Creator. For Muslims, knowing that their brothers and sisters throughout the world are saying the same things, facing in the same direction, at the same times of the day (at least in their time zone), is a powerful reminder of the unity of the Islamic community.

In Muslim regions, the times for prayer are announced

throughout the city by the *muezzin*, an official of the mosque. He calls out, often through a large P.A. system, the words of the *Adhan*, the call to prayer: "God is great (Allahu Akbar). I bear witness that there is no God but the God. I bear witness that Muhammad is the messenger of God. Come to prayer. Come to prayer. Come to success. Come to success. God is great. God is great. There is no God but the God" (Sira §346–47 [Peters]).[1]

Muslims may pray wherever they happen to be at the time—at the workplace, on the side of a road, at home, and so on. Only the Friday midday prayers are meant to be said with other Muslims in the local mosque. At that time, an official (often called the *imam*) usually gives a "sermon" urging people to live in submission to Allah. Both men and women worship together at the mosque, but women usually do so in a separate section of the building (frequently behind a screen). This is designed not for sexist reasons but to avoid any awkwardness as worshippers (male or female) bend over and lie prostrate in front of each other.

What is said during these five daily prayers? Among the most important prayers is a recitation of the opening paragraphs of the Quran. The believer prays: "In the name of God, the compassionate, the most merciful. Praise be to God, Lord of the Universe, The Compassionate, the Merciful, Sovereign of the Day of Judgment! You alone we worship, and to You alone we turn for help. Guide us to the straight path, the path of those whom You have favoured, Not of those who have incurred Your wrath, Nor of those who have gone astray" (Quran 1.1–7 [Dawood]). At the conclusion of

---

1 Cited in Peters, *A Reader on Classical Islam*, 272.

the prayers, the believer says the Shahada (the declaration of faith mentioned earlier).

For Muslims, prayer flows from and exemplifies the believer's desire to submit to Allah. In praying five times a day, Muslims believe they can cleanse themselves of their sins.

The Cleansing Effect of the Daily Prayers

Narrated by Abdullah bin Masud: I asked the Prophet, "Which deed is the dearest to Allah?" He replied, "To offer the prayers at the early stated fixed times." I asked, "What is the next in goodness?" He replied, "To be good and dutiful to your parents." I again asked, "What is the next in goodness?" He replied, "To participate in Jihad (religious fighting) in Allah's cause . . ."

Narrated by: Abu Huraira: I heard the Prophet saying, "If there was a river at the door of anyone of you and he took a bath in it five times a day, would you notice any dirt on him?" They said, "Not a trace of dirt would be left." The Prophet added, "That is the example of the five prayers with which Allah blots out evil deeds."

Sahih al-Bukhari §329–30 (Khan)

THE THIRD PILLAR: TAX FOR THE POOR (ZAKAT)

The third pillar of Islam is both an act of worship toward God and an act of kindness toward fellow Muslims. It is the *zakat*, or poor tax: "Attend to your prayers and render the alms levy (*zakat*).

Whatever good you do shall be recompensed by God. God is watching all your actions" (Quran 2.110 [Dawood]).

As I said earlier, one of the things that disturbed the pagan officials of Mecca about Muhammad was his preaching against their greed and selfishness. In this way, the Prophet was similar to Jesus and the Jewish prophets. Indeed, many scholars believe that the zakat of Islam derives from the Jewish (and Christian) practice of giving alms for the poor. Muslims would reject this socio-historical analysis. The notion of an Islamic tax comes directly from God, not from any existing cultural tradition.

The zakat is usually calculated as an annual tax of about 2.5 percent of a person's total wealth—both income and possessions. In Muslim countries, such as Saudi Arabia, the tax is monitored by the state (even absorbed into normal state taxes). In Western countries, the tax is often collected through the mosque and is voluntary in the sense that no one scrutinises the amount you pay. This is left up to the conscience of the worshipper.

Where does the money collected via the zakat go? The Quran and Sharia law stipulate that the tax may be used for any or all of the following causes: for the relief of the poor and orphans, as a reward for volunteers in military campaigns, and for the spread of Islam throughout the world. In addition to the *zakat*, Muslims are urged in the Quran (and the example of the Prophet) to be generous to needy members of the umma (the Islamic "community"), wherever such are found. As I've said several times, justice and charity toward one's brothers and sisters loom large in Islam: "The righteous man is he . . . who, though he loves it dearly, gives away his wealth to kinsfolk, to orphans, to the destitute" (Quran 2.177 [Dawood]).

THE FOURTH PILLAR: THE FAST OF RAMADAN (*SAUM*)

The fourth critical aspect of Muslim law is a month-long fast during Ramadan, the ninth month of the Islamic (lunar) calendar.

You may remember that it was during the month of Ramadan back in 610 CE that Muhammad is reported to have first heard the call of God to be the Prophet. This was the time when the "recitation" (Quran) began to be revealed. This is what the fast of Ramadan is all about. It is a celebration of the marvel of God's revelation in the Quran: "In the month of Ramadan the Koran was revealed, a book of guidance for mankind with proofs of guidance distinguishing right from wrong. Therefore whoever of you is present in that month let him fast. But he who is ill or on a journey shall fast a similar number of days later on. God desires your well-being, not your discomfort. He desires you to fast the whole month so that you may magnify God and render thanks to Him for giving you His guidance" (Quran 2.184–85 [Dawood]). The point of the fast is clear: it is all about praising Allah for his mercy in giving mankind the guidance we need to walk in God's paths.

The fast of Ramadan begins when an official announces the sighting of the full moon. At this announcement, every Muslim abstains (during *daylight* hours) from food, drink, and sexual activity for the entire month. Families usually enjoy an early breakfast together just before sunrise. This has to keep them going until sunset, when they can enjoy another meal together.

On the twenty-seventh day of the month, Muslims celebrate the night they believe Muhammad first heard the angelic voice. It is called the "Night of Power," for obvious reasons. The fast comes to an end a couple of days later with—not surprisingly—a huge feast. It is called the "Feast of the Breaking of the Fast" (Eid) and it is a time of great joy, equivalent perhaps to Christmas for people in the West. Many Muslims take the opportunity at this time to exchange gifts, mindful always of the greater gift that is the Quran.

THE FIFTH PILLAR: PILGRIMAGE TO MECCA (*HAJJ*)

The final pillar of Islam may seem to Westerners a little burdensome. Muslims would disagree, describing it as one of the greatest privileges of their lives. Every Muslim adult who is physically and financially able must make a pilgrimage (at least once in life) to the birthplace of the Prophet, to Mecca in Saudi Arabia: "Exhort all (Muslim) men to make the pilgrimage. They will come to you on foot and on the backs of swift camels from every distant quarter; they will come to avail themselves of many a benefit, and to pronounce on the appointed days the name of God over the cattle which He has given them for food. Eat of their flesh, and feed the poor and the unfortunate. Then let the pilgrims tidy themselves, make their vows, and circle the Ancient House (the Kaaba). Such is God's commandment. He that reveres the sacred rites of God shall fare better in the sight of his Lord" (Quran 22.27–30 [Dawood]).

During his life, Muhammad made numerous trips to Mecca, where he worshipped his God in the very place he believed Abraham had worshipped God 2,500 years before. The fact that this lengthy pilgrimage is now obligatory for all (able) believers shows just how seriously Muslims take the idea of imitating the example (Sunna) of their Prophet.

Nowadays, the Hajj is a logistical miracle with over two million people each year descending on the Saudi Arabian city for up to a fortnight. The festival takes place during the twelfth month of the Islamic year (Dhul-Hijja) and officially lasts for six days. By coincidence, the Hajj is taking place as I write this chapter.

Several rituals are performed by worshippers during the pilgrimage. First, dressed in white sheets as a symbol of purity, pilgrims make their way to the Kaaba. You may remember that Muhammad "cleansed" the Kaaba when he took over Mecca in 629 CE. He removed its idols and reclaimed it for the one true God. Because of this, the building is a symbol of the statement: "There is no god but Allah." On arriving at the Kaaba, which is situated in the middle of the Great Mosque, pilgrims walk around the structure seven times. (It is worth googling "circling the Kaaba.") This is a picture of the way a Muslim's life revolves around Allah. The court of the Great Mosque where all this happens can apparently squeeze in more than a quarter of a million worshippers at one time. That's one big building.

Another essential part of the Hajj itinerary includes spending an afternoon and evening on the plain of Arafat, near where Muhammad gave his farewell sermon to the Meccans. From midday until sunset, pilgrims call out to Allah for mercy. Many Muslims believe that this part of the Hajj will wash away all previously committed sins. A believer is able to leave this ritual a new person, forgiven by God for past sins. I once heard a Muslim describe this experience as being "born again." I heard another Muslim confess his hope that attending this Arafat ritual would assist the eternal salvation of his father, who had died prior to performing the Hajj. Such is the power of these rituals for modern Muslims.

The Immense Value of the Hajj

Narrated by Abdullah bin Abbas: Al-Fadl (his brother) was riding behind Allah's Messenger and a woman from the tribe of Khath'am came and Al-Fadl started looking at her and she started looking at him. The Prophet turned Al-Fadl's face to the other side. The woman said, "O, Allah's Messenger, the obligation of Hajj enjoined by Allah on his devotees has become due on my father and he is old and weak, and he cannot sit firm on the mount; may I perform Hajj on his behalf?" The Prophet replied, "Yes, you may."

Sahih al-Bukhari §769–72 (Khan)

Another (more minor) ritual associated with the Hajj involves throwing pebbles at large stone pillars. This is known as "stoning the devil" and it is a way for believers to show their hatred for the forces of evil. People are frequently injured during this ritual because the "throwing" can get quite vigorous and the pebbles quite large.

The Hajj concludes with the Feast of Sacrifice. Goats and sheep are sacrificed *en masse* in remembrance of Abraham's sacrifice millennia before. Some of the meat is then eaten by worshippers and the rest, in keeping with Islamic charity, is distributed to the poor. The freezing, packaging, and delivery of these leftovers requires another display of logistical brilliance on the part of the Saudi government.

On returning from the Hajj, pilgrims will usually feel more confident of their standing before God. They will also experience a deepened resolve to submit to Allah in the year to come. Some will complete the Hajj many times, others will do it just once, and still others may never experience it at all. Either way, this great pilgrimage remains one of the five minimum acts of obedience to Islamic law (Sharia).

Muhammad's Own Words about the Five Pillars of Islam

Narrated by Ibn Umar: Allah's Messenger said: Islam is based on the following five principles:

1. (*Shahada*) To testify "None has the right to be worshipped but Allah and Muhammad is the Messenger of Allah."
2. (*Salat*) To offer the compulsory prayers dutifully and perfectly.
3. (*Zakat*) To pay Zakat (the levy).
4. (*Hajj*) To perform Hajj (pilgrimage to Mecca).
5. (*Saum*) To observe fasts during the month of Ramadan.

Sahih al-Bukhari §8 (Khan)

The law of Islam (in the Quran and the example of the Prophet) covers many other parts of life: pork and alcohol are forbidden, modesty of dress is encouraged, inheritance laws are strictly regulated, and so on. The Five Pillars, however, capture the heart of that law (Sharia). Submitting to these five demands ensures God's favour, say both Sunni and Shi'ite Muslims. It makes one ready for the day of judgment, when Allah will condemn evildoers and reward the righteous.

ISLAM ON A PAGE

Islam's key question: What is the correct way to submit to the Almighty in order to please Him and enter into eternal Paradise?

Life of Muhammad

- Born 570 CE
- Called to be Prophet / Quran revealed in 610 CE
- Flees to Medina in 622 (beginning of Muslim calendar)
- Takes back Mecca in 629
- Dies 632

Types of Islam

- Sunni: majority traditional Islam
- Shi'ite: dedicated to Muhammad's family (via Ali)
- Sufi: mystical branch of Islam

Sources of Islamic Faith

- Quran: the very Word of God (in Arabic)
- Sunna: the example of the Prophet (recorded in the Hadiths)

Five Pillars of Islam (the heart of Muslim Sharia, or "law")

1. The declaration of faith (*shahada*): one God; Muhammad is the Prophet.
2. Prayer (*salat*): five times a day; together at the mosque on Fridays.

3. Tax for the poor (*zakat*): 2.5% for the underprivileged and the spread of Islam.
4. The fast of Ramadan (*saum*): month-long commemoration of the coming down of the Quran.
5. Pilgrimage to Mecca (*Hajj*): journey to the birthplace of the Prophet; believed to wash away the Muslim's past sins.

Facts and Figures on Islam Today

- Islam is the second largest religion in the world, with over one billion believers.
- Muslims make up about 20 percent of the world's population.
- Islam is found in more than 200 countries worldwide.
- Around 2.5 million Muslims make the trip to Mecca each year.
- Some countries operate schemes to help people pay for the Hajj. In Malaysia there is a lottery with first prize being an all-expenses paid pilgrimage to Mecca.

Famous Muslims

Malala Yousafzai

Nobel Peace Prize winner Malala Yousafzai became a household name after surviving a gunshot wound to her head in an attempted assassination. She is an outspoken activist for education rights for women and children in Pakistan.

Muhammad Ali

Professional boxer and social activist, Muhammad Ali was the first man to win the heavyweight title 3 times. In 1999, Ali was named the "Greatest Heavyweight Boxer of All Time" and "The Greatest Athlete of the 20th Century" by the popular Sports Illustrated magazine.

Muhammad Hassan Wilkerson

American footballer Muhammad Hassan Wilkerson was drafted to play defensive end by the New York Jets for the 2011–17 seasons. In 2018 he signed a one-year contract with the Green Bay Packers. His season ended when his teammate accidentally leg-whipped him in a tackle, resulting in surgery.

Good Books and Sites on Islam Today

bbc.co.uk/religion/religions/islam/ (a reliable introductory site from the BBC)

sunnah.com (online searchable links to the Hadiths)

islam.uga.edu (a resource centre from the University of Georgia)

http://www.usc.edu/dept/MSA/reference/searchhadith.html (a site for searching all of the Hadiths about Muhammad)

Esposito, J. L. *Islam: the Straight Path*. Oxford: Oxford University Press, 1998.

Rodinson, R. *Muhammad*. New York: The New Press, 2002.

Clarke, P. "Islam: Introduction." *The World's Religions*. Edited by S. Sutherland, et al. London: Routledge, 1988. See pages 307–12.

Baldick, J. "Early Islam." In *The World's Religions.* Edited by S. Sutherland, et al. London: Routledge, 1988. See pages 313–28.

Beckerlege, G., ed. "Islam." *World Religions Reader.* 2nd edition. London: Routledge, 2001. See pages 127–98.

Firestone, R. *Jihad: The Origin of Holy War in Islam.* Oxford University Press, 1999.

Dawood, N. J., trans. *The Koran.* London: Penguin Books, 2003.

Fakhry, M. *An Interpretation of the Quran: English Translation of the Meanings, A Bilingual Edition.* New York University Press, 2000.

Peters, F. E. *A Reader on Classical Islam.* Princeton University Press, 1994.

Ruthven, M. *Islam: A Very Short Introduction.* Oxford University Press, 2012.

Smart, N. and R. Hecht, eds., "Islam." in *Sacred Texts of the World: A Universal Anthology.* New York: Crossroad, 2002. See pages 125–77.

Smart, N. *The World's Religions.* 2nd edition. Cambridge: Cambridge University Press, 2003. On Islam, see pages 285–306.

PART 7
LETTING THE RELIGIONS HAVE THEIR SAY

26

WHAT'S WRONG WITH JESUS

NO DIMMING THE LIGHTS

The title of this chapter is perhaps the opposite of what you might expect from a writer claiming to be a follower of Christ. Surely, a Christian author would want to explain what's wrong with Hinduism, Islam, Judaism, and Buddhism! In fact, no. There are books from the Christian perspective that do just that, as I mentioned in chapter 2. There are Islamic critiques of the religions, too. But this is not that kind of book.

My title is deliberate (if a little exaggerated). Critiquing non-Christian religions has not even been a minor aim of this book. My approach has been to see the great faiths as works of art worthy of display in the best light. I have tried to help readers—Christian or otherwise—to understand and appreciate where the world's vast religious majority is coming from. In what follows, I do not actually intend to criticise Christianity or Jesus himself; Christian readers need not fear! What I hope to do is help readers see what is *distinctive* in each religion by inviting each one—at least hypothetically—to explain how they differ from the world's largest religion (Christianity) and the religion probably best-known to most of my readers. By allowing Hinduism, Buddhism, Judaism, and Islam to set the agenda in the conversation of this chapter, I hope to bring special clarity to the world religions.

Letting the religions critique each other is healthy and clarifying, just as it is healthy and clarifying when political progressives critique conservatives, conservatives critique libertarians, and so on. Whether in religion or politics, it is important to know what each viewpoint sees as its "edge" over the others. I have often said to my students over the years that unless they can articulate what is compelling about Hinduism or Judaism or Conservatism or ancient Stoicism or whatever, they probably do not truly understand the perspective, and they are certainly not in a position to evaluate it. Put another way, we must first know why millions of people are drawn to, say, Buddhism, before we can possibly begin to critique it.

Dimming the lights on Hinduism, Buddhism, Judaism, and Islam, and then turning them up on Christianity, could never be an expression of sincere Christian commitment. It would in fact be an indication of my own uncertainty about Christianity. If I need to obscure other traditions in order to make my own look good, I clearly do not believe Christ can hold his own in the gallery of the faiths. I can think of no better way to express my Christian confidence than to turn the lights on full and let you browse the entire collection for yourself.

"THEY ALL LOOK THE SAME TO ME"

Another benefit of turning the lights on full, so to speak, is that it allows readers to observe the very real differences between the great religions of the world. As I said in chapter 2, it has become increasingly fashionable in our society to emphasise just how similar the world faiths are: "They all speak about a higher power and about being nice to each other. Let's just leave it there!"

But stressing the sameness of the world's religions gives honour to none of them. Imagine attending an art exhibition of the classical masters, turning the lights down low, standing at a distance, and declaring, "They all look pretty much the same to me." Or, to give a musical analogy, imagine your grandma attending a contemporary music festival, listening to all the bands from the back of the crowd with her fingers in her ears, and then declaring authoritatively, "They all sound the same to me."

The only way to pay our respect to different traditions—whether artistic, musical, or religious—is to look closely at them, listen carefully to their emphases, and allow them to convey their different perspectives. Once we have done that for a while, it becomes perfectly clear that, while many of the religions are superficially alike, most of them are fundamentally different.

WHY RELIGIONS DIFFER

There are at least three reasons for the differences between the world religions. First, some of the faiths ask similar questions but arrive at radically different answers. Buddhists and Hindus, for example, both ask, "How can I escape this physical world?" The answers they come up with, however, as should be clear from chapters 3–11, could not be further apart: merging your eternal soul with the soul of the universe is *not* the same thing as relinquishing any notion that there is a self at all.

Second, because of the different cultural backgrounds of the religions, several of them are not even asking the same questions. For example, the Christian question, "How can I find favour with my Creator?" does not even register on the Buddhist radar, where the key question is, "What does it mean to escape the suffering of the world?" Without asking the same question, it is, of course, difficult to arrive at even vaguely similar conclusions.

The third reason for the differences between the religions is the most obvious. Several of the great faiths arose partly in reaction to the perceived errors of what came before. The teaching of the Buddha, as we saw, was set deliberately against his native Hinduism. The rabbis of Classical Judaism in the second and third centuries CE framed their traditions in conscious rejection of the "heresies" of the Essenes, the Sadducees, and the first Christians. A century and a half earlier, Jesus himself had set his own form of Judaism *against* the teachings of the Pharisees. And six centuries later, Islam declared that the Quran was God's final account of the truth, a truth that had been corrupted by Jews and Christians alike.

I want to outline some of the key differences between the religions of the world. Many readers will have spotted these along the way, but a brief run-down of them here in the conclusion to the book will, hopefully, enable us to honour the great faiths by appreciating what is distinctive about them.

It would be perfectly valid, from one point of view, to draw attention to these differences by explaining what Christianity finds "wrong" with the other faiths. I feel more comfortable doing the opposite—showing what is "wrong" with Christianity from the perspective of Hinduism, Buddhism, Judaism, and Islam. I am not trying to be clever here, and I am certainly not trying to upset my fellow Christians. I think this is perhaps the best way for a Christian like myself to reveal the sheer diversity of opinions that exists among the world religions. And having given public lectures in the past with titles such as "What's Wrong with Jesus, According to Islam" (on one occasion in the presence of the Sydney University Muslim Students' Association), I believe this approach allows non-Christians to feel that they have been heard without upsetting the more generous and cheerful Christians in the audience.

WHAT'S WRONG WITH JESUS: HINDUISM

Perhaps the most obvious deficiency in Christianity, from the Hindu perspective, is its belief about the future kingdom of God. Central to Hinduism, of course, is the doctrine of reincarnation— beings are trapped in a circle of rebirth until they merge with Brahman. Jesus, however, taught that every individual would face God's judgment after just one life (and death). This would strike the average Hindu as a complete misreading of the fundamental realities of the universe.

The *physical* nature of the kingdom Jesus envisaged is also problematic. Jesus believed that at the judgment day, the faithful would experience a resurrection from the dead (modelled on his own resurrection) and eternal life in a "new creation." For Hinduism, salvation (*moksha*) is precisely our spirit's liberation *from* individual bodily existence into the non-bodily unity of Brahman.

Perhaps equally troublesome to Hindus is the Christian claim that Jesus is the unique and full incarnation of God. Hindus are usually happy to include Jesus as another avatar of one of the gods (usually Vishnu), but the idea that Christ is the singular human manifestation of the fullness of God is untenable in the Hindu worldview.

Finally, the Christian emphasis on grace runs counter to Hindu notions of human responsibility. Christ taught that sins can be forgiven by God's pure mercy (through his atoning death), whereas the doctrine of karma (in its Hindu form) insists that sinful actions must reap their appropriate consequences, or else be undone through good deeds (karma-yoga) or transcendental oneness (jnana-yoga). Even the path of bhakti-yoga, in which Krishna promises to be our deliverer from endless reincarnations, insists that it is the *degree of our devotion* that will win Lord's Krishna's favour and salvation (see *Bhagavad-Gita* 12.6–7 quoted back on page 51).

WHAT'S WRONG WITH JESUS: BUDDHISM

Buddhism has several disagreements with Hinduism, most notably over the existence of the soul/self (atman) and the reality and worship of Brahman. The differences between Buddhism and Christianity are just as real. Siddhartha Gautama would have shared Hinduism's criticism of the idea of a future bodily resurrection in a new, glorified creation.

In addition, Christ's insistence that humanity's deepest need was what he called "the forgiveness of sins" would have struck the Buddha as a kind of ignorance born of the twin illusions (a) that there is a self who sins and (b) that there is a Creator who forgives. Buddhism is not about guilt and mercy. It is about ignorance and enlightenment.

Another "problem" Buddhism has with Christianity also concerns grace. The Buddha insisted, "By oneself, surely, one is cleansed. One cannot purify another; Purity and impurity are in oneself alone" (*Dhammapada* 165 [Carter]). This emphasis on effort and merit in Buddhism is seen in the distinction between what a layperson can expect from a pious life and what a faithful monk can expect. As Michael Carrithers of Durham University puts it in his *Buddha: A Very Short Introduction*:

> Merit could be laid up [by a lay Buddhist] to secure a better Rebirth. The more merit in the spiritual account, the better the Rebirth. Hence, as there was a high spiritual purpose appropriate to the monk, namely liberation, so there was a lower one appropriate to the layman: better rebirth, and the hope that one would eventually be reborn in circumstances allowing one to become a monk and achieve liberation.[1]

Even the Mahayana tradition, with its many deities and saviour figures teaches that Bodhisattvas (Buddhas-to-be), must ultimately merit their attainment of Buddha status before they can assist others on their way.

Another obvious problem with Jesus, from the Buddhist perspective, is his passion. One of the striking things about the Gospels is that Jesus is deeply moved by many things. He weeps at the death of a friend (John 11:35); he is outraged at the hypocrisies of the temple officials, going so far as to overturn their money-changing tables (John 2:15–17); and he experiences fear and anguish at his impending death (Luke 22:44). From the Buddhist perspective,

---

1 Michael Carrithers, *Buddha: A Very Short Introduction* (Oxford University Press, 2013), 85.

all such emotional reactions to circumstances are at odds with the ideal taught by Siddhartha Gautama that one must stand aloof from all transitory sensations. I mean no disrespect to the Christian Saviour, but the Jesus of the Gospels is not a very good Buddhist!

WHAT'S WRONG WITH JESUS: JUDAISM

What about Judaism? What is wrong with Jesus from the Jewish point of view? At one level, Judaism and Christianity have the most in common of all the religions. They share a belief in God's promises to Abraham and King David. They view God as both Creator and Redeemer. They think of humanity as sinful and in need of divine mercy. They hold similar visions of the future messianic kingdom (Reform Judaism aside). They even share a significant part of their scriptures (the Jewish Tanakh is the Christian Old Testament). For no other two religions is it true to say (at least in theory), "They worship the same God."

On the other hand, no two religions are more directly incompatible with one other than Judaism and Christianity. Perhaps the most basic tenet of Christianity is that Jesus is the "Christ" (Hebrew: Messiah), the Anointed One sent by God in fulfilment of the Old Testament. For Jews, of course, Jesus was nothing of the sort. The Talmud sums up the official Jewish position on the matter: "On the eve of the Passover Yeshu (Jesus) was hanged [i.e., on a cross] . . . because he has practiced sorcery and enticed Israel to apostasy" (Talmud Sanhedrin 43a-c [Neusner]).

Several of the Thirteen Principles of Faith, promulgated by Rabbi Maimonides and found in the Siddur (see pages 152–53), draw a stark dividing line between Judaism and the Christian beliefs that Jesus is the Messiah and the incarnation of the Creator himself.

Contemporary Jews mean no offence to Christians—often, today, Jews and Christians are the closest of religious and geopolitical friends—but the traditions of the Talmud and the Siddur remind us that, for all their shared heritage, Jews and Christians are poles apart on the question of the Messiah!

WHAT'S WRONG WITH JESUS: ISLAM

What about Islam's critique of Christianity? As we have seen, the Quran frequently describes Christians (and Jews) as "People of the Book," that is, people honoured with having received a past revelation from God. One passage declares a close affinity between Muslims and Christians: "The nearest in affection to them [Muslims] are those who say, 'We are Christians.' That is because there are priests and monks among them; and because they are free from pride" (Quran 5.82). I myself have felt this affection from Muslims in my travels through Jordan, Lebanon, the Palestinian Territories, Egypt, and elsewhere in the Islamic world.

The warmth Muslims can show to Christians, and vice versa, is not due to their religious agreement but despite their disagreements. It is a point somehow lost on Cambridge author and academic John Casey in a remarkable Christmas article years ago arguing that Christians and Muslims find unity in their shared love for Jesus: "not the Jesus who was the Son of God, admittedly, and who was crucified, but certainly the Jesus who was Messiah and miracle worker, who conversed regularly with God, who was born of a virgin and who ascended into heaven."[2]

Somehow, Dr. Casey did not notice that he was simply proposing that Christians give up the Jesus they find in their New Testament and accept the Jesus of the Quran. As we have seen, Islam insists that Jesus was *not* God in the flesh, as Christians declare, but was only a great human prophet. Indeed, "They do blaspheme who say: 'God is Christ the son of Mary'" (Quran 5.75 [Ali]). Furthermore, Allah would not have allowed such a holy prophet to suffer the indignity of crucifixion. The Quran is explicit: "They did not kill him, nor did they crucify him" (Quran 4.157 [Dawood]). Two of the central teachings of Christianity—Jesus' status as the incarnation of God and his death on a cross for our sins—are ruled out by Islam.

I once spoke at a university in Sydney on the theme of God's entry into the world in Jesus and his death on a cross. A very polite and articulate Muslim man in the audience advised me during the question time that my lecture was "blasphemous" from the Islamic perspective. He explained that to associate anything human with the Creator was a grave sin. I assured him I meant no offence, and the conversation ended amicably. It brought home to me—and to the slightly uncomfortable audience—just how different the Islamic and Christian conceptions of God are at this point. What is seen as beautiful by Christians (that God would humble himself in human flesh and a sacrificial death) Muslims see as profane and

2 John Casey, "No Offence, but Muslims Love Jesus as Much as Christians Do," Al-Hewar Center: The Center for Arab Culture and Dialog, 2001, http://www.alhewar.com/muslims_love_jesus.htm. https://www.independent.ie/opinion/analysis/muslims-love-jesus-as-much-as-christians-do-26065543.html.

irrational. Because Allah is all-powerful, it is a logical absurdity that he would be subject to weakness, let alone suffering and death.

An additional criticism that Islam levels against Christianity concerns (once again) grace. Islam insists that human beings have the capacity to act in full accordance with the truth. It also insists that it is the individual's responsibility to do so. The Quran states, "Every soul is accountable for what evil it commits, and no soul shall bear the burden of another soul" (Quran 6.164 [Fakhry]). The famed Islamic scholar and translator of the Quran, Abdullah Yusuf Ali, remarks upon this verse, "The doctrine of personal responsibility again. We are fully responsible for our acts ourselves: we cannot transfer the consequences to someone else. Nor can anyone vicariously atone for our sins."[3] The Quran has revealed the path by which human beings may atone for some of their sins, through charity and prayer (see the quotations on pages 254–55, 258). Christianity's claim that salvation is a divine gift made possible only because of the atoning work of Christ on our behalf (his death for our sins) is completely unacceptable.

Further differences between the major faiths could be explored. I suppose I could have offered four more chapters exploring what's wrong with Hinduism, Buddhism, Judaism, and Islam. The fact is, the world's religions all have significant debates with all of the others.

I point this out not because I wish to promote arguments between the religions. Quite the opposite. I believe that when our culture declares, "All religions are basically the same," we are doing religions a disservice. It is a way of silencing them.

---

3 Ali, 339.

27

DUCKS, RABBITS, AND THE ELEPHANT: PLURALISM

Many people who look closely at the world religions end up feeling uncomfortable with the fashionable mantra, "All religions are basically the same." The more acquainted you get with the faiths, the clearer their unique claims become.

But there is a more sophisticated way to affirm the *oneness* of the world's religions. It is an approach called "pluralism," the conviction that while spiritual claims are plural *in form*, they ultimately derive from one unifying source.

The popular version of pluralism, the version you find in the pub or a dinner party, says something like, "The various religions are different paths up the same mountain," or "All roads lead to Rome, and all religions lead to God" (except in the case of Theravada Buddhism, which does not advocate for belief in God).

There are more subtle forms of pluralism that deserve our consideration. One particular question will again emerge: Does emphasising the *oneness* of the great religions give the religions their due respect?

THE BIG TRUTH AND LITTLE FALSEHOODS

One of my world religions students at Macquarie University some years ago put up her hand near the beginning of the first lecture and asked me about the famous Eastern parable of the elephant and the blind men. "Aren't all the religions we're going to be learning about just perceptions of the same ultimate reality?" she asked. "It's just like that story of the six blind men who were invited to inspect an elephant and describe what they thought it was." She proceeded to retell the main lines of the story. The first man touched the head and declared, "It is like a jar." The second felt the ears and said, "It is like a winnowing-basket." The next held the leg and thought it was like a pillar. And so on. According to my student's version of the story, the parable beautifully illustrates that, despite their differences, the world religions are touching the same big truth (the elephant).

The original version of the elephant parable—which comes from the Buddhist scriptures—is far more interesting than this modern retelling. But my student had certainly hit upon a popular way of framing the world religions, as sharing in a deeper, grander truth (the elephant) than any of the specific claims (jar, winnowing-basket, etc.) the religions make.

What is this profound macro-truth? It has little to do with things like Allah requiring five daily prayers, or Buddha advocating the removal of desire, or Jesus dying for the sins of the world. These "truths" are the culturally specific versions of the larger truth that there is some undefinable reality which draws the world toward itself. Here is the crux of religion: something infinite calls us finite beings above and beyond ourselves. This is pluralism.

One striking example of a pluralist argument was made by Chris McGillion, a former religious affairs columnist for a major Australian newspaper. His piece was titled "Groping at Shadows in a Darkened Room," which tells you where he was headed. "The very diversity of religions," he wrote, "speaks to a truth—that all people in every time and place have felt the need to respond to the infinite . . . The various religious traditions are the 'how' of that response . . . All religions are truthful in far more important ways than some of their propositions are false."[1]

McGillion draws a classic pluralist distinction between the small claims of religion and the larger truth of pluralism. Allah's call for prayer, Buddha's doctrine of detachment, and Jesus' atoning death are all small claims—potentially "false" claims—compared to the overarching idea that people through the millennia have "felt the need to respond to the infinite." The *sentiment* of each religion matters more than its *ideas*.

In academic circles, one of the most influential champions of pluralism in the last half century was Professor John Hick of the University of Birmingham (1922–2012). For Professor Hick, religions were not revelations of spiritual reality; they were simply responses to that reality in specific cultural situations. Individual religions are therefore to be thought of as *signposts* to something. They are not the destination.

Hick and other pluralists never discuss how they know that there is a larger truth beyond the actual claims of religions. The

---

1 "Groping at Shadows in a Darkened Room," *The Sydney Morning Herald*, March 18, 2003, https://www.smh.com.au/opinion/groping-at-shadows-in-a-darkened-room-20030318-gdgfzt.html.

point is strongly affirmed and illustrated, but it is never argued. I suspect the force of this way of thinking lies in aesthetics and psychology. It seems more polite and positive to say that all religions are *on to something* (even if they don't quite grasp the *thing* itself).

THE DUCK-RABBIT EXPERIMENT

In his classic *The Rainbow of Faiths*, Professor Hick illustrates his viewpoint by asking readers—as I will ask you now—to look closely at a famous sketch first designed by psychologists studying optical illusions. There are many versions of the same sketch online, but the one below was drawn for us by my daughter Josie:

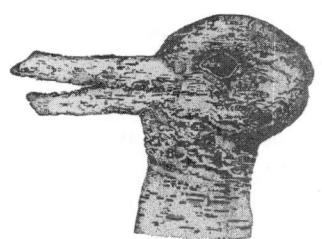

As you can see, the sketch shows an ambiguous figure drawn to look like a duck (facing left) and a rabbit (facing right). Give yourself a moment to see both.

Now imagine conducting the following experiment. If you showed this picture to people who were familiar with ducks but had never seen rabbits, what would they see? Obviously, a duck.

If you showed it to a group that had seen rabbits but not ducks, they would, of course, see a rabbit.

Which group is correct, asks John Hick, the duck group or the rabbit group? He assures us that *both* are correct in their own way. The two groups are entirely justified in describing this image variously as a duck or a rabbit. The contradiction between their opinions is a matter of perception rather than substance.

Hick then compares religious truth with this optical illusion. He says that the great religions of the world contain *perceptions* of reality rather than *descriptions* of reality. Each perspective is culturally determined. Just as the duck-knowing group could only see a duck and the rabbit-knowing group a rabbit, so Muslims see Allah, Hindus see Brahman, Christians see the Trinity, and so on. No one is wrong. It is just a cultural perception, ducks and rabbits.

The analogy is compelling. But there is a problem.

What John Hick does not make explicit is that there is a *third* party in the analogy. There is not just the duck-knowing group and the rabbit-knowing group. There is also the person conducting the experiment. And that person does know the truth. The fact is, the picture is not a sketch of a duck or a sketch of a rabbit. It is an image drawn to look like *both* a duck and a rabbit. The unknowing subjects in the experiment may be justified in merely having a perception of the picture, but the person showing the image is under no such illusion. He knows full well that the sketch is a trick, carefully designed to produce rival-schemata ambiguity—an illusion.

John Hick's analogy succeeds in highlighting an often-overlooked assumption at the heart of the pluralistic perspective. Pluralism suggests that although the world religions are each entitled to their perceptions of reality (believing in Christ, Buddha, etc.), the truth of the situation, known to the pluralist but not to the religionist, is that this reality is ultimately unknowable, and, moreover, that all religious perceptions are, in fact, perceptions, even illusions. The hidden assumption is that pluralists are the only ones *in the know*.

Pluralism ends up claiming to have discovered a *greater truth* that none of the religions has observed before, and then it suggests that the *lesser truths* individual religions thought they could see are mere cultural impressions—ducks and rabbits. By describing religions as true in a manner none of them has ever affirmed before and false in all the ways they have always affirmed, pluralism assumes a questionable intellectual high ground.

THE PRESUMPTION OF PLURALISM

It is true, of course, that most of the religions also claim to possess a set of truths that others do not have. Islam certainly claims this. So does Christianity. And Buddhism, too. In fact, that was precisely the meaning of the original elephant parable. The parable is first found in the Buddhist text known as Verses of Uplift.[2] Buddha offered the story to make the opposite point to the one put forward by my student. In it, the Buddha compares the Hindu gurus of India to "blind men" summoned to inspect an elephant. Each blind man offers his guess but, as Buddha notes, they all contradict each other, and so they cannot all be correct. They are "blind" to the truth. It was not a "jar" but the head of an elephant. It was not a

---

2 Udana 6.4. The full text is available at https://www.dhammatalks.org/suttas/KN/Ud/ud6_4.html.

"winnowing-basket" but the ear of an elephant. And so on. The Buddha was being rigorously logical: contradictory claims cannot be true at the same time. His conclusion is that the blind need someone with sight to reveal the fact of the matter. He insisted that the Four Noble Truths are the fact of the matter. This was a bold claim, to be sure, but it is one that the Buddha *argued for*—he did not merely assert it.

Religious claims do tend to be bold. But they are not presumptuous. First, the world religions do not take credit for their convictions. For the most part, the great faiths insist that a power greater than themselves has revealed truths which are, by nature, beyond human discovery. This is certainly true of Hinduism, Judaism, Christianity, and Islam, all of which emphasise divine revelation. Pluralists take all the credit for themselves. They have apparently discovered the macro-truth that sits above all the religious micro-truths.

There is another substantial criticism that can be levelled at pluralism. Pluralism makes no attempt to justify its premise. When pluralists say that all religions are simply culturally conditioned responses to a reality that is ultimately beyond their reach, we should ask:

1. How do you know that no particular religion grasps reality itself?
2. How do you know that this reality is beyond our reach?

Answers to these questions are never offered in the literature advocating religious pluralism. The chief argument for pluralism seems to be *psychological*, as I say. It is put forward as a more polite and tolerable way to approach religious differences. If you say that religious doctrines are just a matter of perception, no one can be said to be right or wrong.

But pluralism may inadvertently come across as an insult to the religions. It patronises, say, Muslims and Christians by suggesting that their disagreement over the identity and death of Jesus comes down to perception and not truth. This is not exactly polite. I suspect Muslims and Christians would be much better off openly acknowledging—as the Buddha did—that contradictory claims cannot both be right. One of them must be wrong. And it is healthy and honest to acknowledge this, and then to work out how to treat one another respectfully.

TRUE TOLERANCE

The world religions do not teach the same things. Some of their most important beliefs stand in stark contradiction to beliefs held dear by others. This can make us nervous. History is littered with examples of violent intolerance on the part Christians, Hindus, and so on. We all want to avoid such clashes. And pluralism is often thought to be the only way to do so. But there is another way—true tolerance.

Tolerance does not mean that we should try to accept each other's beliefs as true or as equally valid perceptions. That does not do justice to what the religions themselves claim. We have to learn to put up with the fact that Buddhists, for example, cannot accept as true the Hindu doctrine of the eternal soul or atman. That would flatly contradict what the Buddha himself taught. Again, our Jewish friends cannot possibly accept as true the Christian claim that Jesus is the Messiah. That would involve turning off the part of the brain that tries to avoid contradiction.

I love what the great early-twentieth-century English author and public intellectual G. K. Chesterton once said about this weaker form of secular tolerance. He was writing in the wake of the first "Parliament of Religions," a huge international gathering of religious experts (held in Chicago in 1893) who were intent on finding common ground among the faiths. In a cheeky piece for the popular *Illustrated London News*, Chesterton suggested that tolerance for all religions was really an attempt to silence all religions:

> The root difficulty of the Parliament of Religions was this: that it was offered as a place where creeds could agree; whereas its real interest would have been that of a place where they could disagree. Creeds must disagree: it is the whole fun of the thing. If I think the universe is triangular, and you think it is square, there cannot be room for two universes. We may argue politely, we may argue humanely, we may argue with great mutual benefit; but, obviously, we must argue. Modern toleration is really a tyranny. It is a tyranny because it is a silence. To say that I must not deny my opponent's faith is to say I must not discuss it.[3]

This way of thinking about tolerance—as the pursuit of

---

3 G. K. Chesterton, "The History of Religions," *The Collected Works Of G. K. Chesterton:* The Illustrated London News 1908–1910 (Ignatius Press, 1987), 28:194.

agreement—is doomed to fail. But there is a more sensible and workable definition of *tolerance*.

True tolerance is *the noble ability to treat with respect and friendship those with whom we deeply disagree.* A tolerant Hindu is not one who accepts the Buddhist concept of no-self, *anatman*; it is one who can reject this Buddhist idea and still show kindness to Buddhists. Likewise, a tolerant Buddhist will be able to reject the notions of the soul, reincarnation, and Brahman while also displaying respect toward Hindu neighbours. Tolerant Jews should be able to reject Jesus as a false messiah and still have friendships with Christians. A tolerant Christian will be able to declare that Jesus is God in the flesh and still happily befriend a Muslim who believes this idea is a blasphemy. And finally, a tolerant Muslim is not one who accepts as true that Jesus died on a cross for our sins. That contradicts the Quran. A tolerant Muslim is one who can dismiss the cross of Christ and nonetheless live peacefully and respectfully with Christians.

True tolerance, not pluralism, is the path to social harmony. We do not need to agree with each other's ideas or insist they are equal perceptions in order to get along. The real humanitarian spirit is found in being able to love those with whom we profoundly disagree.

ECONOMY OF EFFORT

There is another reason people are sometimes attracted to the idea that all religions are (in some sense) *one*. It is not so much a desire to avoid conflict but a preference for the easy option. Some might call it apathy. Let us call it *economy of effort*.

Suppose you were to ask two Chinese friends how to say "I love you" in Mandarin. One of them replies, "Wo *ai* ni," but the other responds, "Wo *hen* ni." Now you have a problem, which you can resolve in one of two ways. On one hand, you could take the time to research the issue, perhaps speak to another Chinese friend, look up the entry in an English-Mandarin Dictionary, and so on. It would take a bit of effort, but at least you could end up making an informed decision. The other option is far simpler. Rather than dwell on the discrepancy between the two answers—a single syllable difference—you could assume that *both* are correct. Perhaps they are just different ways of saying the same thing, dialect variations of one original expression.

Affirming both answers as true will not only avoid upsetting anyone, it will require no effort at all on your part. It is the perfect economy of effort. The problem is that only one of your friends was correct. "Wo ai ni" means "I love you." "Wo hen ni" means "I hate you."

The point is hopefully clear. When a Hindu affirms the existence of many personal deities and a Jew insists on the existence of just one, it produces a dilemma that you can approach in one of two ways. You can investigate for yourself the historical and philosophical arguments for polytheism versus monotheism. This might involve reading a book or two on the subject, or perhaps just getting alone and thinking through the issues. Alternatively, you can take the simpler option and affirm both claims as valid in their own way: perhaps there are both *many gods* and just *one God*. This might pose a problem for the mathematically minded, but it is clearly the path of least resistance.

When a Buddhist or Muslim (among others) insists that we possess the ability within ourselves to live by the truth and thus merit "salvation," and then a Christian insists these things can only be gifts of God's grace, it raises a problem you can solve in one of two ways. You can explore the grounds for these respective claims and assess whether you personally have the capacity spoken of by Buddhism and Islam. Much easier is to conclude that both are true, in some mysterious way.

To offer a more pointed example: when a Christian affirms that Jesus died on a cross and rose to life, and a Muslim insists that Jesus did neither of those things, it produces a dilemma. On one hand, you could look into it for yourself, assessing what historians think happened to Jesus. (There are more books on this than you might imagine.) Easier by far, however, would be to accept both claims as true in their own way. This may require a degree of mental elasticity on your part—since, in reality, Jesus either did or did not die and rise again—but it is the option requiring the least effort.

What I am suggesting—hopefully not too impolitely—is that the eagerness to affirm all religions as vaguely "true" stems partly from an aversion to having to think deeply about any of them. The "all roads lead to Rome" approach can be a way to justify not strolling down any of the roads. Obviously, none of this applies to you, my dear reader, since you have somehow made it to the end of an entire book about the world religions!

Whether because of the fear of intolerance or because of the temptation to take the easy option, the vague affirmation of all religions has the potential to leave us without any clear convictions. G. K. Chesterton, in the article quoted above, compared a perpetually open mind about religion to a permanently open mouth. It misses the whole point of intellectual (and culinary) openness. There is a "fallacy of the open mind," he said, which imagines that "the object of opening the mind is simply opening the mind." But that is ridiculous. "The object of opening the mind, as of opening the mouth," he concluded, "is to shut it again on something solid." The purpose of an open mind, in other words, is to select something nourishing and feed on it.[4]

I have tried to present the five great faiths in the best light I can. But I close this book by encouraging us all—whether doubters, spectators, or inquirers—to keep exploring the big ideas that have shaped the world's civilisations. Approaching the religions with an economy of effort, or in a pluralist fashion, is a little like Chesterton's all-accepting mouth. Who knows what you'll end up swallowing? One thing seems clear to me: We do not honour the religions by insisting on their sameness or oneness. We honour them by discerning their distinctive flavours and scrutinising their main ingredients. It is in doing so that we might find ourselves feeding on something nourishing.

---

4 G. K. Chesterton, "The History of Religions," 196. In his autobiography, Chesterton wrote another version of this quip, from which I have also drawn above: *The Autobiography of G. K. Chesterton. The Collected Works of G. K. Chesterton:* The Autobiography (Ignatius Press, 1988), 16:212.

GLOSSARY

Agni—Hindu god of fire

Amidah—Jewish *eighteen prayers*

Apostle—*one who is sent out*—Jesus chose 12 apostles who were given the special function to act in his name

Arhat—Buddhist—worthy one who has achieved a state of *karma-less perfection*

Ascetic—one who denies earthly comforts in an effort to strive for mystic consciousness

Atheist—one who believes that God does not exist

Atman—the Hindu soul

Atonement—Jewish concept of God's judgment falling on a sacrificed animal instead of on the person who has disobeyed God

Avatars—incarnations of various Hindu gods

Baptism—Christian cleansing ritual / spiritual bath symbolising the removal of guilt from the believer and providing admission into the Christian church

Bar/bat Mitzvah—Jewish ceremony to mark the transition of a teenager into adulthood

Bhagavad-gita—*The Song of the Lord*—treasured Hindu text

from the *Great Epic of the Bharata Dynasty*

Bhakti yoga—Hindu path of devotion

Bodhi tree—*tree of wisdom* where Buddha discovered enlightenment

Bodhisattva—a Buddha-to-be, or one who delays attainment of *nirvana* in order to assist others

Brahman—Hindu concept—the ultimate and only reality of the universe. All things originate from Brahman

Caliph—Islamic term given to the leader, or deputy, following the death of the prophet Muhammad

Dharma—Hindu duty

Devas—powerful unpredictable beings of the Hindu Vedas

Dvija—Hindu *twice-born* ceremony

Essenes—ultra-devout Jews around the first century who saw themselves as the true people of God. They lived in the desert and diligently followed the scriptures and kept to the Jewish Law.

Eucharist—*Communion or Lord's Supper*—re-enacted meal of Jesus "last supper" with his disciples. The bread and the wine serve as a reminder of Jesus' death and resurrection

Gentiles—non-Jews

Gospel—*grand news*—the New Testament first-century accounts of the life of Jesus

Grace—Christian emphasis on the unmerited gift of God's pardon

Hadiths—collection of the words and deeds of Muhammad

Hajj—Muslim pilgrimage to Mecca

Hanukkah—Jewish festival to mark rededication of the temple by Judas Maccabeus 164 BCE after successful Jewish revolt against Hellenistic rule

Hasmonean Dynasty—century-long dynasty of Jewish priest-kings ruling Jerusalem as free and autonomous state

Hellenistic Empire—Greek empire under Alexander the Great and his successors

Imam—Shi'ite Muslim term for a leader thought to be able to intercede with Allah on behalf of a believer

Indra—Hindu warrior god

Islam—*submission*—surrendering your life to Allah

Jihad—Muslim concept of striving for Allah

Jnana yoga—Hindu path of knowledge

Karma (Hindu)—actions that determine future existence

Karma (Buddhist)—wilful action growing out of desire

Karma yoga—Hindu path of duties

Koran—(Quran)—holy book of Islam

Krishna—incarnation of Hindu god Vishnu

Mahayana Buddhism—*great vehicle*—dominant in Tibet, China, Japan, and Korea

Majjhima Patipada—middle path of the Buddha

Manu—*(Laws of)*—text outlining details of duties of various castes of Hindu society

Margas—Hindu paths to escape birth and rebirth

Mahabharata—epic Hindu poem of Bharata Dynasty

Messiah—*Anointed One*—Jewish belief in the future ultimate and eternal king by whose reign Israel would achieve its purpose

Midrash—Jewish written works devoted to interpreting sections of the Tanak—recasting old texts to have contemporary significance

Mishnah—recorded sayings and legal opinions of first- and second-century rabbis regarded as preserving the spoken instructions to Moses

Moksha—Hindu escape into ultimate reality

Monotheism—belief in *one* God

Muslim—one who submits to Allah

Nirvana—Buddhist notion of extinguishing of all desire—*blowing out* or *extinction*

Palestine—Roman name for land of Israel

Pantheism—everything is god

Pharisees—reform movement in Judaism around first century stressing commitment to preserving and obeying the Law

Pluralism—belief that spiritual truth is *plural* in form, not singular

Polytheism—belief in a great number of gods

Protestantism—Christian churches derived from the sixteenth-century protest movement against the Roman Catholic church's perceived abuses

Ramayana—*Romance of Rama*—epic poem of Hindu smriti writings

Sadducees—faction of conservative Jews under Roman rule—rejected innovation of faith and sought to maintain role of priest and temple; religious aristocracy in Jerusalem

Samsara—Hindu notion of entrapment in birth, death, and rebirth

Sanatana dharma—*Hinduism* or eternal law/religion

Sangha—the Buddhist community

Saivism—devotion to Hindu god Siva

Scruti—"Heard" writings of Hinduism

Sharia—Muslim concept of God's *law*

Shema—Jewish three-line statement of belief

Siddhartha Gautama—founder of Buddhism

Sira—first biography of Muhammad's Life

Smriti—"Remembered" writings of Hinduism

Soma—Hindu god associated with key Vedic ritual

Sunna—the *example* of the prophet Muhammad

Talmud—Jewish set of books interpreting the Mishna

Theravada Buddhism—*school of the elders*—"Classical" Buddhism, found mainly in Sri Lanka, Laos, Cambodia, Thailand, and Myanmar (Burma)

Torah—sacred writing of Judaism—God's instruction to the Israelites on legal, environmental, religious, and social matters; came to refer specifically to first five books of the Jewish Bible

Transubstantiation—Roman Catholic belief that in the ritual of *the Lord's Supper*, the bread and wine change substance and actually become the body and blood of Jesus

Trinity—Christian doctrine of one God in three persons—the Father, Son, and Holy Spirit

Upanishads—sacred writings of Hinduism composed between 1000–300 BCE

Vaishnavism—Hindu devotion to Vishnu

Varnas—Hindu castes

Vedas—earliest writings of Hinduism

Vedism—Aryan religion originally from Persia

Yom Kippur (Day of Atonement)—Jewish festival celebrating the mercy of God toward Israel

Zealots—Jewish faction that violently opposed Roman rule in

the Holy Land

Zen Buddhism—extension of meditative dimension of Buddhism

Zionism—movement within Judaism for a Jewish state in the "Holy Land"

INDEX